ALCOHOL AND OLD AGE

SEMINARS IN PSYCHIATRY

Series Editor

Milton Greenblatt, M.D.

Assistant Dean, School of Medicine
Professor of Psychiatry and
Director of Social and Community Psychiatry
University of California at Los Angeles

Chief of Staff, Veterans Administration Hospital
Brentwood, Los Angeles

Other Books in Series:

Psychiatric Aspects of Neurologic Disease, edited by
        D. Frank Benson, M.D., and Dietrich Blumer, M.D.
Borderline States in Psychiatry, edited by John E. Mack, M.D.
Topics in Psychoendocrinology, edited by Edward J. Sachar, M.D.
Drugs in Combination with Other Therapies, edited by Milton Greenblatt, M.D.
Suicidology: Contemporary Developments, edited by
        Edwin S. Schneidman, Ph.D.
Alcoholism Problems in Women and Children, edited by
        Milton Greenblatt, M.D., and Mark A. Schuckit, M.D.
Ethological Psychiatry: Psychopathology in the Context of
        Evolutionary Biology, edited by Michael T. McGuire, M.D., and
        Lynn A. Fairbanks, Ph.D.
The Family in Mourning: A Guide for Health Professionals, edited by
        Charles E. Hollingsworth, M.D., and Robert O. Pasnau, M.D.
Clinical Aspects of the Rapist, edited by Richard T. Rada, M.D.
Sex Education for the Health Professional: A Curriculum Guide, edited by
        Norman Rosenzweig, M.D., and F. Paul Pearsall, Ph.D.
Methods of Biobehavioral Research, edited by
        E.A. Serafetinides, M.D., Ph.D.
Psychopharmacology Update: New and Neglected Areas, edited by
        John M. Davis, M.D., and David Greenblatt, M.D.

ALCOHOL AND OLD AGE

by
Brian L. Mishara, Ph.D.
Professor, Department of Psychology
University of Quebec at Montreal
Montreal, Quebec
Canada

and
Robert Kastenbaum, Ph.D.
Superintendent, Cushing Hospital
Department of Mental Health
Framingham, Massachusetts

GRUNE & STRATTON
A Subsidiary of Harcourt Brace Jovanovich, Publishers
NEW YORK   LONDON   TORONTO   SYDNEY   SAN FRANCISCO

Grune & Stratton, Inc.
111 Fifth Avenue
New York, New York 10003

Distributed in the United Kingdom by
Academic Press, Inc. (London) Ltd.
24/28 Oval Road, London NW 1

Library of Congress Catalog Number 79-3777
International Standard Book Number 0-8089-1226-7
Printed in the United States of America

Contents

Preface

"One drink is too many for an old person."

"My aunt is 94, she has a glass of sherry every night, and she's still going strong."

"Old people hold their booze better than young people."

"Problem drinking is more (less) common in old age."

"Older problem drinkers have a better (worse) prognosis than the young."

There is no shortage of opinions about alcohol and old age. But which of these opinions have a factual basis, which opinions are in error, miss the point, or require a knowledge base that has yet to be established?

This book attempts to bring together the existing body of knowledge concerning alcohol and old age. We often felt that we were dealing with *two* bodies of knowledge that did not want to have much to do with each other. One position holds that alcohol use is dangerous at any age, in any amount—and even more dangerous in old age. The opposing position suggests that alcohol has therapeutic potential for older people, can be part of the good and satisfying life, and, therefore, should be encouraged. Each of these positions has its distinct literature and advocates. Relatively few people seem to have carefully examined both literatures, the "use" and the "abuse" side of alcohol in old age.

Obviously there are differences in value orientations, as well as assumptions about fact, involved in the two opposing positions. The differences in value orientations (alcohol as beneficial or destructive) have long histories and probably long futures as well. Perhaps, however, we could improve our grasp of the facts (such as they are). The physician, nurse, social worker, minister, nursing home administrator, and many other people concerned with the well-being of the aged can function more effectively with the full range of facts about alcohol and old age at their disposal. Researchers and educators who have previously limited their interest to either the "use" or "abuse" side might find it stimulating and satisfying to learn what has been happening in the area previously neglected. We think this book will have made its contribution if it enables people acquainted chiefly with one side of the alcohol–old age question to achieve an enriched perspective and balance and identify areas where research and clinical effort could usefully be directed.

Our attempt to develop perspective begins in Chapter 1 with a historical survey over the past several millenia of alcohol use by older persons. The deployment of alcoholic beverages for medicinal and sacred purposes is seen as taking some unfortunate turns, leading to major alcoholism problems in large segments of the general population.

Chapter 2 reviews the physiological effects of ethanol and the nonethanol components (congeners) of alcoholic beverages. Major physiological effects are reviewed, and the few studies that have involved elderly participants are discussed.

Chapter 3 is a description and critique of epidemiological data on the extent of alcohol use in old age. We also consider possible explanations of observed differences between younger and older populations.

Chapter 4 concerns problem drinking in old age, beginning with an evaluation of criteria for establishing whether or not an old person has a drinking problem. The population of elderly problem drinkers is described, and a contrast is made between those whose problems began later in life and those who started young and brought the problem with them into old age.

Chapter 5 presents methods of treating alcohol problems, with particular attention to their suitability for helping the older problem drinker. In addition, a small community survey is presented to help explicate the types of help older alcoholics tend to receive these days.

Chapter 6 discusses alcohol and health from two perspectives: the older alcoholic, and the effects of moderate drinking on health status in old age.

Chapter 7 presents a detailed review and critique of studies of possible beneficial effects of alcoholic beverages when made available in moderate amounts to the institutionalized elderly.

Chapter 8 offers new data based on a six-year research series. These previously unpublished findings on community-dwelling elders were generated by a psychobiological theory that raised the possibility that wine, used regularly and in moderation, might improve sleep, sense of well-being, and cognitive and coping skills.

Chapter 9 highlights major conclusions and points to the need for a multidimensional view of alcohol and old age and for continued research on basic issues.

We feel obliged to make it clear at the outset that at numerous points the information needed to present a coherent view of alcohol and old age is not available. The reader at times may become almost as frustrated as the authors! Perhaps, however, this exposure of the gaps and limits of present knowledge will be of some value in leading to more adequate and comprehensive knowledge in the future.

Some readers may wish to approach this book by starting with chapters that are closest to their own areas of interest. Although each chapter is intended to stand independent of the others, a complete (or as-complete-as-now-possible) picture of any one area must take into account findings presented in the other chapters as well. We have tried to integrate data from several sources and, at times, to fill knowledge gaps with speculation. These efforts are identified as such and are chiefly intended to stimulate further attention to questions that will not be answered unless new, substantial knowledge is forthcoming.

ALCOHOL AND OLD AGE

1
Alcohol and the Elderly: Five Thousand Years of Uncontrolled Experimentation

In any consideration of the effects and influence of alcohol on the elderly, certain basic questions arise. Are we acting wisely if we snatch away that mug, goblet, or bottle? Or would it be wiser to offer the aged a drink ourselves? On the other hand, perhaps we should not interfere at all?

In order to answer these questions, one must understand the history of the elderly's relationship to alcohol. Our current assumptions and practices are rooted in centuries of observation and experience. In effect, we have been participating in a largely uncontrolled natural experiment for at least 5000 years. The laboratory is global, encompassing societies at various levels of organization. The variables are many and complex. In focusing attention on old age and alcohol, we must not forget the larger context in which these variables are rooted: the use or nonuse of alcohol depends, to a large extent, on the life-styles and mores of a society at any point in time.

Later in this book, we will consider controlled studies that have been designed to investigate the relationship between alcohol and old age. But first, let us examine the history of this relationship to see how more than 50 centuries of uncontrolled experimentation have set the pattern for our own attitudes today.

THE EARLY DAYS

At the Beginning

Knowledge about the remote past of the human race continues to expand. But *history* begins when it finds a voice, when there are words to reach from one generation to the next. Remarkably, both old age and

1

alcoholic beverages are given pride of place in the earliest records that have come to us from ancient times.

The Epic of Gilgamesh (Anonymous, 1972) is a moral adventure tale that Sumerians entertained each other with 5000 years ago and perhaps longer. Versions of this epic passed from the oral to the written tradition in ancient Babylon. Gilgamesh was a noble, heroic, but very human person who attempted to conquer both old age and death. Neither his courage nor his intellect (nor, for that matter, his "connections") enabled him to pre-serve youth against the onslaught of aging and death. The epic can be interpreted in several ways, emphasizing the heroism, the foolishness, or the vulnerability of humanity when pitted against nature. But it can also be viewed as mankind's first warning to Mother Nature that we are not pleased by all of the universal design and will be laboring mightily to de-velop new options.

Wine plays a curious role in this legend. Before Gilgamesh himself could enter on the scene, there had to be an act or process of cosmic creation. This version of cosmic beginnings featured a stupendous battle between benevolent and malevolent deities. Although the side of good prevailed, heavy casualties were suffered. And it was from their fallen bodies that vines twisted forward through the soil: grape vines, of course. The "blood of the grapes" came to us, then, as our inheritance from the gods who made this world at least moderately secure for mankind. The Sumerian or Babylonian who put the cup to his lips was establishing con-tact with powerful forces of the universe—a form of communion, if you will.

In the same epic tale, then, one of the great areas of human concern was set forth and the origin of wine was celebrated as an intrinsic connec-tion with the origin of our life on earth itself. Perhaps it is not coincidence that early in this epic, wine is introduced as the gift of the dying gods, while humanity fails in its effort to avert its own death or deter the aging process. We have here the basic interplay of ideas and feelings that was captured so memorably by another Mesopotamian in a century far removed both from that of Gilgamesh and our own. Omar Khayyám's *Rubáiyát* remains the definitive statement on wine as solace for humanity's place in an incom-prehensible and blindly spinning universe.

"The Milk of Old Age"

Early historical records strengthen the association between wine and old age. It has long been regarded as the "balm of autumn" or "the milk of old age." While the Gilgamesh epic and the much later poetry of Omar Khayyám present wine as a general elixir for the sorrows attendant upon the human condition, there rapidly developed a more specific tradition involving the elderly. Wine was often viewed both as a psychological comfort and as a practical dietary component for people who were confronted by the impairments and losses associated with advancing age.

To pursue this point further requires some attention to the early prominence of wine as distinguished from other alcoholic beverages. Fermentation is a process that occurs "spontaneously" (without human intention or intervention) when the physical conditions are propitious. There is evidence that people have known about the properties of such "spoiled" food as far back as our knowledge of human society goes. While for most people the word "wine" has come to signify the fermented juice of grapes, the types of wine that can actually be made are much more extensive. Local crops have provided virtually every part of the world with one or more opportunities to discover the effects and uses of wine. One of the reasons for the prominence of wine, then, has been its ready availability. This is not to say that all wines have been found equally palatable. Bad wine could be very bad, indeed. Attempts to establish and maintain reasonable standards of quality occupied considerable attention in antiquity. Many of the wines consumed by Egyptians, Greeks, Romans, and those who came after were heavily adulterated. It is likely that we would find them unpleasant. The good wines were enjoyed, but many were dutifully imbibed much as we make use of nasty-tasting medicine.

Wine also seemed to attract more than its share of symbolism and cultural dynamics. The thriving vineyard was itself an index of the well-favored land and people, of being in good graces with the deities. As Noah stepped from the Ark, for example, he was bidden by the Lord to plant vineyards but was given no instructions about beer and strong spirits. Instead of speculating on the reasons, it may be enough to note that the entire process of developing wine, from planting and tending vineyards to elaborate social and religious rituals for using the product, has given wine a distinctive place in the spectrum of alcoholic beverages from early times forward (but with strong competition later, as we will see). Beer, as another product of fermentation, also was well known in antiquity and was often a staple item in the diet. However, beer seldom seemed to attract the imagination and the mythmakers as much as wine did.

Many of the favorable effects attributed to wine appeared to be especially valuable for the aged. Then as now, the elderly were apt to view their diminishing physical prowess with dismay. How could they resist availing themselves of a beverage that "digesteth food and disperseth care and dispelleth flatulence and clarifieth the blood and cleareth the complexion and quickeneth the body and hearteneth the hen-hearted and fortifieth the sexual power"? (Anonymous) As this passage from the *Arabian Nights* suggests, wine was in excellent favor as an aid to digestion and as an all-around booster of sagging biology and lagging libido.

The use of wine as an outright medicine was also favored, as was its use as an agent in which to suspend other medical ingredients. Fifty centuries ago, clay tablets contained medical prescriptions specifying wine as the menstruum. The old person, being somewhat more vulnerable to illness, was an active customer for wine-as-medicine as well as for wine-as-solace-and-booster.

We must also take account of the significance played by religious celebrations and rituals in some of the major cultures of the ancient world. The libation was a pervasive and central aspect of ceremonials in ancient Egypt, for example. The pharoah, from his golden goblet, sipped the wine that would consolidate his relationship with the (other) deities. Common folk took their libations from lesser vessels, but the nation's partaking of wine was an important affirmation of its integrity as a group and its fortunate place in the cosmic scheme of things.

A practice of this kind would seem to have had particular benefits for the old person. During its better years, Egypt achieved high standards of human concern. Family and community affection were valued. The medical profession reached new heights. And those who might in less favorable situations have been rejected and abandoned—such as the ailing old person—were still counted as valuable members of family and community. The ritualistic libations helped to emphasize the togetherness of all people, including the aged. The old person, in fact, had a distinctive place in the proceedings. For a moment's perspective, compare two mental images: the aged Egyptian who participates honorably in libations that symbolize unity of community and unity with deity, and the aged man on a twentieth-century skid row who sits in a filthy doorway with only a bottle of cheap wine for company.

Respect for the aged and the pervasive use of wine for domestic and religious occasions were also features of the Hebrews of biblical times. They acknowledged the same basic advantages of wine as those already noted. In addition, wine was clearly specified as an antiseptic. The use of wine as a topical anti-infection agent continued for centuries, while the stronger alcoholic beverages also were recruited for this purpose.

Then as now, however, wine was used primarily as a beverage. Two consecutive passages in Proverbs (31: 6, 7) specified conditions in which alcoholic beverages were especially appropriate:

> Give strong drink unto him that is ready to perish, and wine unto those that be of heavy hearts.
> Let him drink, and forget his poverty, and remember his misery no more.

These recommendations were not limited to the aged but were considered appropriate for all those confronted with loss, misfortune, or the advent of death. Alcoholic beverages are characterized in these passages as antidepressants and obliterators of painful memory and consciousness. Some modern readers might find it difficult to reconcile "poverty" and "misery" with the condition of old people in biblical times. The Scriptures, after all, commanded us to honor our fathers and mothers. But poverty, misery, and fear of abandonment were realities to many aging people of the time (Griffin, 1946; Kastenbaum & Ross, 1975, pp. 421–449). The biblical injunctions can be regarded as a moral campaign mounted to overcome the problems experienced by elders of the time, an expression of an ideal code rather than a description of existing reality. That a few old people were respected and treasured does not demonstrate that this was the good fortune of all elders in biblical times any more than in our own. If one could not enjoy health, love, and security in advanced age, one might at least be passed the comforting jug.

The distinction between "wine" and "strong drink," as made in the above passages and in many other ancient sources, remains somewhat unclear. Alex Waugh (1959) claims that "the liquid which Mahommed [sic] prohibited was not the fermented juice of the grape but spirits, a distillation of dates and raisins." The ancients often did seem to distinguish between wine and stronger beverages, although it is not always easy to determine what type of beverage is being cited in a particular statement.

A society's attitude toward alcoholic beverages has often made a firm distinction between moderate and immoderate use. Another passage in Proverbs, for example, warns that kings and princes might while under the influence "forget the law, and pervert the judgment of any of the afflicted" (31:5). Some of today's elders can recall being warned in their youth to resist the blandishments of "demon rum." But two millenia ago, wine and possibly other alcoholic beverages were seen as vehicles for the misbehavior of actual demons who would insinuate themselves into the drink and cause our lapses from good judgment. This was an especially prevalent concept in the Arabic world. In both the Judaic-Christian and Moslem traditions, there was awareness that alcohol abuse posed a threat to the individual and the community, but there were also times, places and circumstances where a drink was the "treatment of choice." The concept of alcohol as treatment and the distinction between unacceptable and acceptable uses of this substance emerge even more clearly as we move from ancient days to our own time.

ALCOHOL, MEDICINE, AND MORALITY

Keepers of the Flame

Arabian scholars preserved and extended much of the knowledge gained in the world of antiquity until it was rediscovered and disseminated throughout Europe as the "Dark Ages" gave way to "the Enlightenment" (to use the extravagantly oversimplified characterizations of these eras that remain so popular). The sophisticated medical practices of the Arabians included the frequent but highly differentiated use of alcoholic beverages. Avicenna, a tenth-century Persian, exercised a major influence in medical practice for approximately eight centuries. A number of his rules focus upon the use of alcoholic beverages. Specific to old age, we find, for example, Rule 860 (Gruner, 1930):

> The wine which is best for elderly persons is old, red, with warming effect, and diuretic. New and white sweet wine should be avoided, unless a bath is taken after a meal at which such wine is taken, and unless there is thirst. In that case it is allowable to take white wine which is light without much body in it, thus taking the place of plain water. Elderly persons must shun sweet wines which are likely to prove oppilative (but wines prepared with honey may be allowed even in cases where gout is threatened). Young persons should take it |wine| with moderation. But elderly persons may take as much as they can tolerate. Wine is borne better in a cold country than in a hot one. (pp. 409–410)

Whether or not a contemporary physician would choose to follow this particular rule, it is evident that the eminent Avicenna gave high priority to proper care of the elderly and to appropriate use of alcohol.

Avicenna also wrote in detail about the correct type of wine for specific ailments and conditions affecting all age ranges. He offered careful observations in areas that only recently have undergone controlled empirical research (e.g., absorption of alcohol into the bloodstream).

In the Arabic tradition, we find clear recognition of the difference between constructive and harmful use of alcoholic beverages. Side by side with medical and protoscientific writings on the proper side of alcohol, there appeared diatribes against improper use. This is reflected in a long-standing distinction that might seem to represent a contradiction to the outsider: the Koran forbids the use of wine by true believers; nevertheless, Islamic law historically has been interpreted to condone the use of wine as medicine (Lucia, 1963).

The Moderate Life

The wise use of alcoholic beverages was also specified in a significant European tradition. Gruman, in his classic study of humankind's quest for the prolongation of life, distinguishes between those who have sought a super life span and those whose goal has been the achievement of the outer limit of life that is part of nature's basic endowment to our species. Luigi Di Cornaro was an influential advocate of the latter position. This affluent gentleman of the fifteenth century had, by his own admission, lived so indulgently that by his fourth decade he was a shattered, prematurely aged hulk of a person (Cornaro, 1979). Cornaro reformed his ways. He adopted a new life-style marked by the classical virtues of discipline and moderation.

The fact that this articulate wastrel-turned-sage proceeded to live vigorously well into his ninth decade did much to cause widespread dissemination (if not necessarily emulation) of his views. The Cornaro approach included the daily, moderate use of wine as a source of nutrition, aid to digestion, and inducement to serenity.

As a notable figure in the prehistory of modern geriatrics, Cornaro illustrates the tradition that holds (1) that individuals have it within their power to influence their health and longevity in the second half of life; (2) that moderation in all spheres is a wise approach; and (3) that wine contributes positively to this life span.

The ground rules laid down by Cornaro and others in this tradition are important to bear in mind. Excessive use of alcoholic beverages was condemned. A person was ill-advised if he thought he could make up for a failed or failing life by turning to the jug. The use of alcoholic beverages by the elderly thus was neither good nor bad in itself. *How* the beverages were used was the significant point—as part of a constructive life-style or as symbol of psycho-moral deterioration and capitulation.

Assertions, Not Evidence

Attention has been called to the differentiation made in both the European and Arabian traditions between proper and improper use of alcoholic beverages. Yet from time to time, disapproval has been expressed of *any* use of alcoholic beverages, even if for such limited purposes as comforting the aged and ill. Even the Arabian physicians with their scrupulous specifications and qualifications occasionally were accused of trying to make old people drunk. Disapproval, distrust, and anger concerning the use of alcoholic beverages in the later years of life remains a component of our contemporary attitudinal mix and will be touched upon again later in this book.

The reputed benefits of alcohol were not limited to the elderly, of course. Physicians recommended strong drink for those suffering pain or shock (as during surgery in the preanesthesia days). Beverages were served to those who had lost blood or were otherwise fatigued and debilitated. Fastidious people in the fourteenth century were advised to use alcoholic beverages as mouthwashes (which may have been preferable to actually imbibing some of the crude concoctions of the times). Well in advance of modern conceptions of infection, some thirteenth-century medical authorities applied alcohol to the site of wounds and incisions for antiseptic purposes. Such a use had already been adumbrated by descriptions in the *Iliad* and *Odyssey,* which also mentioned the sedative and nutritional values of alcohol (wine, specifically).

Despite their long tradition of sanctioned use, however, the objective efficacy of alcoholic beverages remains open to question. A clear example

is the prescription of sherry-sack to prevent plague during London's cata-
strophic 1665 epidemic. This serves to remind us that claims for the salutary
effects of alcoholic beverages (and other presumably therapeutic substances) must be viewed critically, no matter what their place in history.

At the one extreme, it is easy to dismiss the sherry-sack claim as a
desperate projection beyond actual knowledge. At the other extreme, it is
easy to accept the statements of many older people through the years to the
effect that they felt alcoholic beverages made life more tolerable or satisfying to them. The area of serious question encompasses the vast range
between the two extremes. From history we learn that alcoholic beverages
were recommended for many problems and disorders, including those of
the elderly. Precisely how effective such beverages were for their various
purposes cannot be gleaned from history; still less are we able to determine
the modality of action: how do these beverages work, if they actually do
work? These questions will be examined later in the light of current
knowledge.

Destructive Effects of Alcohol

The dangers of alcohol abuse have been known for centuries, at least in
their more obvious aspects. But the widespread effects of alcohol abuse are
largely a more recent development. Like many other problems that have
burgeoned along with the growth of the "modern" life-style, alcohol abuse
was set into motion by a combination of technological and socioeconomic
circumstances.

One of the necessary elements was the availability of an alcoholic
beverage stronger than wine or beer. While other alchemists worked to
transmute lead into gold, a ninth-century Arabian, Jabir ibn Hayyan, developed an effective process of distillation. He is also credited as the person
who gave this substance the name that it has carried through all the suc-
ceeding centuries. "Alkuhl" referred originally to a cosmetic preparation
made of powdered antimony. It was a finely ground and therefore subtle
material. Beverages that unleashed a potent but invisible force could be
thought of as having a spiritual essence as subtle as "alkuhl." Interestingly,
a competing derivation of this term has also been proposed by some historians, but this also comes from the Arabic. "Alguhul" referred to an evil
spirit or malicious ghost.

If Hayyan invented an effective distillation process, it remained for
others to comprehend its "market value." Near the end of the thirteenth
century, a professor of medicine at the University of Montpellier burst
forth with the discovery that here, indeed, was the "water of immortality"
that people had been seeking for centuries. Arnaldus de Villanova labeled
this wondrous substance *aqua vitae,* "and this name is remarkably suit-
able, since it is really a water of immortality. It prolongs life, clears away

ill-humors, revives the heart, and maintains youth'' (*Arnald*, 1943), Apparently this triumph of medicine (conceived as a gift from the deity) is the preparation known today as brandy. Claims for its powers were extensive.

At this point, however, strong spirits were envisioned by alchemists and physicians as a major breakthrough for human health and well-being. The usual warnings about overindulgence were issued. It took another breakthrough for the medical triumph to capsize into social catastrophe, and it took another professor of medicine to achieve it. Franciscus Sylvius, a seventeenth-century professor at the University of Leyden, succeeded (whether by intent or accident is not known) in concocting a substance that was so relentlessly distilled that it consisted of very little else but alcohol. The Dutch called it *junever*, referring to the juniper herb that was used in an effort to mask the raw, unpleasant taste. The British called it gin.

Here is where economic considerations came to the fore. The new and powerful distilled spirits were made from grain. And it became obvious that money was to be made from changing grain into gin (or vodka). In 1690, the British government passed ''An Act for the Encouraging of the Distillation of Brandy and Spirits from Corn.'' As Roueché reports, nearly a million gallons were produced annually within four years, and this amount soon doubled and tripled (Keller et al., 1974). By 1742, about 20 million gallons were being produced—and consumed!

The availability of gin and other powerful spirits came at a time when rural people were heading toward London and other cities in search of a better life. Many found misery instead. Impoverished, rootless, diseased, subject to pollution and violence, they became the forerunners of many slum dwellers in centuries to come. The new life held more confusion, deprivation, and terror than promise. Comfort would be taken where it could be found.

The famous graphics of Hogarth in his Gin Alley and Rake's Progress depictions illustrate better than words the impact of strong spirits on a dis-spirited population. Alcohol solved problems for the moment, or dissolved the impulse to care about them. Over a period of time, however, alcohol bred patterns of long-range destruction in human lives. That juncture of history at which cheap, strong drink was newly available and humans were trapped in new and unbearable life circumstances provided an excellent breeding ground for abolitionists. Indeed, a temperance reaction did establish itself within a few years but was unable to stem the tide. The governments learned to make their own adjustments: if strong drink could not easily be eliminated, why not make the most of it? Taxes were steadily increased until revenue from sale of alcoholic beverages became a sort of addiction for the government itself (thereby compromising its ability to take effective action against alcohol abuse).

Other strong spirits became available. One further example is worth citing. Rumbullion, the alcoholic essence of fermented molasses, was distilled in Boston as early as 1657. It enjoyed a phenomenal success. The result was the making of many fortunes and the development of a rum-driven industry with significant international components. The process of procuring and shipping molasses from the West Indies soon became linked with the slave trade. It is too simple to blame the rise of slavery on American shores on rum and its profit motive, but there is probably no other single reason that was more important. The misery and degradation associated with slavery over the years, and with its long, painful lingerings into our own day, must be counted among the destructive effects of alcoholic beverages. It is easiest to recognize the destructive potential of alcohol when we see a person disabled by drink. But the social consequences are broader and perhaps even more destructive if not quite as obvious to the eye.

It has been estimated that the economic cost associated with alcohol abuse in the United States is in the range of $25 billion a year (Keller et al., 1974). Any such estimate can only be approximate because comprehensive and dependable data are not fully available on many of the component factors that contribute to this cost, such as absenteeism and poor job performance, medical costs, accidents, and welfare payments. Furthermore, the cost factor, staggering as it is, serves as an index for other destructive consequences of alcohol abuse that one cannot really calculate in financial terms. The National Highway Traffic Safety Administration has estimated that between $6 and $7 billion a year in expenses can be directly related to vehicular accidents and alcohol alone, but this figure barely hints at the human suffering and loss inovlved. As in many other spheres of alcohol effect, the destructive consequences are not limited to the person who has misused alcohol but extend often to family, friends, colleagues, employers, as well as to complete strangers (such as in the case of car accidents). There is no disputing the general pattern of destructive effects related to the abuse of alcohol in the United States and in a number of other comparable nations. These effects reach into many areas of our lives as individuals and as a society. New data are continuing to emerge on specific alcohol-related problems, such as alcohol's effect on the unborn child. While knowledge will continue to develop in many specific areas of alcohol-related destructiveness and while trends may come and go in the scope and magnitude of these problems, it is clear that alcohol abuse is among this nation's major health, economic, and social problems. This is not to say that we would be free from major problems if alcoholic beverages were unknown or that the availability of alcohol is an adequate explanation for the problems. It is perhaps most appropriate to see alcohol as both a "cause" and an "effect" in a complex interactive system.

It is no wonder, then, that antipathy and fear have become among the most dominant attitudes associated with the use of alcoholic beverages. On the other hand, the moderate use of alcoholic beverages also enjoys a long tradition. To paraphrase the cliche, it might not be sensible to throw out the aged with the aqua vitae.

Under what conditions and for what purposes can alcoholic beverages be condoned or even recommended for use by the elderly? And under what conditions should the destructive potential of alcohol generate appropriate alarm in us? These are among the major questions that will be explored throughout this book.

REFERENCES

Anonymous. *The book of the thousand nights and a night* (fourteenth century from ninth-century sources). Several versions currently available.

Anonymous, *The epic of Gilgamesh* (circa 3000 B.C.) (H. Mason. trans.). New York: New American Library (Mentor), 1972.

Arnald of Villanova's Book on Wine (1310, Naples) (H. E. Sigerist, trans.). New York: Schuman, 1943.

Cornaro, L. *Sure and certain methods of attaining a long and healthy life* (1563). New York: Arno Press, 1979.

Griffin, J. J. The Bible and old age. *Journal of Gerontology*, 1946, *1*, 464–472.

Gruner, O. C. *A treatise on the canon of medicine of Avicenna.* London: Luzac, 1930.

Kastenbaum, R., & Ross, B. Historical perspectives on care of the aged. In J. G. Howells (Ed.), *Modern perspectives in the psychiatry of old age.* New York: Brunner/Mazel, 1975.

Keller, M., Promisel, D. M., Spiegler, D., Light, L., & Davies, M. N. (Eds.). *Alcohol and health.* Washington D.C.: U.S. Department of Health, Education, and Welfare, 1974.

Lucia, S. P. *A history of wine as therapy.* Philadelphia: J. P. Lippincott, 1963.

Waugh, A. *In praise of wine and certain noble spirits.* NY: Sloane, 1959.

2
Physiological Effects of Alcohol, with Particular Reference to the Aged

Alcoholic beverages are complex substances that have complex effects on us. Before examining the question of abuse versus constructive use of alcohol in old age, it will be useful to review what is known about the basic physiological action of alcohol in general. This will help provide a foundation for evaluating the personal, situational, and sociocultural factors that play important roles in the overall pattern of alcohol use and its consequences. It will also help us avoid either overestimating or underestimating the significance of chronological age per se.

ALCOHOLIC BEVERAGES: BASIC FACTS

Ethanol (Ethyl Alcohol)

The type of alcohol used in beverages is but one of many specific compounds that share the generic name. It is a compound comprised of carbon and hydrogen atoms, with one or more hydroxyl (hydrogen and oxygen) groups attached. Ethanol is simpler in structure (Ch_3CH_2OH) than most of the other forms of alcohol. In its pure form, ethanol is a clear liquid that resembles water but has a faint odor and a strong, burning taste. It flows easily and is readily dissolved in water.

Ethanol and other forms of alcohol to which it is most closely related (methyl and ethylene) have many industrial and commercial uses. Antifreeze and rubbing alcohol are among the most familiar uses around the household, but they also have significant applications as industrial solvents and in the manufacture of inks, dyes, synthetic rubber, and so on. The so-called higher alcohols (those with more atoms in the molecule) are used in cosmetics, soaps, lubricants, and other products. The alcohol family would be an important one, then, even if nobody ever had thought of treating it as a beverage. From this point on, we will be concerned only with ethanol and only with its properties as an agent taken internally.

The Alcohol Content of Beverages

Beverages differ appreciably in their alcohol content. The ethanol content of a particular beverage is expressed by weight and by volume, the latter being in more common usage. Another familiar term of measurement is *proof*. It is easiest to use the United States proof scale as the reference point here: the proof value is derived simply by multiplying the content-by-volume by 2. Thus, a swig of 100% alcohol (not recommended!) would carry a 200-proof rating. The proof rating of a beverage most often comes to the fore when attention is directed to "hard liquor" where the concentration of alcohol is relatively high.

The ethanol content of broad classes of beverages is given in Table 2.1. The classifications include the beer family, table wines, dessert or cocktail wines, liquors, distilled beverages, and a sampling of other fermented beverages that have been favored by particular national or ethnic groups. The ethanol content is expressed here in terms of percent by volume.

To keep the alcohol content of a beverage within perspective, it is necessary to remind ourselves that the typical serving varies in amount from one type to another. A shot of whiskey, for example, generally consists of between 1 and 1½ oz. of liquor, while beer is usually consumed in 8- or 12-oz. servings. Obviously, then, we will find different physiological effects if we compare two identical "doses" than if we compare two typical "servings" of different beverages. It is also obvious that the typical serving of beverages with higher alcohol concentrations is usually smaller.

Congeners: The Nonethanol Constituents

There is more to beverages than their ethanol content. The nonethanol constituents are usually grouped together under the rubric *congeners,* although not everybody is happy with that term. By whatever term the nonethanol constituents are known, however, they contribute much both to the taste and to the biochemical effect. The nonethanol constituents can be subdivided into traces of other forms of alcohol and a variety of other nonalcoholic components. Laboratory studies that utilize various concentrations of ethanol without congeners have methodological rectitude on

Table 2.1
Alcohol Content (Percent by Volume)
in Various Beverages[a]

Beverage	Alcohol % by Volume	
Beers	4.8	
Lager	4.8	
Malt	6.4	
Bock	5.7	
Stout	7.0	
Table wines		
White, dry	11.9	
White, sweet	12.4	
Red	12.2	
Rose	12.2	
Champagne	12.5	
Dessert wines		
Port	19.8	
Muscatel	19.7	
Sherry[b]	20	
Vermouth, dry	17.7	
Vermouth, sweet	17.1	
Liquers (selected)		
Benedictine	43	
Cointreau	40	
Creme de menthe	29	
Irish or Scotch-based	39–40	
Ouzo	46	
Rock-and-rye	32	
Distilled spirits		
Brandy	43[c]	50[c]
Gin	40	50
Rum	40	50
Tequila	40	50
Vodka	40	50
Whiskey	43	50
Fermented beverages favored by particular ethnic groups		
Apple cider	3.5–13.5	
Mead (honey wine)	10[d]	
Pulque (cactus wine)	6	
Sake (rice-based)	12–16	

[a] Based on data compiled by Leake and Silverman (1966).

[b] Percentage is almost identical for all forms of sherry.

[c] Distilled spirits most commonly are available in two standard concentrations (e.g., 80 or 100 proof), although exceptions can be found.

[d] Commecial producers of mead, one of the most ancient of alcoholic beverages, sometimes add distilled spirits that increase the alcohol content. All the fermented beverages in this group have a fairly variable level of alcohol content when made on a noncommercial basis.

their side. They provide the clearest opportunity to study direct effects of ethanol on the body or its subsystems. Such studies can be generalized to "real-life" consumption and effects of typical beverages only with some risk, however, as the congeners in beverages affect both their appeal and their effects on the individual.

All beverages that consist of more than ethanol and water contain some mixture of congeners. Our preferences for one class of beverage over another or for one particular brand or variety are often based on the blend of congeners that create distinctive color, aroma, and taste. The research literature in this area has increased in quantity and sophistication since the late 1950s, when the gas-liquid chromatography method of analysis was first applied. It was found, for example, that scotch has appreciably fewer congeners than do rye and bourbon. Specific differences were noted between "old" (pre-Prohibition era samples) and modern bourbon and between raw and matured ("aged") samples, and so on.

In his pioneering research, R. B. Carroll identified and measured the compounds known as acetaldehyde, ethyl formate, ethyl acetate, methanol, n-propanol, and isoamyl alcohol in whisky, vodka, gin, and wine. The content of these congeners varied appreciably among the different types of beverage. Vodka was the "purest" (most congener-free) of the beverages tested, with only 3 g of all the above per 100 liters, while bourbon showed 285 g per 100 liters. The obtained difference was mostly due to ethyl acetate and isoamyl alcohol components (Carroll, 1970). It became clear that equivalent servings of vodka (or gin) and whisky contain significantly different concentrations of nonethanol components. This, of course, tends to support the experiences of drinkers who feel that the two classes of beverage affect them in different ways.

An even broader range of congeners has been set forth by Leake and Silverman (1966). The specific values cannot be assumed to have remained entirely constant (the same should be said of the Carroll data), as the nature of the beverages themselves shift to some extent over the years as methods of production are altered. The data remain useful as instructive guides, however, and the reader is referred to the detailed tables presented by Leake and Silverman. For our immediate purposes, it may be sufficient just to note the diversity of nonethanol and nonalcoholic components that has been identified in various concentrations in the more popular types of beverage.

In beer, for example, we can find carbon dioxide, flouride, hydrogen sulfide, phosphate, sulfur dioxide, calcium, copper, iron, magnesium, potassium, sodium, lactic acid, tannins, amino acids, ammonia, thiamine, riboflavin, panththenic acid, pyridoxine, nicotinic acid and biotin. Beer contains peptides, which are protein-degradation products, and energy-producing sugars and maltodextrins. While concentrations of acid in beer conventionally are subsumed under the "lactic" rubric, they actually include traces of many specific acids including citric and tartaric. Beer obviously contains much more than just ethanol.

Wine has many of the same components, in different concentrations. There are some important differences among wines that reflect the nature of the soil in which the grapes were grown. These differences show up particularly in the traces of inorganic compounds such as manganese, potassium, iodine, and the ferrous form of iron that is ready for physiological utilization. The congeners of wine appear to be especially complex. This complexity plays a significant role in the differences that sensitive consumers observe between one wine and another. Scientists are also challenged by the complexity of wine and have continued to examine its components and their physiological effects. We will touch base with a few of the findings and hypotheses at appropriate places in this book.

One of the important physiological differences between wine and hard liquors is associated with their respective nonethanol components. Wines are relatively rich in tannins. Beers and wines also have a relatively high concentration of various kinds of solids. The tannins and solids seem to be operative in maintaining a relatively slow absorption rate of alcohol. The alcohol in whisky, brandy, vodka, and gin is absorbed more rapidly. This means that the classes of beverage that have higher concentrations of alcohol to begin with also tend to have faster absorption rates. It comes as no surprise, then, to learn that physiological (and behavioral) responses differ depending on the particular type of beverage used.

MAJOR PHYSIOLOGICAL EFFECTS OF ALCOHOL BEVERAGES

Most contemporary researchers emphasize the complexity of effects related to the ingestion of alcohol. In addition, we would also like to emphasize the distinction between results based on administration of ethanol in various concentrations (a common research strategy) and the effects of the more complex beverages that are actually consumed outside of the laboratory. The real-life physiological effects are certainly related to the congeners as well as to the ethanol, but they may also be related to social context, personal expectations, and other variables that differentiate a laboratory from a naturalistic situation. The gap between animal research and conclusions about physiological effects in humans must be kept in mind as well. Furthermore, since there have been few systematic studies of alcohol effects on the *aged,* one must be cautious about generalizations in this direction as well. In addition, there are many empirical and theoretical questions about the physiological effects of alcoholic beverages that are far from settled today. One must be ready to revise conclusions—and attitudes—as new data continue to be developed.

One more caveat: Researchers and those who support or fail to support their work and who publish or decline to publish their findings all are part of a society that has a mixture of attitudes toward alcohol. There are people among us who believe alcoholic beverages to be amiable companions and enhancers of life, while others view brewed, fermented, and distilled spirits as hazardous and wicked. It would be more than a little naive to assume that the interplay of widely disseminated attitudes has somehow bypassed the scientific community. Research and theory in many other areas have been influenced by cultural expectations and pressures. The person who is careful about drawing conclusions will bear these dynamics in mind as one more possible source of complexity in understanding the effects of alcoholic beverages. We are not speaking of improprieties in the design, conduct, or reporting of the studies themselves. We simply wonder how equitable a balance has been achieved between studies mostly aimed at demonstrating deleterious effects and those aimed at demonstrating positive effects of alcohol, and whether bias in one direction or the other has not intruded inadvertently into studies intended to be cast in a completely nonjudgmental orientation. Each person who examines the literature will have to come to his or her own conclusion.

Effects on the Nervous System

It is somewhat artificial to examine the effects of a particular agent, such as ethanol, upon any one organ or system in abstraction from the others. The body does not operate that simply. With due caution, however, we can attend to major effects of ethanol on both the cellular level and on the integrative action of the nervous system.

There is a fairly well known distinction between the effects people sometimes seek or seem to attain with the use of alcoholic beverages and the basic action of ethanol itself. Some individuals drink for a "high," and yet alcohol is known physiologically as a depressant. In other words, the ingestion of alcohol is associated with a decrease in physiological function. In this sense, ethanol can be classified among the narcotics, agents that produce a reversible decrement in physiological activity. It should be noted, however, that even on the physiological level alone, it is not appropriate to assume that alcohol or any other narcotic-like substance has an identical effect on all components of the cell. Ethanol might reduce or, let us say, inhibit the activity of some cellular components and thereby increase or "release" the functioning of others. This situation could prevail on the multicellular level as well. Ethanol could depress physiological functioning in some sybsystems with a resulting increased activation of others.

The person who feels more highly aroused after consuming alcohol might, then, be responding to bodily feedback from subsystems that have been temporarily heightened in activity through the inhibition of other physiological mechanisms. This, of course, is not the only possible explanation of the subjective and behavioral outcomes of drinking. It does suggest, however, a physiological reality for the paradoxial sense of "feeling high" when using an agent that basically *decreases* functioning.

The relationship between physiological effect and personal experience can be pursued further. Consider dosage level, for example. It has been known since the late eighteenth century that a low concentration of ethanol increases the excitability of neurons. A higher concentration, however, will have the opposite effect (Knutsson, 1961). This significant physiological phenomenon seems to find its counterpart in the experience and behavior of people who move from light to moderate to heavy intake of alcoholic beverages. (Reference is made here to a limited time frame, such as an evening's "social drinking," but there may also be applicability to long-term patterns as well.)

An important research observation, now well confirmed, adds still another dimension. Ethanol has a *biphasic* effect on brain acetylcholine level (Hunt & Dalton, 1976). Acetycholine is a neurotransmitter; therefore, variations in brain level might be expected to be associated with more pervasive effects throughout the nervous system. A single dose of ethanol leads first to an increase and then to a decrease in the acetylcholine level. Perhaps this should be known as a triphasic effect, because the acetycholine level subsequently rebounds when the concentration of ethanol further declines. Thus, there are *phases* of relative excitation and inhibition even with a single dose or drink of ethanol, as well as with continued ingestion. It seems less surprising as we examine the physiological side of drinking that a person might experience differential effects rather than one simple response.

Still another factor that must be considered is the accumulative effect of ethanol on cellular structures. Until recently, most physiological research has focused on the acute or short-range effects. In the realm of human thought, behavior, and interaction, we are often interested in long-term patterns of response. The cell or organism with a history of ethanol intake is likely to respond differentially to the same dose that is administered to one who has never so indulged.

Detailed reviews of the research literature (e.g., Mullins, 1954; Wallgren & Barry, 1970; Grenell, 1971; Ellingboe, 1978) offer a wealth of information for those who are interested in the whole, emerging story of alcohol effects on the nervous system. We have selected several points for their intrinsic significance and for their sociobehavioral implications:

1. Ethanol passes through the blood-brain barrier. How much passes through depends on a number of factors, among which the efficiency of the liver can be cited as of particular importance. The liver has been estimated to be about 5000 times more powerful than the brain in breaking down ethanol into its metabolic products (Raskin & Sokoloff, 1972).

2. Ethanol has a *variety* of effects on the central nervous system (CNS), whether we are considering the individual neuron or the larger system. Which effects are "primary" and which "secondary," and which effects have the most substantial influence on the behavioral level are difficult to determine.

3. The effects of ethanol appear to be most powerful on cell membranes and their biochemical fields. When a sufficient concentration of ethanol has developed, there is a decrease in the permeability of neuronal membranes and in ion conductance. Calcium level is also affected, thereby altering the release of acetycholine at synapses. Although other direct and indirect consequences of ethanol have been found on the cellular level, it is probable that the effects on conductance of nervous impulses hold the key to the systemic influence of alcohol (e.g., Wallgren & Barry, 1970).

4. The effect on synaptic transmission has an important bearing on ethanol as an *anesthetic* agent. The anesthetic effects of alcohol are physiological as well as subjective.

5. Studies using the evoked potential method[1] indicate that ethanol may suppress both the excitatory and the inhibitory functions of the nervous system (Weiss, Mendelson, & LaDou, 1964; Begleiter & Platz, 1972). This suppression effect is not the same for both, however, as there is greater suppression of excitation. Furthermore, as greater concentrations of ethanol build up, the differential increases—the more ethanol, the greater suppression of excitatory as contrasted with inhibitory functions.

6. Electroencephalographic (EEG) studies demonstrate a general slowing of wave frequencies and an increase in the percentage time of alpha activity. These basic findings have been reported for three decades, beginning with the pilot work of Davis et al. (1941). To the extent that EEG readings provide dependable information about the electrical functioning of the human brain, it would appear that alcohol induces more synchrony and stability in the total pattern of cerebral electrical activity. Such a pattern is associated in general with a "resting" or "less responsive" state of the organism. Some researchers

---

[1]The deliberate stimulation of the brain or some component of its sensory system to detect possible changes in electrical activity.

believe the EEG pattern more closely resembles mild (and reversible) anoxia rather than light sleep. There are numerous research observations indicative of relationship between EEG changes and subjective/behavioral alterations with the ingestion of alcohol in humans (e.g., Varga & Nagy, 1960), but there is also good reason to be cautious in taking either set of changes to be a reliable index, let alone a "cause" of the other.

7. Marked individual differences have repeatedly been observed in both the electrical activity of the brain and the more-or-less accompanying behavioral changes. Some of these differences can be attributed to the individual's history of alcohol use: both true alcoholism and experimentally produced conditions of temporary alcoholism (e.g., Isbell et al. 1955) lead to higher levels of *toleration*. There must be more ethanol ingested to yield the effects that a lesser amount has on a person with a more limited history of drinking. This is not an adequate explanation for the total range of variation, however. EEG patterns differ appreciably among individuals before, during, and after the use of alcohol. Accordingly, the research literature includes many cautionary statements against the hasty application of "general" findings, since one of the general findings is that people are so different from each other!

8. Low concentrations of ethanol have differential effects throughout the CNS, but high concentrations have a diffuse effect. This is still another physiological support for the drinker's experience that "going easy" can produce subtle and varied body feedback, while "serious drinking" may court the "blotto effect."

9. "There is little evidence for a stimulant or beneficial effect of any alcohol dose on any sensory capability"—so concluded Wallgren & Barry (1970, p. 315) after an extensive review of the literature. Detrimental effects on sensory fucntion are the rule, but these differ in magnitude. There is not much effect on the detection of weak visual and auditory signals, for example, but a more marked effect on the ability to discriminate between different intensities in the same modality.

10. It has already been implied in this section that the differential inhibition of certain structures or subsystems can "release" or "disinhibit" other functions. Examples have been demonstrated in the realm of sensory functioning. Binocular vision requires that the image obtained through one eye be subordinated to the other. Ethanol can interfere with this process, so that both images are seen at the same time. This is one more illustration of the oversimplification involved when we speak of alcohol as a depressant or an inhibitor, although there is something to be said for these concepts in a very broad sense.

Sleep

Although sleep could be included under the general rubric of ethanol effects on the nervous system, this is an organismic state of such relevance to the problems examined in this book that it deserves separate attention. Some of our own research on possible beneficial effects of alcoholic beverages for elderly people has centered on sleep and its correlates. In this brief section, we will try to limit attention to physiological aspects, although, in practice, these are best considered in conjunction with the behavioral and situational.

In their valuable review of the alcohol–sleep connection, Williams and Salamy (1972) also capture the gist of the general awakening of research interest in sleep: "Along with advances in electrophysiological, pharmacological, and behavioral technology which occurred during the past two decades, there emerged a conviction that sleep was not simply a passive, resting state, somewhere near the lower pole of a continuum of vigilance. Instead, sleep was seen as a complex, constantly changing but cyclic succession of active psychophysiological phenomena, qualitatively, not quantitatively, different from those of waking" (p. 435). They quickly added that "Despite the extraordinary growth of research on sleep, its phenomenology, its mechanisms, and its response to drugs, there have been remarkably few systematic studies of the acute or chronic effects of alcohol on this complex state, either in humans or animals" (p. 436). They note that two of the major limiting factors in our knowledge have been the lack of clarity about the neural sites of action and biochemical targets of alcohol and the paucity of systematic conceptions about the basic neurobiological mechanisms of sleep. As we will see below, research on the neural receptors of various substances that affect the functioning of the CNS has yielded some provocative findings since the Williams and Salamy review. Conceptions of the neurobiological mechanisms of sleep are still in transition, as might be expected in a field that is still so new and active.

Many facts about sleep have been established in recent years, chiefly through analysis of electroencephalographic (EEC) patterns. This information has been widely disseminated, but it might be helpful to offer a very brief summary. Human sleep can be understood as consisting of four stages (Dement & Kleitman, 1957) through a normal night's repose. For the awake individual the EEG typically shows an alpha rhythm dominance in the range of 8–12 cycles/sec (cps), most saliently associated with the occipital region. During stage 1 sleep, EEG waves become slower and stronger. Alpha gradually is replaced by 4–6 cps theta waves. Stage 2 is marked by 12–15 cps spindles known as sigma waves. While the "background" waves are of low voltage, another form of electrical activity streaks across in spontaneous or seemingly random episodes. These are high voltage patterns known as K-complexes. Some researchers believe that stage 2 is the beginning of "true" sleep, with stage 1 being a drowsy in-between state. The K-complexes are thought to be temporary arousal states that are related to the detection of stimuli—perhaps the physiological substrate for the dog slumbering by the fireside with one ear up and one eye half open.

Stage 3 brings with it higher-voltage slow-moving delta waves at about 1–4 cps. This is followed by stage 4 in which the delta waves that ripple through the existing background of electrical activity become the dominant pattern.

The total four-stage cycle lasts for about 90 minutes in adults. The amount of time spent in each stage changes, however, throughout the night. Delta sleep has its longest stay in the first cycle, typically enduring for about 30 minutes. With every repetition of the cycle, the individual spends less time in the delta stage—which many characterize as the deepest valley of sleep. By contrast, there is a steady increase in the amount of time spent in the rapid eye movement (REM) phase. This phase of sleep takes its name from bursts of rapid eye movements that occur during "unsettled," low-voltage stage 1 activity. REM occurs during stage 1, but not at every moment in that stage. Most people today know that interruption of the sleeper during the REM phase often results in the reporting of dreams. This observation (Aserinsky & Kleitman, 1953) stimulated the development of contemporary approaches to the study of the biology of both sleeping and dreaming. It should also be appreciated that the REM phase is marked by a more general alteration in the state of the organism. Through the sleep cycle, most physiological indices show stable or reduced levels. During the REM phase, however, there is an upheaval and increased variability in physiological functions. Changes in respiration seem to be one of the most dependable as well as obvious indices of REM sleep, apart from data on the rapid eye movements themselves. The altered pattern of psychophysiological functioning with REM is perhaps the most "dramatic" observable occurrence during the normal sleep cycle and has attracted much of the research and theory-making. (However, particular attention will be directed to delta sleep in dealing with aging.)

It is also relevant to remind ourselves that the basic paradigm of the stages of sleep, and much of the detailed research that followed, centers on the functioning of healthy young adults, usually males. This was certainly a reasonable subpopulation with which to inaugurate systematic research. We should not be too hasty, however, in transposing these findings to the total range of human variability.

What, then, is the effect of alcohol on sleep? Research has generally followed the format of contemporary sleep studies into the broader range of phenomena. The participant becomes comfortable with the surroundings of a sleep laboratory for a few nights and baseline data are collected, followed by whatever experimental manipulation has been planned. In this instance, the experimental manipulation consists of asking the participant to ingest a certain amount of ethanol and then go to sleep as usual. EEG and measures of autonomic activity monitor the response throughout the night, and other types of observation may be made as well. The participants, as usual, have been normal, healthy young men. The basic studies have been conducted in several different laboratories with different research teams. Results have been consistent enough to suggest that they can be taken as "true-until-proved-otherwise," despite the small number of participants in any one study.

Studies of this type with healthy young men (e.g., Yules et al., 1967) indicate that a moderate dose of alcohol leads to earlier onset of sleep. There is less motility during sleep and a slight increase in the cardiorespiratory rate. REM sleep declines during the first half of the first "alcohol night." There tends to be a rebound effect during the second half of the night. In fact, when the study is continued over a longer period of time, REM sleep not only rebounds but may exceed its baseline level. Normal (healthy and nonalcoholic) participants seem to adapt quickly to the alcohol effects: the suppression of REM sleep during the first half of the night tends to diminish or disappear in subsequent "alcohol nights" (Knowles et al., 1968). "Slow-wave" sleep tends to increase in the first half of the night and then to decrease in the second half when the alcohol condition is introduced. It appears, then, that moderate intake of alcohol has mirror-image effects on the two major types of sleep, REM and slow wave. The effects on slow-wave sleep usually do not seem to be as substantial as the REM effects. The sleep alterations summarized above can be related, at least in part, to the level of blood alcohol concentration (e.g., Rundell et al., 1972). The basic cycling of sleep through its stages does not seem to be affected by the moderate use of alcohol. It is chiefly the duration of time spent in each phase, as well as some of the autonomic correlates, that shows alteration. Individual differences are also important here as in other types of physiological research with humans.

Naturally, researchers have also been interested in the sleep patterns of people with histories of alcoholism. Individuals with chronic intoxication show suppression of REM sleep (e.g., Zarcone et al., 1975). Furthermore, their sleep tends to become fragmented. There are frequent awakenings and frequent changes in the EEG state (e.g., Mello & Mendelson, 1971). When alcoholics are in a withdrawal period, there is usually a further increase in the severity of sleep fragmentation.

The pattern of slow-wave sleep with alcoholics seems to be more complex. When compared with alcohol-free periods of time, some addicts show more slow-wave sleep when they are drinking heavily, while others show less. These differences have now been related to the baseline level of slow-wave sleep during their alcohol-free periods (Gross & Hastey, 1975). Alcoholics with relatively low levels of slow-wave sleep during baseline periods show a further reduction in slow-wave sleep when they have been drinking heavily, while those with relatively high baseline levels tend to show an increase. But alcoholics who continue to drink heavily over a period of several days tend to show a reduction in slow-wave sleep whatever their baseline levels had been—thus, if one drinks heavily and consistently enough, slow-wave sleep will be diminished. Researchers are continuing to explore the relationship between baseline and intoxication sleeping patterns in alcoholics.

There has been particular interest—and controversy—concerning the overall effects of withdrawal on the sleep patterns of alcoholics. The alcoholic who is in a period of abstinence often suffers from insomnia (e.g., Victor, 1966). It has been thought by some observers that REM deprivation and insomnia must be closely related to the development of hallucinosis during the withdrawal period (e.g., Feinberg & Evarts, 1969). The leading hypothesis was that when REM rebounds, it becomes so strong that it somehow bursts its way into the waking state. The hallucinations of the "drying-out" alcoholic, then, might represent the displacement of REM activity. The alcoholic is dreaming while he is awake, and the combination of states is an unsettling one, to say the least. There has been some support for this view. Highly disturbing nightmares, for example, have been reported shortly before the onset of outright hallucinations in alcoholics during the withdrawal period (Johnson et al., 1970). Subsequent research, however, suggests that REM does not rebound in all alcoholics (e.g., Gross & Hastey, 1975). Nancy Mello, a leading researcher in this area, concludes that one can no longer assume a close parallel between dreams and REM activity (Mello, 1978). She reports ". . . there is no invariant association between vivid dreams and hallucinatory episodes and REM activity. Neither did there appear to be a continuum of sequential changes which progressed from perceptual alteration, to illusions, to vivid dreams, to hallucinations during chronic intoxication and withdrawal. An alcohol-induced suppression of REM activity followed by REM hyperactivity during alcohol withdrawal was not consistently observed. Most important, hallucinations were observed during intoxication as well as during alcohol withdrawal" (Mello, 1978, p. 1632).

The two broad types of research we have sampled here—normal versus alcoholic participants—have made it clear that the effects of moderate and excessive use of alcohol must be distinguished. Williams and Salamy (1972) review evidence that strongly suggests the differential may be related to brain damage among alcoholics. Animal experiments, for example, have indicated that slow-wave sleep requires an intact cerebrum (Jouvet et al., 1964, and in several other studies). REM sleep appears to be mostly dependent on other CNS structures, some of which may also be damaged or out of synchrony in many alcoholics. It is unwise to assume that alcohol has the same effect on sleeping patterns of normal and alcoholic individuals.

How much is "special" about the effect of ethanol on the sleep pattern of normal and alcoholic individuals is not yet entirely clear. Many researchers have noted that ethanol effects on sleep resemble those of other drugs in some respects and also that stress, illness, and any generalized "challenge" to the CNS can have effects that are in some way comparable. The differential, then, between normal and alcoholic individuals in their response to alcohol may come down to the difference between people with intact and those with damaged nervous systems in adapting to *any* challenge. This is by no means to deny an important degree of specificity related to alcohol as such. It is simply to caution against automatically assuming that the effects of alcohol are completely distinctive and therefore can be evaluated without taking into account the individual's ability to cope with stimulation and challenge along a broader spectrum. One major vein of research here has been the effort to distinguish alcohol from barbiturate effects on sleeping and on brain functioning in general. This work has generated several hypotheses related to the nature and processes of sleep in general. We will pick up on some of this material in a later chapter, where attention is given specifically to sleep patterns in the aged.

This brief and selected review of a very complex set of phenomena— the alcohol–sleep connection—should not conclude without at least a mention of the biogenic amines in regulating sleep. Researchers now tend to agree that sleep is an active process and that it may not be too farfetched to speak of a "sleep arousal system." It is not just that other things stop happening in our CNS, and we then "fall" asleep. Certain positive changes must occur as well. Among the physiologically active agents that have been linked to sleep arousal, we find increasing reference to a set of amino acids. *Serotonin* is one of the leading candidates, as Williams and Salamy put it, for the role of the major "hypnogogic" agent. For the moment, it is enough to file away the thought that our bodies may naturally produce sleep-inducing elixirs whose availability and levels can have much to do with the quantity and quality of repose we enjoy. This topic does not necessarily bring ethanol to mind. A "dose" of properly diluted ethanol administered as part of an experiment does not in itself contain biogenic amines, although it is appropriate to examine possible effects on such amines. The possible role of alcoholic *beverages,* however, becomes more interesting in this respect when we recall that these beverages usually comprise a variety of congeners as well. In turn, this line of inquiry will lead us in a later chapter to consider possible effects of wine on sleeping patterns.

If nothing else, perhaps this discussion has established that the relationship between alcohol and sleeping patterns is a relevant one to consider as we continue to pursue the use and abuse of alcohol in old age.

Sedation

People sometimes drink "for relaxation," although this is not always the effect achieved. The possibility that alcohol has a sedative effect deserves separate attention here because, like sleep, it is one of the topics that has been fairly systematically pursued in the clinical research literature examined later in this book.

Conceptually and methodologically, it is not easy to establish the precise relationship between the use of alcoholic beverages and effects that could be called tranquilizing or sedative. Naitoh (1972), for example, has pointed out that it is naive to assume that "an increase or decrease of one autonomic activity will directly and unambiguously reflect a certain physiological or psychological state . . . (or) warrant a uniform psychological interpretation, such as an increase or decrease of the level of anxiety" (p. 422). In other words, we confront the familiar problem of an imperfect correspondence between the "objective" (if that is what the physiological status of an individual is) and the "subjective" (inner experience or its more overt messenger, self-report). A person might *feel* as though he or she is more relaxed with a drink in hand, although physiological indices of reduced tension may be ambiguous, weak, or contradictory. Similarly, physiological indices of reduced tension do not necessarily mean that the individual feels more relaxed or in a better state of mind. We can choose to believe the physiological *or* the subjective *or* the behavioral (the individual as observed by others) indices. The three sources of information will not always converge into a consistent picture.

The *situation* in which the use of alcohol occurs has been shown to be an influential variable in the effect of ethanol on the autonomic nervous system as well as on self-reported anxiety (e.g., McDonnell & Carpenter, 1959). It makes a difference, for example, whether one drinks alone or with others. One cannot generalize securely from a measure such as skin conductance level (often interpreted as a physiological index of arousal or tension) to the individual's self-reported experience.

Efforts to specify precisely *how* alcohol achieves a sedative or anxiety-reduction outcome can seem premature when there is so much difficulty in determining if such an effect is actually present. Coopersmith and Woodrow (1967), for example, found that the usual "young, adult males" showed a lowered skin conductance level and presumably a lowered level of arousal/anxiety after a shot of whiskey. This effect occurred in a situation in which the participants were thought to be experiencing some mild and vague distress prior to the drink. A previous study by Coopersmith (1964) had demonstrated that the same kind of participants were better able to pay attention to the demands of a task when their anxiety level presumably had been lowered by a drink. The sensitive observer, however, would probably distinguish between arousal level and anxiety in such performances. A moderate serving of whisky might have the effect of lowering anxiety and heightening arousal in the same situation. This can sound contradictory and paradoxical—it rather depends on definitions and our sensitivity to the phenomena. As students of human behavior, we might be able to appreciate the difference between a tense, uncomfortable form of arousal that could be called "anxiety," and a state of alert, exuberant arousal for which a more positive term might be sought. It is for reasons such as these that it is difficult to come up with a simple set of conclusions on the alcohol-sedation link.

For the moment, we suggest that the physiological changes associated with use of alcohol can be interpreted in various ways by the individual. Whether the overall perceived effect is one of tension decrease or increase depends on individual history and expectations, the nature of the situation, and everything else that goes into making the person what he or she is. There is no reason to doubt that some individuals under some circumstances experience a tranquilizing or sedative effect from the use of alcoholic beverages. Others, as we know all too well, become dangerously aggressive and violent. This is a reaction we do not ordinarily associate with relaxed well-being. Because it is so difficult to examine the purely physiological connection between alcohol and sedation when the psychosocial phenomena are so pervasive, we will reserve further discussion of this point for specific contexts, particularly involving the aged.

Metabolism and Nutrition

The role of alcohol as a nutrient and as an active agent in the metabolic process has not always received the attention it deserves. Alcohol is readily absorbed through all mucous membranes. In humans, it is the small intestine that absorbs most of the alcohol taken in as part of beverage ingestion (about 80 percent), while the remainder is absorbed from the stomach. We have already mentioned that the rate of absorption is influenced by the alcohol concentration and the type and amount of congeners in the beverage; the condition of the gastric mucosa and the emptying time of the stomach also affect absorption rate. The absorption rate is important for its impact on general physiological and behavioral effects. We can see the role of situation and even of ethnic-cultural background here. The person who drinks on an empty stomach will feel the effects of alcohol more quickly and more potently than the person who consumes the beverage along with a meal. Life-style factors that encourage solitary and alienated drinking behavior increase the "punch" of alcohol, often with increased risk to physiological integrity and behavior control. Cultural patterns in which people sit down together and share food and conversation as well as drink result in a more gradual release of alcohol into the general metabolism. The release of alcohol into the bloodstream leads to quick distribution throughout the body and the attainment of an equilibrium with the water content of the tissues.

The alcohol itself serves as a direct nutrient. It is generally accepted that approximately 7 calories of energy are yielded by a gram of alcohol (Leake & Silverman, 1966). The metabolization of alcohol speeds up with increasing doses. The type of beverage also makes a difference: most people metabolize beer and wine faster than whiskey. The metabolization (or oxidation) of alcohol is carried out mostly in the liver. The body does find use for most of the alcohol it takes in under normal circumstances, upwards of 90 percent. The rest is excreted not only through urine but also by breath, saliva, and sweat. The rate of both oxidation and excretion varies appreciably among individuals and probably accounts for some of the psychological differences experienced by drinkers.

The energy made available by alcohol has been estimated to be in the range of 50 calories per hour, although this figure is variable. A person who used only ethanol as a source of nutrition would have only a fraction of the energy needed for hard work. Goldberg (1963) notes that when alcohol becomes part of the daily diet, it can have opposite effects on body weight. If alcohol is added to the established menu, then body weight will likely increase. Prolonged intake, however, sometimes leads to decrease in the utilization of other foods. The person may have enough energy to get by if daily life is not especially demanding of high physical output, but persistence in such a pattern can lead to a number of deficiency diseases. The alcohol itself does not "cause" the ailments, but it becomes part of a dietary pattern that is unbalanced and that invites disorder.

There is, however, a more direct way in which prolonged and excessive use of alcohol can impair nutrition. Forsander (1963) explains this clearly:

Alcohol is an elegant substrate, and it is oxidized in a very simple enzyme system. If alcohol is oxidized in large amounts for a relatively long period, the normal enzyme equipment is not used, and may well degenerate in the same way as other tissues, for instance, an unused muscle. Everything is in order and no disturbances occur as long as alcohol continues to be present as a substrate; but when the excessive drinker attempts to return to a normal diet, difficulties may appear. The drinker is poorly equipped with the enzyme systems needed to utilize the food in a normal diet, and at this point medical aid is advisable. Fortunately the human body is usually able to adapt itself to new conditions, and it can often resume normal functions even without medicines. However, if the changes are irreversible, as in cirrhosis of the liver, then a return to normal is no longer possible. (p. 57)

This situation with respect to metabolism also illustrates the addiction or dependency of the chronic, excessive drinker.

When we consider the total beverage rather than its alcoholic component alone, the dietary picture is, of course, enriched. Minerals and vitamins occur in some beverages but not in others. Grain and fruit-based beverages have sustenance to offer that is related to their earth-grown sources, unless a distilling process has left little but the ethanol. Some of these factors will be considered when we examine wine and health in the aged.

Cardiovascular Effects

One of the most important realms of alcohol effect is also one of the most controversial. Knott and Beard (1972) note that "the literature is abundant with reports extolling the salutary effects of alcohol on the heart and blood vessels; many reports also exist outlining the cardiotoxicity of the drug and condemning its clinical use—and in some instances its social use. Confusion has been the natural consequence" (p. 347). We would prefer not to add to this confusion. Differences in methodology and conceptual orientation account for some of the reported differences (e.g., whether the ethanol is administered intravenously or orally), but there are also gaps in substantive knowledge toward which current research efforts are being directed. The following points are among the most significant ones to keep in mind when considering the positive and negative aspects of alcohol use in old age:

1. The "good feelings" a person may experience when using alcohol do not necessarily mean that the cardiovascular effects are entirely favorable; it is possible for harm to be done while being masked by a temporarily improved subjective condition. The relationship between the subjective and the objective state cannot be assumed.

2. The *functional reserve* of the cardiovascular system may be particularly vulnerable to alcohol. Research by Knott and Beard and others suggests that trauma, heightened stress, and increased work load may be more difficult to handle for people who use alcohol. This would be especially true when "excessive" amounts of alcohol are involved, but it also tends to beg the question as to what constitutes "excessive" use. When there is a clear intoxication-plus-stress configuration, then there is also a clear danger signal that cardiovascular functioning may not be equal to the challenge.

3. It has been known for a long time that alcohol dilates blood vessels. Now, however, it appears to be well established that the opposite effect also occurs. Blood flow tends to be increased in vessels close to the skin (this is probably a contributing factor to the subjective experience of feeling warm and cheery, if the effect is not extreme). At about the same time, however, there is vasoconstriction in deeper layers, such as muscular masses. Perhaps it can be said that we must "pay for" one effect with the other. There are various theories about the mechanisms involved, usually working on the possibility that alcohol has a depressant effect in central organismic systems but a secondary stimulatory effect on the periphery. Theories apart, it no longer seems adequate to assume that alcohol is a vasodilator and only a vasodilator (Wallgren & Barry, 1970).

4. There is a body of data, stretching back over many years, indicating alcohol at first leads to stimulation and hyperexcitability of cardiac function but is then followed by the opposite effect. The biphasic change in electrical activity seems to be related to alcohol-induced alterations in sodium concentration around cell membranes, although the full story is probably more complicated.

5. Circulatory failure is one of the primary routes of death when alcohol concentrations reach intolerable levels. Death by hypotension or circulatory failure is most likely to occur when the accumulation of alcohol in the blood requires hours to have its lethal effect. More rapid deaths tend to be associated with respiratory failure.

It is obvious that alcohol does affect the cardiovascular system in significant ways. How much alcohol, if any, is safe for a particular individual requires serious attention, especially in the presence of physiological and environmental hazards to health.

THE EFFECTS OF ALCOHOL ON AGING AND THE AGED

Some Cautions and Distinctions

There is not yet a substantial body of research specific to the physiological effects of alcoholic beverages on aging and the aged. As already mentioned, most laboratory research has relied on young adults, whether mice or men. This paucity of research is confined to what might be called the "pure" or "normal" relationship between alcohol use and its physiological consequences. It is a different story when attention is turned to pathology and disease entities. Alcohol has been both implicated as a trigger or intensifier of various pathological conditions and touted as a preventive or cure. Some studies concerned with the alcohol–illness link have included the elderly, and these will be considered in Chapter 4. It is important to bear in mind, however, that we are deficient in knowledge of the basic relationships between alcoholic beverages and physiological functioning in aging and the aged. This deficiency necessarily limits the generalizations one might like to make about the impact of alcohol along the illness–health dimension.

The distinction made here may seem peculiar to those who are accustomed to assuming that aging *is* illness. Progress in gerontological research, however, has led to increasing differentiation between those changes with age that appear to be intrinsic and those that can be attributed to diseases and impairments that are suffered in the course of life's journey. One general effect of these continuing studies has been to indicate that some of the so-called inevitable degenerative changes associated with aging can be delayed, prevented, or ameliorated. Not all impairment and distress must be tolerated simply because the individual has reached a relatively advanced age. Another general effect of research has been to focus particular attention on those phenomena that do, indeed, seem at the core of age-related changes as distinguished from "accidents" of illness and impairment.

It is difficult to conduct research that cleanly separates "pure aging" from the superimposition of "accidental" illness and impairment. One of the most notable efforts was the pioneering research of a National Institute of Mental Health team headed by James E. Birren (1969). This multidisciplinary team compared healthy and very healthy old men with each other and with a sample of healthy young men. Differences between old and young were less frequent and salient than common opinion would have expected. When a clear difference was discovered, however, it became the focus for subsequent attention. An important example is the lower amplitude of peak EEG activity for the older men. This phenomenon appeared (and still appears) to be more closely related to intrinsic changes with age than to acquired impairments. It would be logical, then, to conduct a series of studies of alcohol effects on the electric activity of the CNS with aging, but systematic research of this kind has not yet been pursued.

Another distinction familiar to gerontologists must also be mentioned here. The status of the aged person (or of any of his component systems) should not be mixed up with the *process* of aging. It is well known, for example, that some characteristics of aged people are attributable to their immediate situations or their developmental histories rather than to the process of aging per se. Each generation has a developmental history with certain unique features (nutritional status, type of child rearing, educational level, career opportunities, exposure to war, economic disaster, etc.). Furthermore, each generation has opportunities and deprivations in the later years of life that are relatively distinctive. The person entering old age today encounters a different situation than did the person who reached this phase two decades ago, and the process of historical change shows no signs of stopping. This means that we cannot really observe old people at a particular moment in history and conclude that "this is what *aging* is all about."

Unfortunately, there is very little evidence available that would help us distinguish between the effects of alcohol on aging and in old age. At the least, one would require longitudinal investigations. Preferably, these would be studies that also would include the more sophisticated *cross-sequential* designs in which longitudinal and cross-sectional components are integrated. In cross-sequential designs (of which there are several varieties), individuals are followed over a period of time while new recruits are added to the study at specified intervals. This provides the opportunity, through sophisticated data analysis techniques, to distinguish the relative contribution of two sources of variance: changes over time, and differences related to the sociohistorical context.

At least one more distinction should be made. Research usually has followed common practice by treating age in simple chronological terms. Furthermore, the chronology has almost always been expressed in terms of age since birth. The convenience and other advantages of this approach do not require defense. This practice is so pervasive, however, that we sometimes forget there are alternatives. In recent years, the concept of *functional age* has received increasing attention (e.g., Fozard, 1972). Empirically, it can be demonstrated that individuals at the same chronological age differ from each other in functional age along a number of dimensions. These are sometimes grouped into subrealms of physiological, psychological, and social functioning. Thus, when we speak of alcohol effects as related to age, and mean by this only chronological age, we are introducing a large and unspecified error term. It would be useful—perhaps critical—to employ the alternative criterion of functional age as well.

Some Hints and Fragments

We will now consider briefly (as befits the limited data available) some observations relevant to the alcohol–aging/aged relationship apart from problems closely associated with pathological states. Obviously, there will be no effects to consider unless the alcohol is ingested in the first place. One of the few studies of relatively old animals found a decrease in alcohol consumption with age. Fitzgerald, Barfield, and Warrington (1968) studied chimpanzees and orangutans aged 4 to 44 years. The apes were given either fruit juice or a 10% alcohol/fruit juice solution using either vodka or ethanol. The participants had their decided preferences. Alcohol with grape juice was a more popular combination than with either orange or grapefruit juice. Paralleling consumption patterns among humans in the United States, the male chimpanzees drank more than the females and also tended to become intoxicated more frequently. For those chimps with well-documented life histories, their drinking behavior increased up until the fourth decade. At that point, there was an abrupt decline. Caution is needed in the interpretation of these results, however, since consumption of the placebo cocktail also dropped at that age, although not as sharply. While amount of consumption is an important component of alcohol effects, the study did not concentrate further on age-related physiological differences.

Vestal et al. (1975) studied age differences in the distribution and elimination of ethanol in humans. Fifty healthy adults aged 21 to 81 years received continuous intravenous infusion of alcohol for 1 hour. The intake was at the rate of 375 mg/m^2 of surface area per minute. This is equivalent to an average dose of .57 g/kg of body weight. Blood samples were drawn at 15- to 30-minute intervals for up to 4 hours after the ethanol infusion. Overall, the investigators found no age effect in the rate of ethanol elimination. Peak ethanol concentrations in the blood at the end of the infusion period, however, were correlated significantly with age ($r = .55p < .001$). Furthermore, lean body mass and total volume of ethanol distribution were both negatively correlated with age.

The researchers reached the following conclusions:

> The smaller volume of body water and the decreased lean body mass in the old subjects most likely explains the higher peak ethanol levels in blood water . . . as compared with young subjects. Age differences in peak plasma or serum levels of several drugs have been reported and these differences have been attributed to differences in metabolism or distribution. This study demonstrates that the compositional changes in the body play an important role in the interpretation of pharmacokinetic data, especially when age is a significant variable. The administration of doses of ethanol, based on the usual measurements of body size (body weight or surface area) may result in increased pharmacologic effects in older subjects due to increased blood levels resulting from changes in body composition rather than, or in addition to, alteration in metabolism or brain sensitivity.

Perhaps the differences found by Vestal et al. also become known through an internal biofeedback mechanism to the old people themselves. This could be a factor in reduced or otherwise altered patterns of alcohol consumption with age.

It should also be noted that this research team administered alcohol by a method that is not used by most people in daily life. Intravenous versus oral ingestion of alcohol (not to mention differences related to congeners) require some caution in the direct application of results to the situation of the elderly in "real life."

A follow-up study in the same laboratory by Vestal and his colleagues has directed attention to the effect of age on the response of the hypothalamic-hypophyseal-renal axis (Helderman et al, 1978). The participants were relatively healthy adults ranging in age from 21 to 92 and divided, for purposes of analysis, into younger (21–49) and older (54–92) subjects. The intravenous method of introducing ethanol was again employed. Ethanol was used as an inhibitory agent for the secretion of arginine vasopressin (AVP), a plasma antidiuretic hormone. The inhibitory effect was shown across the entire age range in this study, indicating that ethanol produces a water diuretic effect by inhibiting AVP secretion. Age differences were found in the pattern of response, however. The younger participants "responded in what may be termed the classical manner with a prompt and continued inhibition of the secretion of AVP through the period of rising blood ethanol levels. . . . Response in the old group . . . was paradoxical. Initially, during the first half of the 1-hour intravenous ethanol load, the AVP levels were inhibited. But, despite continued increase of blood ethanol concentration, the hormone levels returned to baseline by the end of the infusion and rebounded to nearly twice the basal value by the end of the study period. Thus there is a loss of, or escape from, the inhibitory effects of the ethanol molecule during a period in which further suppression would have been expected" (p. 45).

The ethanol load can be regarded as a kind of stress test. Helderman and colleagues note that the "escape" from the expected inhibitory effect in the physiological response of the older participants might possibly have been related to differences in cardiovascular functioning. This suggests another promising line of inquiry and perhaps some thought on the part of geriatric clinicians as well.

This study raises several other points. It is becoming increasingly evident through gerontological research on a broad front that challenge or stress to the organism often yields findings one would not obtain through simple observational methods. Ethanol can serve as a useful means of inducing carefully controlled "doses of stress." From the clinical standpoint, however, alcohol may have stress effects in the elderly that differ from that which occurs in the young. While it is premature to draw firm conclusions from a research area that is still so new, it seems already clear that we cannot assume physiological response to be the same when alcohol enters the bodies of the young and the old.

It would be useful to have research of this type in many other physiological realms. We might expect to find differences in the utilization of alcohol with aging because of fairly well established data indicating that general metabolism decreases (e.g., Barrows & Roeder, 1977). The differences here might be mediated in part by the level of physical activity, which also tends to decrease with age. Unfortunately, we could find no research on this question—or on many others that might be posed.

The studies already described involved the administration of ethanol under controlled conditions. One might also examine physiological differences related to age for people who differ in their use and nonuse of alcoholic beverages in every day life. Men who could be classified primarily as wine drinkers, beer drinkers, hard liquor drinkers, or abstainers were distinguished within the ranks of participants in a Veterans Administration longitudinal study of normal aging. While the overall study is longitudinal (as is the case with the research of Vesta et al. but involving different samples and methods), the available data come from a one-time sampling of their drinking behavior and physiological status.[2] In this case, the subpopulation available for analysis included 152 nondrinkers, 195 beer drinkers, 64 wine drinkers, and 215 hard liquor drinkers. There were no differences in mean chronological age among these four categories with one exception: the beer drinkers (mean age 45) were about 7 years younger than the others. Age variance was larger in the nondrinker group, however. This suggests that few of the old participants were nondrinkers, and subsequent analyses were conducted with age as a covariate.

A sampling of 42 laboratory variables was examined for possible group differences. Pulmonary functioning and blood pressure were also examined. Of a total 44 biomedical variables, only 3 showed significant differences among the four groups. Wine drinkers as a group were highest on reaction, a measure of pH or the acidity–alkalinity of the urine; on total bilirubin, a measure of liver function; and on monocytes, a subpopulation of circulating white blood cells.

In general, then, laboratory tests of biomedical functioning did not distinguish between drinkers and nondrinkers. These standard measures perhaps are 'not sensitive enough to the effects of alcohol in a basically healthy population. Other possibilities are that there is systematic error in self-reports of drinking behavior or (the simplest possibility of all) that there are few substantial differences in physiological status between those who do and those who do not use alcoholic beverages. The few obtained differences on biomedical variables could be set aside as

[2]We appreciate the access to unpublished data of the Veterans Administration Normative Aging Study in Boston.

"chance significant" findings unless demonstrated again in other populations.

In this study, it was possible to examine functional as well as chronological age differences with drinking, although not as thoroughly as might be desired. There was no evidence that drinkers were functionally older (or younger) than nondrinkers across the broad span of biomedical variables. Whatever this "nonfinding" might eventually come to mean in the light of subsequent research, it would appear that there is no support here for the more extreme positions that alcohol use either leads to premature debilitation or preserves one in a singularly youthful condition. It should be recognized that these data were collected with broad research objectives in mind rather than specifically studying the relationship between age differences and the effect of alcohol, and therefore they do not lend themselves to the purpose with the clarity and scope that other types of design might have yielded.

The person who seeks an integrated understanding of the effects of alcohol on the physiological status of the aged person or on the process of aging obviously should plan on living a long time, since it is going to take awhile before sufficient knowledge becomes available. And whether or not one's patience with the unpredictable pace and vicissitudes of research should be enhanced by the use of alcoholic beverages—well, that will just have to be a personal decision!

REFERENCES

Aserinsky, E., & Kleitman, N. Regularly occurring periods of eye motility and concomittant phenomena during sleep. *Science, 1953, 118,* 273–280.

Barrows, C. H., & Roeder, L. M. Nutrition. In C. E. Finch & L. Hayflick (Eds.), *Handbook of the biology of aging.* New York: Van Nostrand Reinhold, 1977, pp. 561–581.

Begleiter, H., & Platz, A. The effects of alcohol on the central nervous system in humans. In B. Kissin & H. Begleiter (Eds.), *The biology of alcoholism.* New York: Plenum Press, 1972, pp. 293–344.

Birren, J. E., Butler, R. N., Greenhouse, S. W., Sokoloff, L., & Yarrow, M. R. *Human aging: A biological and behavioral study.* Washington, D.C.: National Institute on Mental Health, 1969.

Carroll, R. B. Analysis of alcoholic beverages by gas-liquid chromatography. Studies of congeners in alcoholic beverages. *Quarterly Journal Studies on Alcoholism,* 1970, Suppl. 5.

Coopersmith, S. The effects of alcohol on reactions to affective stimuli. *Quarterly Journal Studies on Alcoholism,* 1964, *25,* 459–66.

Coopersmith, S., & Woodrow, K. Basal conductance levels of normals and alcoholics. *Quarterly Journal Studies on Alcoholism,* 1967, *28,* 27–32.

Davis, P. A., Gibbs, F. A., Davis, H., Jetter, W. W., & Trowbridge, L. S. The effects of alcohol upon the electroencephalogram (brain waves). *Quarterly Journal Studies on Alcoholism,* 1941, *1,* 628–630.

Dement, W., & Kleitman, N. Cyclic variations in EEG during sleep and their relation to eye movements, body motility, and dreaming. *Electroencephalography and Clinical Neurophysiology,* 1957, 9, 273–277.

Ellingboe, J. Effects of alcohol on neurochemical processes. In M. A. Lipton, A. DeMascio, & K. F. Killam (Eds.), *Psychopharmacology: A decade of progress.* New York: Raven Press, 1978, pp. 1653–1664.

Feinberg, I., & Evarts, E. V. Some implications of sleep research for psychiatry. In J. Zubin & C. Shagass (Eds.), *Neurobiological aspects of psychopathology.* New York: Grune & Stratton, 1969, pp. 334–393.

Forsander, O. A. Influence of alcohol on the general metabolism of the body. In S. P. Lucia (Ed.), *Alcohol and civilization.* New York: McGraw-Hill, 1963, pp. 43–60.

Fozard, J. L. Predicting age in the adult years from psychological assessments of abilities and personality. *Human Development,* 1972, *3,* 175–182.

Goldberg, L. The metabolism of alcohol. In S. P. Lucia (Ed.), *Alcohol and civilization.* New York: McGraw-Hill, 1963, pp. 23–42.

Grenell, R. G. Effects of alcohol on the neuron. In N. Kissen & H. Begleiter (Eds.), *The biology of alcoholism.* (Vol. 2) *Physiology and behavior.* New York: Plenum, 1972, pp. 1–20.

Gross, M. M., & Hastey, J. M. Sleep disturbances in alcoholism, in R. E. Tarter & A. A. Sugarman (Eds.), *Alcoholism: Interdisciplinary approaches to an enduring program.* Reading, Mass.: Addison Wesley, 1976, pp. 257–307.

Helderman, J. H., Vestal, R. E., Rowe, J. W., Tobin, J. D., Andres, R., & Robertson, G. L. The response of arginine vasopressin to intravenous ethanol and hypertonic saline in man: The impact of aging. *Journal of Gerontology,* 1978, *33,* 39–47.

Hunt, W. A., & Dalton, T. K. Regional brain acetycheline levels in rats acutely treated with ethanol and rendered ethanol-dependent. *Brain Research,* 1976, *109,* 628–631.

Isbell, H., Fraser, H., Wikler, A., Belleville, R., & Eisenman, A. An experimental study of etiology of "rum fits" and delirium tremens. *Quarterly Journal Studies on Alcoholism,* 1955, *16,* 1–8.

Johnson, L. C., Burdick, J., & Smith, J. Sleep during alcohol intake and withdrawal in the chronic alcoholic. *Archives of General Psychiatry,* 1970, *22,* 406–412.

Jouvet, M. Mechanisms of the states of sleep. In S. S. Kety, E. V. Evarts, H. L. Williams (Eds.), *Sleep and altered states of consciousness.* Baltimore: Williams & Wilkins, 1967.

Jouvet, M., Vimont, P., & Delorme, F. Étude de la privation selective de la phase paradoxale du sommeil chez le chat. *Comptes Rendus des Seances de la Societe de Biologie et de Ses Filiales* (Paris), 1964, *158,* 756–762.

Knowles, J. B., Laverty, S. G., & Kuechler, H. A. Effects of alcohol on REM sleep. *Quarterly Journal Studies on Alcohol,* 1968, *29,* 342–347.

Knott, D. H., & Beard, J. D. Changes in cardiovascular activity as a function of alcohol intake. In B. Kissen & H. Begleiter (Eds.), *The biology of alcoholism.* New York: Plenum Press, 1972, pp. 345–366.

Knutsson, E. Effects of ethanol on the membrane potential and membrane resistance of frog muscle fibres. *Acta Physiologica Scandinavica,* 1961, *52,* 242–253.

Leake, C. D., & Silverman, M. *Alcoholic beverages in clinical medicine.* Chicago: Year Book Medical Publishers, 1966.

McDonnell, G. J., & Carpenter, J. A. Anxiety, skin conductance and alcohol. A study of the relation between anxiety and skin conductance and the effect of alcohol on the conductance of subjects in a group. *Quarterly Journal Studies on Alcohol,* 1959, *20,* 38–42.

Mello, N. K. Alcoholism and the behavioral pharmacology of alcohol: 1967–1977. In M. A. Lipton, A. DiMascio & K. F. Killam (Eds.), *Psychopharmacology: A generation of progress.* New York: Raven Press, 1978, pp. 1619–1638.

Mello, N. K., & Mendelson, J. S. (Eds.). *Recent advances in studies of alcoholism.* Washington, D.C.: U.S. Government Printing Office, 1971.

Mendelson, J. H., & LaDou, J. Experimentally induced chronic intoxication and withdrawal in alcoholics. Part I: Background and experimental design. *Quarterly Journal Studies on Alcoholism,* 1964, Suppl. 2.

Mullins, L. J. Some physical mechanics in narcosis. *Chemical Review,* 1954, *54,* 289–323.

Mullins, L. J., Kleitman, N., & Cooperman, N. R. The effect of alcohol and caffein on motility and body temperature during sleep. American Journal of Physiology, 1953, *106,* 478–485.

Naitoh, P. The effect of alcohol on the autonomic nervous system of humans: Psychophysiological approach. In B. Kissen & H. Begleiter (Eds.), *The biology of alcoholism.* New York: Plenum Press, 1972, pp. 367–433.

Raskin, N. H., & Sokoloff, L. J. Enzymes catalysing ethanol metabolism in neural and somatic tissues of the rat. *Neurochemistry,* 1972, pp. 273–282.

Rundell, O. H., Lester, B. K., Griffiths, W. J., & Williams, H. L. *Psychopharmacologia,* 1972, *26,* 201–218.

Varga, B., & Nagy, T. Analysis of alpha rhythm in the electroencephalogram of alcoholics. *Electroencephalography and Clinical Neurophysiology,* 1960, *12,* 933–939.

Vestal, R. E., McGuire, E. A., Tobin, J. D., Andres, R., Norris, A. H., & Mezey, R. Aging and ethanol metabolism in man. *Clinical Pharmacology and Therapeutics,* 1977, *21,* 343–354.

Victor, M. Treatment of alcoholic intoxication and the withdrawal syndrome: A critical analysis of the use of drugs and other forms of therapy. *Psychosomatic Medicine* 1966, *28,* 636–650.

Wallgren, H., & Barry, H. Actions of alcohol (vol. 1). Amsterdam: Elsevier, 1970. 1970.

Williams, H. L., & Salamy, A. Alcohol and sleep. In B. Kissen & H. Begleiter

(Eds.), *The biology of alcoholism.* New York: Plenum Press, 1972, pp. 435–483.

Zarcone, V., Barchas, J., Hoddes, E., Montplaisir, J., Sack, R., & Wilson, R. Alcohol intoxication and withdrawal: Experimental studies. In M. M. Gross (Ed.): *Advances in experimental medicine and biology.* New York: Plenum Press, 1975, pp. 431–451.

3
The Extent of Alcohol Use in Old Age

Do individuals change their patterns of drinking as they mature? Do elderly people drink more or less than other age groups? Are there more problem drinkers or more abstainers among older Americans? Answers to questions such as these may be found in epidemiological studies of the frequency, quantity, variability, and patterns of drinking throughout the age spectrum. This chapter reviews relevant epidemiological data on drinking patterns in old age. However, before presenting the data, we will (1) briefly review studies of general drinking patterns in our society and (2) examine important methodological issues involved in the epidemiological studies. Readers already well versed on the general subject of drinking in our society might prefer to turn directly to the later sections of this chapter, which examine the validity of epidemiological studies and review research on alcohol on old age.

REVIEW OF DRINKING BEHAVIOR IN OUR SOCIETY

Approximately two out of every three adults in the United States (68 percent) use alcoholic beverages to some extent (Cahalan, Cison, & Crossley, 1969). Men (77 percent) show a higher percentage of drinkers than do women (60 percent). Since the end of World War II, the percentage of men who drink has remained relatively constant. There has been a gradual increase, however, in the percentage of women who report being users of alcoholic beverages. "Heavier" drinkers—defined as people who ingest more than an ounce a day—are found most often among men aged 18 to 20 and 35 to 39, and among women in the age range of 21 to 29. These differential patterns for the two sexes certainly invite further study, preferably with research designs that integrate physiological, psychological, and sociological variables.

Throughout the total adult age range, about 1 person in 11 can be classified as a "heavier" drinker using the above definition. Survey data by Harris & Associates, Inc. indicate that 9 percent of adults in the United States are "heavier" drinkers, while another 18 percent qualify as "moderate" drinkers (between 0.22 and 0.99 oz.). Another 31 percent are "lighter" drinkers, consuming less than 0.22 oz. per day on the average. This leaves 42 percent of the adult population who are either total abstainers or drink less than once per month (Harris, 1972–1974).

It should be made clear that classifications such as those used by the Harris survey research group do not necessarily reflect the prevalence of "problem drinking." One individual might ingest an ounce or more a day without giving any indication that there are deleterious effects either for himself or others, while another person might in some way suffer ill effects from what is objectively a more moderate or a less frequent use of alcohol. It is easier to establish statistical criteria for drinking behavior based upon frequency and extent of use than to agree on precisely what constitutes either "problem drinking" or "alcoholism." There are appreciable individual differences in tolerance for alcohol in an individual. Furthermore, difficulties in specifying social and behavioral outcomes and relating them directly to the use of alcohol must be acknowledged.

Nevertheless, it is obvious that a wide range of human distress is associated with the use of alcoholic beverages. Some observers prefer the simple view that alcohol "causes" the problems, while others see more complex patterns in which it might be more appropriate to regard alcohol effects as *intensifying* difficulties for the individual and others in society.

Regional Variations

Alcohol consumption varies across the United States. The differences include both the extent and the type of beverage consumed. Adults in and around the Tennessee area consumed 1.81 gal. of absolute alcohol per capita in 1972. This was the lowest reported consumption in the nation. For the other extreme, we would move to the far western states of California, Oregon, and Washington (along with Alaska and Hawaii), where per capita use was reported at 3.10 gal. (Efron, Keller, & Gurioli, 1974).

There are indications of regional differences in the type of beverage consumed. There is what might be called a "beer belt" that comprises Texas, Oklahoma, Mississippi, and Tennessee in particular. New Englanders and those in the South Atlantic regions prefer distilled spirits. The Pacific region consumes the most substantial amount of wine, perhaps because it is also a major area for the production of this beverage.

Across the nation, beer (46 percent) and distilled spirits (42 percent) are of nearly equal popularity, with wine consumption encompassing only 12 percent of the total (Chafetz, 1974).

Ethnic and Demographic Variations Other than Geography

Drinking practices vary according to ethnic background, religious affiliation, amount of education, socioeconomic status, and occupation. This general finding should not be surprising, for life-styles in general shows the mark of all these influences.

The available data indicate that Irish-Americans have more alcoholism problems than other ethnic groups of the same social class (Plant, 1967). By contrast, first-generation Italian-Americans drink frequently but have few alcohol-related problems (Lolli et al., 1958). Later generation Italian-Americans are more frequently involved in problem drinking, however (Jessor et al., 1970). It has also been reported that Chinese-Americans and those of Jewish background have few drinking problems (Milgram, 1975).

These ethnic differences usually are interpreted as reflections of social attitudes toward drinking. In groups where drunkenness is tolerated, there tends to be more inebriation, while in ethnic groups that do not have a history of tolerance for inebriation, this phenomenon is less common. As ethnic differences tend to diminish from first to later generations in the United States (but not necessarily with the same rate of negative acceleration for all ethnic groups), some of the group influences that may moderate drinking practices may become attenuated and less effective.

The range of possible dynamics and functions of drinking behavior in relation to individual behavior and group forces is a subject that deserves more extensive consideration than what is possible here. It might, however, be useful to summarize one attempt to construct a general approach to this subject, an approach that could apply not only to groups defined in terms of national origin but for all combinations of ethnic–religious–educational and other influences.

Horton (1943) examined the influence of alcoholic beverages in a variety of so-called primitive societies. Two common features of alcohol effects emerged clearly, in his view at least. The use of alcoholic beverages seemed to reduce feelings of anxiety. This reduction of anxiety was experienced as pleasurable and rewarding. Naturally, the person who felt better after drinking would be inclined to drink again; on a group level, drinking behavior became a social custom. Drinking, however, also tends to encourage behaviors that transgress other social norms. Sexual and aggressive impulses, in particular, are likely to emerge, and these call forth the enforcement of social sanctions on the individual—punishment rather than reinforcement. What feels good, then, because it reduces anxiety, may elicit punishment or threat of punishment from society—and may thus lead to heightened anxiety. The heightened anxiety might, of course, tempt the individual to drink again! This line of analysis, pursued further by Horton, suggests a rather widespread ambivalence or contradiction in both the individual and the group. Perhaps, then, every ethnic or other socially constructed group in the United States could be understood in terms of the particular balance it strikes between supporting drinking behavior as an anxiety-reducing custom and restricting drinking behavior because it may unleash forbidden or inappropriate impulses. Horton's view is not presented here as the only or the most comprehensive approach that could be taken to this problem, but as an example of how one might start to examine the function and process of drinking behavior in relationship to the individual's primary social reference groups.

Religious practices may have an important influence on drinking behavior, particularly where articles of faith require abstention. Followers of the Mohammedan religion are not allowed to use alcohol (although medicinal use has been approved and advocated for some purposes by Moslem physicians; see Chapter 2). Although orthodox Moslems may abstain from alcohol, the sales of alcoholic beverages in such predominantly Moslem nations as Turkey indicate that abstinence is no longer the rule among some contemporary Moslem populations.

Recent survey findings indicate some differences among Protestants, Catholics, and Jews in extent of drinking behavior (Harris, 1972–1974). There have been relatively higher proportions of drinkers and heavy drinkers among Catholics. Jews, though rarely abstainers, had the lowest proportion of heavy drinkers. Since 1965, however, the proportion of people who indicate "no religious affiliation" has about doubled. This confuses the distinction between the three major religious groups. Furthermore, ethnic background is often confounded with religious affiliation. The Irish-Americans, for example, are mostly Catholics (but, of course, not all Catholics are Irish-Americans).

Relationships have been found between education and the consumption of alcoholic beverages. Most abstainers (62 percent) are people with less than an eighth-grade education (Cahalan et al., 1969). Highly educated people are more likely to be among the "heavier" drinkers. Similarly, people in the lower socioeconomic levels are more likely to be abstainers than those in the upper levels (Harris, 1972–1974).

Men with semiprofessional jobs have the highest proportion of heavy drinkers. Among employed women, the heaviest drinkers in general are those with jobs in the service fields. Relatively few executives of large manufacturing companies in the United States abstain from drinking, although these executives tend to remain in light and moderate rather than heavy usage patterns (Caravan, 1972).

The possibility that alcoholism may be related to genetic influences has been raised on a number of occasions. Most studies in this area, however, have failed to confirm this hypothesis (Chafetz, 1974). Recently, though, the study of children who were raised by nonalcoholic foster parents after being taken from their alcoholic parents suggests that heredity may be a factor in some severe forms of alcoholism. There is no large-scale research at the present time to substantiate a firm genetic basis for alcoholism, although the hypothesis still remains viable.

It is important to bear in mind that the data for all the factors bearing on alcohol consumption mentioned above come from a relatively small number of studies. Furthermore, there is a particular caution to be sounded about the time factor. Conclusions drawn about ethnic and regional variations in alcohol consumption, for example, may not retain their validity beyond a particular period in the life of our society. There is need for continued updating if we are to avoid the error of perpetuating stereotypes.

ARE EPIDEMIOLOGICAL DATA VALID?

Studies on the extent of alcohol use by the elderly rely upon epidemiological techniques. In epidemiological studies, individuals were either given a written questionnaire to complete or asked predetermined questions by a skilled interviewer. Since the intention is for all people to be interviewed under basically the same circumstances, asked the same questions, and guaranteed total anonymity, it is usually assumed that the results will be valid and that any errors will be randomly distributed among the different subgroups. Are these legitimate assumptions, particularly when considering an elderly sample?

The basic problem with interview and questionnaire approach is that it trusts that the respondent will give accurate answers. The researcher, however, usually has no way of knowing if the answers do correspond to actual circumstances. Does the elderly woman who "never touched a drop of alcohol in my whole life" have a bottle stashed in the cupboard? Is the older man who said he "drinks only occasionally and not more than two drinks" going to run off to the local tavern for an all-night drunken spree after the interviewer leaves? We have no way of knowing for sure. But how the respondent perceives the interviewer may influence the honesty of the answers. Individuals might believe that they are being helpful by overstating the amount of drinking they do so that the nice young interviewers will have something to write down and not lose their jobs.

Nowadays, Americans are growing up in an atmosphere where polls and questionnaires abound. However, many of the elderly are not accustomed to being questioned by strangers about intimate aspects of their lives. A high proportion of elderly people are receiving some form of government medical aid, insurance benefits, social security, welfare, or other forms of assistance. They might suspect that the government or some other service agency was interested in knowing about their health status or concerned that they might be a poor risk. Under these circumstances, one might expect that elders could be more reluctant to disclose aspects of their life, such as drinking behavior, that might be looked upon with disapproval by others.

Many elderly people have been characterized as lonely and isolated (Butler, 1975). Some welcome the opportunity for social interaction even if the person is just a stranger who is taking an opinion poll. After the initial suspicion wears off, it is not uncommon for interviewers to be invited into the home of the elder for a cordial chat which may veer into many topics that are not on the interviewer's agenda. Interviewers have often reported that they felt that the old person "just wanted someone to talk to." Under circumstances where the old person is desirous of having the interviewer stay, the elder might be quite motivated to give responses that he or she thinks would be pleasing or interesting to the interviewer. Such a response bias may have a decisive effect upon the nature of the interview results.

Sampling biases are always an issue in epidemiological studies. Do the people sampled represent the general population of elderly individuals? Perhaps, rather than generalizing about "the elderly alcoholic," it is more useful to talk about various ethnic, economic, or geographic subgroups.

Since systematic epidemiological studies were only begun in the past two decades, all the data are only applicable to the current generation of elderly people living today. We do not know if current results apply to the elders of past and future generations. Also, since there have been no long-range longitudinal studies that collect data on the same individuals as they grow older, it is not easy to determine if people change their drinking behavior as they age, since we are just looking at generational differences. Until longitudinal studies are conducted, we must rely upon self-reports of past drinking practices that may be of questionable accuracy.

Despite these possible sources of bias, epidemiological studies probably offer a useful basis for studying the general phenomena of alcohol use in old age. However, the reader should bear in mind that the numbers obtained do not necessarily indicate behavior but only reflect what people *say* they do. Memory difficulties, dishonesty in responding, and response biases to the interviewer (who is usually of a different generation than the elderly respondent) are all factors that should be kept in mind. Furthermore, questions may be worded in such a way as to elicit responses that do not truly reflect the respondent's behavior (e.g., a particular person may not consider taking a glass of beer now and then to be drinking). It is hoped that future studies will incorporate methods that enable actual behavioral observations to be made. For example, within a given neighborhood, what proportion of the customers at the local liquor store are over age 60? What beverages do they buy, and in what quantity? What proportion of the members of an elderly housing project can be found each evening in the local bar? How much do they drink there, and how do they react? Although such topological behavior observations have problems of their own, this type of information would be essential to check the validity of results determined from epidemiological studies.

THE EXTENT OF DRINKING IN OLD AGE

The most extensive recent study of American drinking practices was conducted by Cahalan, Cisin, and Crossley (1969). They conducted 2746 interviews from a national probability sample drawn so that the findings would be representative of the total population of per person aged 21 years or older living in households within the contiguous United States (exclusive of Alaska and Hawaii). They found that 47 percent of their sample age over 60 did not drink at all or more than once a year. This compares with 40 percent abstainers age 50 to 59, 29 percent age 40 to 49, 22 percent age 30 to 39, and 24 percent age 21 to 29. They classified drinking behavior into five categories ranging from abstainers to heavy drinkers and based upon the factors of quantity consumed, frequency of drinking, and the variability of drinking. People who drank greater amounts per occasion were rated as heavier drinkers than those who drank the same volume but smaller quantities spread out over time.

Table 3.1 shows a comparison of men and women by age on the five

Table 3.1
Percentage of Respondents in Q–F–V Groups, by Sex and Age

	N^2	Abst.	Drinkers Infreq.	Light + Mod.	Heavy	% Heavy of All Drinkers
Total sample	2746	32	15	41	12	18
Men	1177	23	10	46	21	28
Women	1569	40	18	37	5	8
Age 21–29	472	24	15	47	14	18
30–39	588	22	17	46	15	19
40–49	597	29	12	44	15	21
50–59	462	40	14	36	10	25
60+	624	47	15	32	6	11
Age not given	3^b					
Men						
Age 21–24	100	16	8	54	22	26
25–29	116	17	8	51	24	29
30–34	109	12	7	51	30	34
35–39	134	16	12	50	22	26
40–44	150	18	8	54	20	24
45–49	114	25	7	38	30	40
50–54	116	25	13	41	21	28
55–59	81	30	14	34	22	31
60–64	82	30	5	41	24	35
65+	175	38	16	39	7	11
Women						
Age 21–24	112	32	20	39	9	13
25–29	144	29	21	45	5	7
30–34	156	29	23	42	6	8
35–39	189	27	22	44	7	10
40–44	189	35	16	43	6	9
45–49	144	36	14	40	10	15
50–54	147	51	16	32	1	3
55–59	118	50	14	35	1	3
60–64	110	47	20	31	2	3
65+	257	60	15	24	1	2

This table is reprinted courtesy of Cahalan et al., 1969.

^2N = the number of actual cases in each base group (unweighted). Percentages are calculated on weighted numbers; the weighted base for the total sample is 5321 which represents the total number of adults in the 2746 households.

[b]The three respondents (all women) who did not give their ages are omitted from all subsequent age tables.

quantity–frequency–variability groups. It is clear that women in the elderly group more frequently drank less or not at all as compared to elderly men. These results are similar to an earlier study by Mulford (1964), which found a sharp drop in the rates of drinkers at age 40 to 50. Cahalan et al. (1969) summarized Gallup poll findings that indicated an increase in the percentage of drinkers at all age levels in recent years but a decrease in drinking after the age 50. These findings reflect a pattern that has been consistent since polls taken in 1957. The results clearly indicate that people over 50 years of age tend to drink less than when they were younger (or at least report to the interviewer that they drink less).

Studies of Other Countries

The results of the study by Cahalan and co-workers indicating less drinking among the elderly was consistent with those of a study of drinking in a London suburb conducted by Edwards et al. (1972). They found fewer drinking problems with increasing age. The study by Encel, Kotowicz, and Resler (1972) in Sydney, Australia, indicated only slight age differences in the quantity and frequency of drinking up to age 60. After age 60, however, men were more frequently light or infrequent drinkers or abstainers. These age differences were more marked in females, who showed a dramatic decrease in drinking after age 60.

Similarly, Wallace (1972) found more abstainers among people aged 61 and over in Norway. He reported, however, that between 1962 and 1966, there was an increase in the proportion of drinkers in the general population and that this increase was largest in proportion in the oldest age groups (over age 50).

Regional Variations

Wallace (1972) found great regional variations within Norway. In Oslo, 34 percent of the respondents were regular drinkers and 30 percent abstained. By contrast, in the eastern regions, only 12 percent were regular drinkers and 40 percent abstained; in the south and west, 13 percent were regular drinkers and 61 percent abstained; and in the north, 7 percent were regular drinkers and 51 percent abstained. He found that major factors in abstinence were rural background, religious influences, and higher incomes. Regional differences have also been found in the United States. Room (1972) compared results in San Francisco and national samples from other parts of the United States. He found, for example, that 37 percent of San Francisco males and 58 percent of San

Francisco females over age 60 abstained from drinking. This compared to national sample results of 48 percent of males abstaining and 73 percent of the females abstaining. Other regional differences were found between central coastal cities with populations over 1 million, coastal central cities with less than 1 million population, and interior central cities of less than 1 million. Therefore, regional variations, particularly rural–urban distinctions, should be important factors to consider when studying the extent of alcohol use.

Reasons for Less Consumption Among the Elderly

Why do elderly people drink less? The first possible explanation is that they do not actually drink less, they just *say* that they do. Reports of less drinking may be the result of any of the inherent biases in the research techniques that were mentioned in the earlier discussion of epidemiological data. Reports of less alcohol consumption by elderly people may also reflect failure to be conscious of the extent of behavior that is considered unacceptable. Perhaps elderly people do not consciously realize the effect of their drinking behavior. For a variety of possibly unconscious motives, elderly people may not know that their alcohol consumption is occasionally excessive, a behavior that is inconsistent with a self-image of being quite sober individuals.

Haberman (1970) suggested in a self-report study of a New York City sample that the high proportions of persons indicating abstinence from alcoholic beverages showed denial by people that they were actually drinking. If denial of drinking does occur, it would be interesting to determine if the denial is an artifact of the data-gathering procedure, where the respondent deliberately gives inaccurate data to the interviewer, or reflects unconscious psychological processes within the individual.

Even if denial does exist, it would only affect differences between older and younger groups if denial is disproportionately present among the elders. Is there more reason for elderly people to respond inaccurately than there is for young people? To date, no evidence has been presented indicating that older or younger respondents are any more honest or less biased in their responses to survey studies or show more denial of drinking.

There are at least two alternative explanations for this phenomenon. One alternative argument was presented by Drew (1968). He argued that alcoholism is a self-limiting disease, since it is associated with increased mortality. His study in Victoria, Australia, looked at the actual prevalence of alcoholism problems based upon admissions to a Victoria hospital and compared it to a predicted prevalence based upon known cumulative incidence statistics. Drew found that after 40, the actual prevalence increasingly dropped far below predicted prevalence. In his review of 21 independent studies of alcoholism, he noted only 2 investigations in which the proportion of alcoholics by age group had not begun to decrease by age 50. Drew suggested that since many alcoholics die at a relatively young age or suffer from various disorders that may result in long-term institutionalization, people with alcohol problems may not be prevalent among a sample of households. Therefore, the alcoholics who either die young or are hidden away in institutions would be included in the surveys by Cahalan et al. or in similar studies.

A number of studies have documented that chronic alcoholics have higher death rates than the general population (Belloc, 1973; Room & Day, 1974; Shurtleff, 1970). This is not an indictment of drinking in general. The higher mortality is concentrated on frequent heavy drinkers and those with a current and large drinking-related problem. In fact, the Shurtleff (1970) study indicated that at older ages, people who abstained from alcoholic beverages showed a *greater* mortality than those who drank moderately. The proportion of the total adult population of problem drinkers who have increased mortality related to drinking is only between 2 and 3 percent. Thus, this higher mortality could only account for a small proportion of the abstinence among elders. Furthermore, the finding relating abstinence to increased mortality actually works against the observed finding that older people abstain more. This finding was replicated in the study by Belloc (1973), in which there was a slight tendency for light drinkers to show the lowest mortality of all the drinking and nondrinking groups.

Drew (1968) also suggests that beneficial effects of treatment may account for a small proportion of reduction in alcoholism among the elderly. Long-term positive results from treatment programs are scarce, however, and this area is controversial at best. Still, the known proportion of individuals whose problem is so severe that they require treatment is quite small compared to the extent of the reduction in drinking observed in older people.

An alternative hypothesis is that as people grow older, they decrease their alcohol intake. Amark (1951) concluded from his own findings and from a number of other Swedish and German authors that "many alcoholics, at the age of 50 years, improved spontaneously to such an extent that they are no longer in need of being taken in charge." Moore (1964) observed that in Japan, "most alcoholics reach a peak of consumption between age 20 and 40, with tapering off after 40." More recently, Wallgren and Barry (1970) reviewed reports of problem drinkers who, in their old age, either gave up drinking completely or imbibed only moderately.

Age Differences or Age Changes?

All of these speculations raise the following question: Do the data indicating less drinking among elderly people reflect lifelong drinking practices, or do they reflect changes in drinking patterns as a result of age? If elderly people stop or cut down on their drinking later in life, then these data probably reflect some changes associated with old age. If, however, the lower proportion of drinkers among the elderly is often a continuation of lifelong abstinence, then what we are observing may be a generational difference. We would therefore expect that as the present generation of younger, heavier drinkers matures into old age, they will continue to drink more heavily, except for those who die before growing old.

We indicated earlier that Gallup poll data has shown consistently less drinking among older people since 1947. These results support the hypothesis that there is an age-associated change in consumption level. Another way to determine lifetime drinking patterns is simply to ask people not only about their current drinking habits but also about their past behaviors. Knupfer and Room (1950) conducted such a study in the San Francisco area in 1964. They found that the small proportion of former drinkers who abstain rises slightly with age (of male former drinkers who are from age 21 to 39, 3 percent abstain; of men 60 and over, 11 percent abstain—of women who are 21 to 39, 6 percent abstain; of women 60 and over, 9 percent abstain). However, the proportion of lifelong virtual abstainers increases dramatically among those aged over 60 (among men from age 21 to 39, 6 percent abstain; over 60 years old, 20 percent abstain—in women from age 21 to 39, 20 percent abstain; over age 60, 56 percent abstain).

Knupfer and Room suggest that this difference between age groups may be a function of "selective forgetting of youthful foibles on the part of those further removed from them" (p. 115). They point out that those who were over 60 at the time of the study (in 1964) were at least 30 years old when Prohibition was repealed and thus may have been less likely to begin drinking patterns while in their twenties. However, it is interesting to note the sharp differences in drinking patterns among the age groups. Their results indicate, for example, that while only 6 to 7 percent of men aged 21 to 39 abstain from drinking, 56 percent of elderly women report abstinence. Since societal attitudes toward women drinking in public have improved greatly in recent years, perhaps the proportion of elderly female abstainers will be less when the present middle-aged generation matures into old age. Also, it would verify if these San Francisco results were replicated in other parts of the country.

Factors Affecting Drinking Behavior

Although Knupfer and Room (1950) went on to ask respondents why they abstained from drinking, they did not break down these analyses according to age groups. Their findings suggested that "moralistic" reasons were fairly prevalent, but 90 percent of the lifelong abstainers also indicated other reasons. They found that 52 percent of the lifelong virtual abstainers had incomes of less than $5000 per year. This suggests an interesting relationship that should be explored further, since the median income for elderly people in the United States was less than $5000 according to 1969 U.S. Census data. Perhaps some elderly people abstain because they cannot afford the costs of imbibing.

A small recent study by Johnson (1974) surveyed 169 people over age 65 living in households on the Upper East Side of Manhattan in New York City. The results confirmed other survey data, although a higher proportion of abstainers (44 percent) was found among men than in other studies, while the proportion of abstainers among women (53 percent) was comparable. This study included a high proportion of lower socioeconomic groups living alone or in small households. They found that 61 percent of the men and 29 percent of the women were currently abstainers but formerly drank at least occasionally. These findings are at odds with those reported by Knupfer and Room (1950) for a larger sample in San Francisco that included a broader range of socioeconomic groups.

Johnson found that among the current nondrinkers who formerly drank, 50 percent had reported that they stopped because it made them sick or thought it was bad for their health. These abstainers, however, reported being in as good health as those who had always abstained. There was also a relationship between level of current drinking and self-reports about health. Healthier respondents were more likely to drink than were those who reported poor health.

This relationship between drinking and health failed to be replicated in another study of institutionalized elders by Mishara et al. (1974) using the same questionnaires. They found no relationships between current reports of health and former drinking practices. In the Johnson (1974) study, consumption of alcoholic beverages was also associated with greater activity levels, including such things as shopping, reading, playing games, and social or cultural functions.

In the Cahalan et al. (1969) study, an Index of Social Position (ISP) showed an interesting association with drinking in the general population. There was generally a decrease in the proportion of light and moderate drinkers as one goes down the socioeconomic scale. This decrease in light and moderate drinkers also occurred among the elderly: those with the highest ISP (52 percent of males and 35 percent of females over age 60) were more frequently light and moderate drinkers than those with the lowest ISP (36 percent of males and 21 percent of females). Parallel differences could be seen in the percentage of respondents who abstained from drinking. In males, the highest ISP counted for 21 percent abstainers; upper-middle, 36 percent; lower-middle, 42 percent; and lowest, 36 percent. For females over age 60, the highest ISP had 41 percent abstainers; upper-middle, 58 percent; lower-middle, 52 percent; and lowest, 66 percent.

In the Cahalan et al. (1969) study, 61 percent of the abstainers indicated that they formerly drank. Of these, 10 percent said they stopped before age 25, and 14 percent had considered themselves at least fairly heavy drinkers. Among the women who abstained from drinking, 18 percent formerly drank, 2 percent stopped before age 25, and only 1 percent considered themselves at least fairly heavy drinkers. Major reasons for abstaining for males over age 60 included concern for health (30 percent); dislike of drink (24 percent); no need or desire (22 percent); religious or moral reasons (19 percent); bad example in the past (13 percent); financial reasons (13 percent); and upbringing (11 percent). Among women over age 60, religious or moral reasons for abstaining were highest (30 percent); followed by no need or desire (28 percent); upbringing (27 percent); dislike of drink (20 percent); bad example in past (20 percent); concern for health (18 percent); and financial reasons (6 percent). These figures differ somewhat from those of younger age groups. Among the males, religious or moral reasons were cited more frequently in ages 30 to 49. Among women, religious or moral reasons were generally highest from age 30 onward, but the women aged 60 and over were slightly more frequently brought up not to drink as compared to middle-aged women. Similar age differences in religious and moral reasons were not observed for the males.

Cahalan et al. (1969) classified drinkers as nonescape drinkers, escape drinkers, and heavy escape drinkers. These classifications were based upon questions about why people drink. Escapist answers indicated drinking to help relax, to ease tenseness, to help cheer up, to help forget worries, or to forget everything. In addition, respondents were classified as scoring high or low on an alienation scale. In general, heavy drinkers had higher scores on the alienation scale. It was then hypothesized that a higher alienation score would be related to tendencies to drink for escape reasons. Table 3.2 indicates the percentage of escape and heavy escape drinkers by alienation score and sex. Among

Table 3.2
Percentage of Escape and Heavy Escape Drinkers, by Alienation
Score[a] and Sex

	N	Abstainers + Infreq. Drinkers	Light, Mod. + Heavy		Heavy Escape Drinkers[b]
			Nonescape Drinkers	Escape Drinkers	
Total sample	2746	47	35	18	6
Men					
Age 21–39					
Low score	321	25	54	21	9
High score	138	23	46	31	17
Age 40–59					
Low score	331	32	45	23	11
High score	130	36	37	27	13
Age 60+					
Low score	139	42	44	14	4
High score	118	54	20	26	9
Women					
Age 21–39					
Low score	400	52	34	14	2
High score	201	48	25	27	9
Age 40–59					
Low score	382	53	35	12	3
High score	216	65	21	14	3
Age 60+					
Low score	194	68	23	9	c
High score	173	79	11	10	1

This table is reprinted courtesy of Cahalan et al., 1969.
[a] High Alienation = agreed with two or more of four statements from Alienation scale.
[b] Base: total sample
[c] Less than 0.5%.

persons under age 40 and among men of all ages, more of those with
higher alienation scores were heavier escape drinkers. Cahalan et al.
concluded that "a higher tendency towards feelings of alienation related
to a higher likelihood of drinking for reasons of escape from one's
personal problems or moods (such as anxiety of depression)" (p. 170).

CONCLUSIONS

Overall, the results indicate that old people drink less than younger people. According to these data, among old people, there are few very heavy drinkers. A considerable number of people seem to reduce the extent of their alcohol consumption as they grow older, usually after age 50. No single reason for this reduction has been corroborated. It is likely that a combination of factors are involved: Elderly people may stop or reduce imbibing because they feel that alcohol may have some negative effect on their health. Some quit for financial reasons; the luxury of buying alcohol beverages may be beyond their limited financial means. Some of the reported reduction of alcohol intake may be a distortion of the facts, however. Elderly people, for whatever reasons, may not report the true extent of their consumption. Perhaps those who say they never drank throughout their life are forgetting, quite conveniently, the foibles of their youth. Since alcohol consumption in the general U.S. population is rising, we might expect that elders in future years will be drinking more.

Perhaps the reason that elderly people consume less alcohol relates to their knowledge about the effects of drinking. Subjective reports of the effects of drinking indicate that many people feel alcohol helps them to forget or escape from their present reality. These characteristics of alcoholic beverages may result in problem drinking, which is discussed in the next chapter. However, numerous laboratory and clinical studies (e.g., Wallgren & Barry, 1970) indicate that alcohol may lower a person's performance on cognitive and motor tasks. Aging is often associated with the reductions in cognitive and psychomotor performance (Bromley, 1974). Increased performance difficulties appear to be well documented, although there is lively current controversy over the extent, causation, and reversibility of apparent age-related deficits (Horn & Donaldson, 1976; Baltes & Schaie, 1976). Perhaps older people who are fearful of their own bodily decline are reluctant to engage in behavior that might exacerbate their difficulties.

One interpretation of human behavior is that our potential to perform various tasks generally exceeds what is required of us in most situations. We are able to do our work easily without using anywhere near the maximum of our reasoning powers. As people get older, according to this view, the gap between what is required of them and the potential they have to draw upon may diminish to the point where performance in daily activities may require close to the maximum potential an individual has on hand. Under such circumstances, elderly people or people who are approaching old age may be quite wary of engaging in an activity such as drinking that they feel could inhibit or disrupt their behavior. They would no longer have the competence to control their actions in an effective manner or even carry out the simplest daily tasks. Perhaps it is this stereotype of the effects of alcohol that lead many people to stop this behavior as they approach their old age.

The stereotype may work through another mechanism as well. Elders may fear that their *reputations* as competent people might be compromised if they continue to use alcoholic beverages. Fears of this type have been expressed by some of the elders who have been approached to participate in alcohol-use studies by the authors.

The fear of ill health from drinking has been reported as a frequent reason for stopping. In this regard, it is interesting to note that at least one study showed that those who stopped because of fear of ill health had no more health problems than those who abstained. Furthermore, recent evidence (Shurtleff, 1970) suggests that mortality risks in old age are somewhat greater for people who abstain than for those who drink moderate amounts.

REFERENCES

Amark, C. A study in alcoholism. *Acta Psychiatrica Scandinavia,* 1951, Suppl. *70,* 273.

Baltes, P. B., & Schaie, K. W. On the plasticity of intelligence in adulthood and old age. *American Psychologist,* 1976, *31,* 720–725.

Belloc, N. Relationship of health practices and mortality. *Preventive Medicine,* 1973, *2,* 67–81.

Bromley, D. B. *The psychology of human ageing.* Middlesex, Eng.: Penguin, 1974.

Butler, E. *Why survive? Being old in America.* New York: Harper & Row, 1975.

Cahalan, D., Cisin, I. H., & Crossley, H. M. *American drinking practices; A national study of drinking behavior and attitudes* (Monograph No. 6). New Brunswick, N.J.: Rutgers Center of Alcohol Studies, 1969.

Caravan Surveys Inc. *Executives' knowledge, attitudes, and behavior regarding alcoholism and alcohol abuse.* Report prepared for National Institute on Alcohol Abuse and Alcoholism. Princeton, N.J.: ORC Caravan Surveys, 1972.

Chafetz, M. E. *U.S. Department of Health, Education and Welfare, Public Health Service, alcohol and health second special report to the U.S. Congress.* Washington: U.S. Government Printing Office, 1974.

Drew, L. R. H. Alcohol as a self-limiting disease. *Quarterly Journal of Studies on Alcoholism,* 1968, *29,* 956–967.

Edwards, G., Chandler, J., Hensman, C., & Peto, J. Drinking in a London suburb. II. Correlates of trouble with drinking among men. *Quarterly Journal of Studies on Alcoholism,* 1972, *6,* 94– 119.

Efron, V., Keller, M., & Gurioli, C. *Statistics on consumption of alcohol and on alcoholism.* New Brunswick, N.J.: Rutgers Center of Alcohol Studies, 1974.

Encel, S., Kotowicz, K. C., & Resler, H. E. Drinking patterns in Sydney, Australia. *Quarterly Journal of Studies on Alcoholism,* 1972, Suppl. *6,* 1–27.

Haberman, P. W. Denial of drinking in a household survey. *Quarterly Journal of Studies on Alcoholism,* 1970, *31,* 710– 717.

Harris, L., & Associates, Inc. *Public awareness of the National Institute on Alcohol Abuse and Alcoholism advertising campaign and public attitudes toward drinking and alcohol abuse* (Phase 1: Fall 1972, Study No. 2224; Phase 2: Spring 1973, Study No. 1218; Phase 3: Fall, 1973, Study No. 2342; and Phase 4: Winter 1974 and overall summary, Study No. 2355.) Reports prepared for the National Institute on Alcohol Abuse and Alcoholism.

Horn, J. L., & Donaldson, G. On the myth of intellectual decline in adulthood. *American Psychologist,* 1976, *31,* 701–719.

Horton, D. The functions of alcohol in primitive societies: A cross-cultural study. *Quarterly Journal of Studies on Alcoholism* 1943, *4,* 199–320.

Jessor, R., Young, H. B., Young, E. B., & Tesi, G. Perceived opportunity, alienation, and drinking behavior among Italian and American youth. *Journal of Personality and Social Psychology,* 1970, *15,* 215–222.

Johnson, L. A. Use of alcohol by persons 65 years and over, Upper East Side of Manhattan. Final report on Contract HSM-43-73-38 NIA. Submitted to National Institute on Alcohol Abuse and Alcoholism, January 1974.

Knupfer, G., & Room. R. Abstainers in a metropolitan community. *Quarterly Journal of Studies on Alcoholism,* 1970, *31,* 108– 131.

Lolli, G., Serianni, E., Golder, G. M., & Luzzatto-Fegiz, P. *Alcohol in Italian culture: Food and wine in relation to sobriety among Italians and Italian Americans* (Monograph No. 3). New Brunswick, N.J.: Rutgers Center of Alcohol Studies, 1958.

Milgram, G. G. *What is alcohol? and why do people drink!* New Brunswick, N.J.: Center for Alcohol Studies, Rutgers University, 1975.

Mishara, B. L., Kastenbaum, R., Patterson, R., & Baker, F. A study of alcohol effects in old age (Phase II). Final report on Contract #NO1-AA-3-0103. Submitted to National Institute on Alcohol Abuse and Alcoholism, 1974.

Moore, R. A. Alcoholism in Japan. *Quarterly Journal of Studies on Alcoholism,* 1964, *25,* 142– 150.

Mulford, H. A. Drinking and deviant drinking, U.S.A., 1963. *Quarterly Journal of Studies on Alcoholism,* 1964, *25,* 39–53.

Plaut, T. F. A. *Alcohol problems: A report to the nation by the Cooperative Commission on the Study of Alcoholism.* New York: Oxford University Press, 1967.

Room, R. Drinking patterns in large U.S. cities; a comparison of San Francisco and national samples. *Quarterly Journal of Studies on Alcoholism,* 1972, Suppl., *6,* 28– 57.

Room, R., & Day, N. *Alcohol and mortality.* Special report to the National Institute on Alcohol Abuse and Alcoholism, March 1974.

Shurtleff, D. Some characteristics related to the incidence of cardiovascular disease and death: Framingham study, a 16-year follow-up. In W. B. Kannel & T. Gordon (Eds.), *The Framingham Study,* Section 26. Washington, DC: U.S. Government Printing Office, 1970.

Wallace, J. G. Drinkers and abstainers in Norway. *Quarterly Journal of Studies on Alcoholism,* 1972, Suppl., *6,* 129–151.

Wallgren, H., & Barry, H. III. *Actions of alcohol,* Vol I: *Biochemical, physiologicål, and psychological aspects;* Vol. II: *Chronic and chemical aspects.* New York: Elsevier, 1970.

4
Problem Drinking

The prevalence of problem drinking seems to be lower in the elderly than in other age groups (see Chapter 3); still, significant numbers of elderly experience difficulties related to alcohol consumption. This chapter reviews studies on the extent and nature of alcoholism and alcohol-related problems in older groups.

WHAT IS AN ALCOHOL "PROBLEM" IN OLD AGE?

A social worker once told the story of an elderly client who came into a clinic and said that he had a drinking problem. When asked to describe the problem, he said that since he had retired, he no longer could afford to drink as much as he had in the past and that was his problem! If it were left to the client to identify whether a drinking problem exists, many of the people who are characterized as "problem drinkers" would neither realize they had a problem nor admit to it. The diagnosis of alcohol-related troubles has generally been made on the basis of outside rather than self-report evaluation. Carruth (1973) has suggested that in old age, drinking problems include nine constellations of symptoms reported for the general population by Cahalan et al. (1969):

1. Symptoms developed as a result of drinking, such as debilitating hangovers, blackouts, memory loss, and "shakes."

2. Psychological dependence on alcohol, defined as the inability to conduct normal everyday tasks without drinking or planning one's life around drinking.
3. Health problems related to alcohol use, including accidents resulting from and existing health problems being compounded by drinking.
4. Financial problems related to alcohol use.
5. Problems with spouse or relatives as a result of alcohol use.
6. Problems with friends or neighbors as a result of alcohol use.
7. Problems on the job as a result of drinking.
8. Belligerance associated with drinking.
9. Problems with police or the law as a result of drinking.

The above difficulties are not always mutually exclusive, and most people are defined as problem drinkers when they exhibit more than one symptom from this list. For example, in the detailed studies of the elderly by Williams et al. (1973), problem drinkers were defined as persons experiencing difficulties in three or more of the above nine symptoms.

People may have some of the above symptoms without anyone knowing they are problem drinkers. Survey results suggest that the elderly tend to drink either alone or in family groups more than younger people do (Cahalan et al., 1969). Thus, these symptoms in the elderly are less likely to be noticed than with younger people who drink in public places. Since elderly people tend to have more health problems in general, this may obscure the effect of alcohol on existing difficulties. Many elders experience financial problems because they live on fixed incomes from retirement or social security benefits, and so buying liquor often becomes a financial burden. Elderly women in particular are much more likely to have experienced the loss of a spouse, so current marital problems might not be associated with drinking. Compared to younger adults, a relatively small proportion of the elderly hold jobs, so problems on the job as a result of drinking would be less frequent. Williams (1973) suggests that there are many older individuals who are not diagnosed or treated as problem drinkers because they have (1) avoided contact with agencies who could provide care, (2) stopped contact with the care-providing system before their drinking problem was detected, or (3) managed to receive treatment for other symptoms while their alcohol-related problems remained undiagnosed and untreated.

THE EXTENT OF ALCOHOL PROBLEMS IN OLD AGE

As we have seen in Chapter 3, national population surveys found fewer heavy drinkers among the elderly than in other age groups. Older people also were less likely to report drinking-related problems than younger adults. For example, high "current problem scores," which indicate psychological, health, economic or drinking pattern difficulties, occurred in only 8 percent of men over age 60 and in 1 percent of women over age 60, as compared to 15 percent of men aged 40 to 59, 20 percent of men aged 21 to 39, 5 percent of women aged 40 to 59, and 5 percent of women aged 21 to 39 (Cahalan et al., 1969). It should be noted, as we discussed in detail in Chapter 3, that survey results may be subject to numerous methodological problems that may bias the results for different groups toward either overreporting or underreporting.

Although survey findings indicate that the extent of alcohol consumption in old age is fairly small, research literature on alcohol use by the elderly is dominated by studies reporting the dire conditions of elderly alcoholics and their need for help. For example, an article in the *New England Journal of Medicine* entitled "A Paradoxical Refuge" (1951) discussed the special problems of alcoholism in old age cause by retirement, our social treatment of the elderly, and the elderly person's physical changes. The findings were in sharp contrast to articles by Drew (1968) and Von Mering and Weniger (1959) which conclude that alcohol abuse among the aged does *not* constitute a major social problem. Perhaps the difference in opinion stems from one's perspective. Researchers may find that compared to other age groups, alcohol poses very little problem for most elderly people or that among all the problems elderly people face, alcohol is one of the less important difficulties. This is no solace to the practitioner who is trying to help an older person with his alcohol problems or a general hospital director faced with a high proportion of hospital admissions consisting of older people with alcohol-related complications. Even if, as the survey data suggest, alcoholism and alcohol abuse are less frequent, it still exists and can pose a serious disruption to the life of the older person. It also affects a large constellation of friends, family members, and medical and social service agencies.

This chapter summarizes studies that have documented the extent of alcohol-related problems among institutional admissions and treatment programs. All the studies suffer from the common limitation that each was sampled from a specific population at a specific institution (or institutions). This makes it difficult to generalize about the applicability of their findings to institutions in different geographic locations or to agencies serving populations with different characteristics. The variability among the different studies suggests strongly that factors such as socioeconomic level, ethnic and cultural differences, and geographical location (urban versus rural) may play an important mediating role in alcohol-related difficulties in old age.

One must keep in mind that all agency studies involve only those people who come to their attention. Some agencies work primarily with individuals who seek help voluntarily. Other agencies mainly serve people who are brought in for help involuntarily by police or emergency ambulances. These studies indicate nothing about the person who remains outside the network of agencies for whatever reason, for example, those with symptoms were not diagnosed accurately enough to lead them to an agency where appropriate treatment was available. The studies totally ignore people who keep their problems to themselves and display no dramatic external public symptoms that lead to their being apprehended.

ALCOHOLISM AMONG THE INSTITUTIONALIZED ELDERLY

Table 4.1 summarizes studies on the proportion of elderly people seeking treatment at various agencies. Favre and Meuron (1963) studied all clients who came to an alcohol clinic in Geneva, Switzerland, during the year 1960. It was found that 10.3 percent of the 252 males and 12.5 percent of the 48 females were over age 60. Alcoholism was defined in this study as the incapacity to stop drinking once having begun or the inability to abstain from drinking in the first place. Of the 25 people in their sixties, 11 were diagnosed as primary alcoholics: their addiction appeared to be a matter of long-standing habit that was begun before age 45. The remaining 14 were classified as having secondary alcoholism that was a reaction to either psychotic or neurotic difficulties. Of those 25 people in their sixties, 12 were married, 5 were single, 6 widowed, and 2 divorced. They reported that 2 male clients began their drinking in old age as a reaction to growing older. But in contrast to this, one woman stopped drinking entirely as a reaction to growing older.

Perhaps the most extensive survey in terms of number of residences covered was conducted by Gaillard and Perrin (1969) in France. They sent survey questionnaires to the medical directors of 161 rest homes. Overall, they found a remarkable amount of alcoholism, particularly among the homes for men. Among the 128 rest homes for men, the average report was that 25 percent of the residents were acute al-

Table 4.1
Studies of the Proportion of Elderly People Seeking Treatment
at Various Agencies and Living in the General Population

Authors	Population/ Agency	Sampling Method	Sample Size	Results
Cahalan, Cisin, & Crossley (1969)	U.S. population	Probability sample	624 people over 60	6% of elderly, heavy drinkers
Chu (1972)	San Francisco Chinese community	Survey	41 Chinese men, age 52–85	7.3% of elderly, heavy drinkers
Favre & Meuron (1963)	Geneva Alcoholism Agency	All clients seen in 1960	252, male; 48, female	10.3% of male clients and 12.5% of female clients were over age 60
Gaillard & Perrin (1969)	Rest homes in France	Physician's reports	All residents in 174 homes	25% of males; 11% of females chronic alcoholics
Gaitz & Baer (1971)	Texas psychiatric screening ward	Consecutive admissions	100 admissions, over age 60	Alcoholism diagnosed in 53% of males and 30% of females
Gillis & Keet (1969)	Cape Town, S. Africa Treatment Program (Alcoholism)	Consecutive admissions 1959–1964	797 (all white; 86% male)	2% of clients were over age 60
Graux (1969)	Rest home in Lille, France	All residents	Not given	33% of males and 10% of females over 60, alcoholics
Harrington & Price (1962)	Mississippi Veterans Administration Domiciliary	All admissions	236, age 61–70; 33, over 70	14% aged 61–70 and 1.4% over 70, history of alcoholism

Table 4.1 (continued)

Authors	Population/ Agency	Sampling Method	Sample Size	Results
Hoffman (1970)	Minnesota State Hospital	Consecutive admissions for alcoholism	377 out of 400	22% were aged 56–72
Kramer (1969)	279 U.S. state and county mental hospitals	All admissions in 1967	153 male, 314 female	Of new admissions: 30% aged 55–64; 9% age 65–74, and 1% over 75, major diagnosis of alcoholism
Lennon et al. (1970)	Massachusetts Chronic Disease Hospital	Consecutive admissions for tuberculosis	530 male	58% of those over age 60 had been arrested for drunkenness
Lutterotti (1969)	Italian Rural Hospital Internal Medicine Department	Alcoholics seen	400	36% were over age 60
Myerson & Mayer (1966)	Halfway House in Massachusetts	Skid row alcoholics	208 male	Median age was 46, 30% were in their 50s, 54% in their 40s
Pequignot et al. (1969)	Paris Hospital	Patients over age 60	905	9.2% were alcoholics, 4.3% in acute alcoholic states
Rosin & Glatt (1971)	English Nursing Home for Female Alcoholics and Drug Addicts	Consecutive admissions	706 admissions, 1950–1966	3.7% were over age 70

Table 4.1 (continued)

Authors	Population/ Agency	Sampling Method	Sample Size	Results
Schuckit & Miller (1976)	California Veterans Administration Hospital	Consecutive admissions to acute medical unit	113 of 194 male admissions over age 65	7.9% were active alcoholics
Simon, Epstein & Reynolds (1968)	San Francisco General Hospital	First admission psychiatric patients	534 age 60 and over	23% diagnosed as alcoholics
Wax (1975)	Baltimore, Maryland residents	Population sample	Not reported	5% of those over age 55, problem drinkers

coholics. Only 5 of the responding institutions indicated no alcoholism in their facility. The authors suggest that the 25 percent figure is perhaps the underestimation of the number of active elders who have alcoholism problems, since this figure was derived from a sample that includes bedridden patients who would have a difficult time becoming addicted to alcohol. Acute alcoholism among women was found in only 11 of 161 institutions. The prevalence of women with acute alcoholism in these 11 establishments ranged from 1 to 10 percent, with an average of 3.5 percent. For both men and women, it was reported that acute alcoholism resulted in sleep disturbance of other residents owing to inebriated speech and bellowing brawls between residents (sometimes with injuries), soiling of clothing from vomiting or incontinence, and aggressiveness of lack of discipline with regard to the staff.

Acute alcoholism was distinguished from chronic alcoholism, which was defined as regular addiction to alcoholic beverages. Overall, 41 percent of the men in 128 institutions reporting were considered chronic alcoholics. More than half of the male residents in 47 institutions were regarded by the medical directors as chronic alcoholics. The average institution reported that 11.6 percent of its women were chronic alcoholics.

In their discussion of reasons for this high prevalence of alcoholism in French rest homes, the authors cited the cultural practice of drinking at a young age and the low educational levels of many of the residents. It was also stated that most of the homes provided little in the way of recreation; there was little to do other than sit around and drink. There were numerous cafes in the vicinity of rest homes (e.g., 36 cafes in a town of 2000 inhabitants). The staff was cited for encouraging or being indifferent to elders who drink, and physicians were criticized for allowing residents to consume large quantities of alcoholic beverages. In fact, 89 percent of the institutions themselves served wine with limits of from 1 glass to 1 liter per day per person. Two percent of the institutions served a full liter of wine per person per day, and 23 percent served a half liter of wine per day. In addition to legal or condoned consumption on the premises, it was common to smuggle alcoholic beverages into the institutions. It is interesting to note that in 53 percent of the homes, wine was prescribed by physicians in doses usually between one-quarter and one-half a liter each day. The physicians who prescribed wine for elderly residents gave the following reasons for doing so: "French tradition does not allow one to give them anything else but wine." "All the other beverages except wine are not well accepted by the elderly." "It seems cruel to me to eliminate the daily ration of wine because they are accustomed to it and it is their only source of comfort."

Overall, 57 percent of the physicians surveyed felt it was "impossible," "difficult," or "very difficult" to change the drinking patterns in their institutions. Forty-three percent of the physicians who felt that it was possible to reduce drinking problems among the elderly suggested that first one would have to establish a system of strict surveillance of visitors and of elders when they returned from excursions outside of the institutions. Second most frequent among their possible solutions was the provision for more recreational activities such as game rooms, television, libraries, and planned manual activities in sheltered workshops. Among the less frequent suggestions were the elimination of cafes in close proximity to institutions for the elderly, control of money given to elders, and elimination of wine on the premises. One physician suggested that the doctors should practice what they preach and set an example by not drinking themselves. Another suggested that elders who work should not be paid with supplements of wine. The skeptical physicians who felt it was impossible or difficult to limit alcohol consumption in institutions for the elderly saw the problem in the elderly as inseparable from the general national policy toward alcohol consumption.

Overall, the authors conclude that alcoholism among the institutionalized elderly is not so much a medical as it is a social problem. In order to prevent alcoholism in old age, it would be helpful to have elders continue the pursuit of activities that allow them to maintain their physical and mental health. They stressed the need for preparation for retirement as well as education against alcoholism, not just for the elderly but for people of all ages.

Gaitz and Baer (1971) studied 100 consecutive admissions of persons over age 60 to a psychiatric screening board in Texas. They found that 44 of these elderly patients were diagnosed as having some type of alcoholism. Primary alcoholism (36 cases) was more common than secondary alcoholism (8 cases). Only 5 of the 44 patients diagnosed as alcoholics began their excessive drinking after age 50. The authors state, however, that even for these patients, the duration of excessive drinking ranged from 2 to 22 years. In addition, they felt that it is difficult to obtain precise data about when they began drinking excessively or when their drinking became a serious problem.

In the Gaitz and Baer study, alcoholics with diagnosed organic brain syndrome (OBS) were compared with alcoholics without OBS and with nonalcoholic psychiatric patients with OBS. Alcoholics without OBS generally were in better health and showed fewer other psychiatric problems. Interestingly, alcoholics with OBS tended to be younger than other patients with OBS who did not have alcohol-related difficulties. Overall, 61 percent of the alcoholics among the elderly were diagnosed as having OBS. Mortality for alcoholics with OBS was higher than that for alcoholics without OBS, as it was for psychiatric patients with OBS. They concluded that "the presence of OBS with alcoholism drastically affects survival . . . among non-OBS alcoholics mortality was consistent with actuarial rates for their age levels" (Gaitz & Baer, 1971, p. 378).

One of the most thorough surveys of diagnoses of people admitted to state and county mental hospitals was reported by Kramer (1969). In his study of all admissions (153,314) to 279 institutions in 1967, he found that 19 percent were diagnosed as having some type of alcoholism. Among persons aged 54 and younger, 28 percent were admitted for alcoholism. This figure is comparable to the 30 percent admitted between ages 55 and 64. It constitutes a drop from the 37 percent in the previous decade for ages 45 to 54. Still, in what is generally considered old age, alcoholism is an infrequent diagnosis for new admissions: among people aged 65 to 74 admitted to mental hospitals, only 9 percent were diagnosed as having alcoholism. Over age 75, this figure dropped to 1 percent. It is possible that more people were admitted with alcoholism problems, but their diagnosis was not made accurately. Considering Gaitz and Baer's findings that 61 percent of their small sample of mental hospital admissions with diagnoses of alcoholism also had OBS, perhaps many people with alcohol-related problems in the Kramer survey might instead have been placed in this more general category of OBS.

Simon, Epstein, and Reynolds (1968) studied 534 admissions to a psychiatric screening ward in San Francisco. Among those patients aged 60 and over, 28 percent had a serious drinking problem at the time they were admitted. Simon and Neal (1971) reported that among the same sample, over 50 percent of those who drank to excess suffered from OBS. The authors felt that since alcoholism problems were often present at the same time as other psychiatric conditions, such as OBS, it was often difficult to determine a diagnosis of alcoholism.

In a study of 797 consecutive admissions to a hospital treatment program for alcoholics between 1959 and 1964 in Cape Town (Gillis & Keet, 1969), only 2 percent of the clients were over age 60. This hospital was highly selective as to whom they would treat, however. Only voluntary white clients were admitted for treatment, excluding those "without motivation" and with "gross brain damage." There is no way of telling how many elderly people who may have needed help were turned away because of "gross brain damage."

The study by Graux (1969) confirmed the results by Favre and Meuron (1963) that alcoholism is quite frequent in rest homes in France. Graux studied rest homes in Lille. He found that among pensioners aged 45 to 60, 90 percent of the men and 80 percent of the women were alcoholics. Among residents over age 65, one-third of the men and 10 percent of the women were alcoholics. He cited the sordid atmosphere and called for increased activities, the provision of other beverages such as coffee and fruit juices, and better medical attention.

Harrington and Price (1962) commented that there were relatively few admissions of people over age 60 with diagnoses of alcoholism. They suggested, however, that most people with alcohol-related problems are admitted earlier in life, usually before age 61.

There have been a number of other admission studies that give some indication of the elderly alcoholics receiving treatment. Hoffman (1970) studied 377 of 400 consecutive males admitted for treatment of alcoholism to a Minnesota hospital.

In this sample, 22 percent were between the ages of 56 and 72. Lennon et al. (1970) studied 530 males admitted for treatment of tuberculosis at a Massachusetts chronic disease hospital. He found that 58 percent had a history of previous arrests for drunkenness. Lennon and his associates pointed out the hidden problems of alcoholism among individuals admitted for other medical difficulties. In a study of 400 alcoholics admitted to an Italian hospital's internal medicine service, Lutterotti (1969) found that 36 percent were over age 60. Lutterotti suggested that, at least in his population of farmers and working-class people, alcoholism is a far greater problem among the elderly than has been previously suggested in the literature.

Other studies report data from which it is difficult to determine the exact number of people who might be termed "elderly." For example, Myerson and Mayer (1966) studied 208 men who were classified as "skid row" alcoholics reporting for treatment at a halfway-house program initiated by a Massachusetts hospital. They reported a median age of 46 and a range from the early twenties to the early sixties, and noted that 53.5 percent were in their forties and 29.7 percent were in their fifties. No information was provided as to how many were over age 50 and how many were under 40. Rosin and Glatt (1971) observed that of the 706 alcoholic patients admitted to a nursing home near London dealing exclusively with alcoholics and drug addicts, only 3.7 percent were over the age of 70. Unfortunately, it is difficult to determine how many of those over age 70 might have fallen into the category of "drug addicts" rather than alcoholics. Simon et al. (1968) studied psychiatric admissions to a San Francisco general hospital. They included only people aged 60 and over who were first admissions for a psychiatric problem and who had no history of arrests. They found that 23 percent were diagnosed as alcoholics. In addition, 5 percent of those who had no diagnosis of alcoholism were classified as "heavy social drinkers."

Wax (1975) reported preliminary findings on a study of the elderly in the Baltimore, Maryland, area. She reported a 5 percent prevalence of "problem drinking." However, she commented that this prevalence might be higher in winter, as homeless alcoholics seek shelter, although this would not be relevant to some of her subsamples. Her observation about seasonal variations might well apply in many other locales as well.

Schuckit and Miller (1976) studied 113 of 194 consecutive admissions of males over age 65 to the acute medical ward of a California veteran's administration hospital. They found that 20 of the men could be classified as having been alcoholics at some time in their life but that only 9 of the 20 could be termed "active alcoholics." A few of the other 11 reported occasional current drinking, but none indicated any difficulties.

Several studies of special ethnic or national groups are of interest. Chu (1972) studied 41 Chinese men living in San Francisco, 38 of whom were born in China. These men were aged 52 to 85. He found that 7.3 percent could be classified as "heavy drinkers," which he termed one or two drinks daily or three or four drinks on occasion at least once a month. Chu concluded that there is a low rate of alcoholism among Chinese in America as compared to whites because there is a high

abstinence level (26 of these 41 men studied) among the former. Pequignot and associates (1969) studied patients over the age of 60 who were
admitted to the Cochin Hospital in Paris between 1966 and 1968. They
found that 9.2 percent were alcoholics and 4.3 percent were in acute
alcoholic states at the time of their hospitalization.

These studies of the incidence of alcoholism and problem drinking
brought to the attention of different agencies show a great diversity of
findings. If one looks just at people over age 60 or 65 who are admitted
for alcohol-related disorders, we find that these make up between 5 and
54 percent of admissions to the institutions surveyed. Reasons for the
great discrepancies from study to study include the following: (1) the
unique nature of each facility—some places have a reputation for the
treatment of alcoholism and thus attract more people with alcohol-
related problems than other facilities; (2) ethnic and cultural difference in
the population that various institutions serve; (3) differences in the
abilities of various agencies to find and attract individuals with specific
types of problems; and (4) regional variations in the incidence of alcoholism among the elderly.

If one looks instead at the percentage of *all* people treated for
alcoholism difficulties, then the picture changes. A fairly small proportion of people treated for alcoholism are over age 60 or 65. Although
there are probably exceptions among special populations (e.g., residents
of French rest homes), it seems that a fairly low proportion of alcoholics
who come to the attention of institutions for treatment are elderly. These
findings may reflect either a low incidence of alcohol-related problems
among the elderly or the fact that elderly people are not treated in many
agencies because of institutional practices and prejudices or because the
elderly themselves do not seek treatment. Another possibility is that
alcoholism may not be adequately diagnosed among some elderly people
who receive treatment for other medical or psychiatric problems.

National Institute of Mental Health Statistical Notes

Statistical data compiled by the U.S. National Institute of Mental
Health (NIMH) include tabulations of the diagnoses of patients admitted
for treatment in various facilities. Data collected in 1969 (U.S. NIMH,
1971a) indicated that 6 percent of people over age 65 admitted to state
and county mental hospitals were diagnosed as suffering from alcoholism. Another survey (U.S. NIMH, 1969) indicated that 6 percent of
all people discharged over age 65 from general hospitals had alcohol-
related diagnoses. Among people over age 65 admitted to private mental

hospitals, 9 percent of the admission diagnoses were for alcohol disorders (U.S. NIMH, 1972).

In general, elderly people constitute quite a small percentage of those who receive outpatient psychiatric services and treatment on an outpatient basis in community mental health centers. People aged 65 and over constitute only 2 to 4 percent of all outpatient psychiatric services (U.S. NIMH, 1971b). Among this small number of people who received outpatient treatment, 12 percent were diagnosed as having alcohol-related problems.

INPATIENT TREATMENT CENTERS

Statistical data compiled by the NIMH indicate that among all admissions to inpatient facilities for the treatment of alcoholism, people age 65 and over are most likely to be admitted to a general hospital (U.S. NIMH, 1970). Half (49.8 percent) of the people 65 and over admitted for alcoholism treatment were treated at general hospitals. The next most likely treatment center is a Veteran's Administration hospital, where 27.7 percent of older people treated for alcoholism sought help. Less frequent sources of inpatient help for the elderly are state and county mental hospitals (9.7 percent), private mental hospitals (8.8 percent)[1] and outpatient services at community mental health centers (4.0 percent).

This reflects a pattern different from that of younger alcoholics. Younger alcoholics in all age brackets are most frequently treated at state and county mental hospitals, accounting for almost 50 percent of admissions. Private hospitals for other age groups account for between 3 and 5 percent, community mental health centers account for slightly less than 4 percent, and general hospitals compete with VA hospitals for the balance. This different pattern of admissions for alcoholism may reflect the fact that elderly alcoholics more frequently have medical complications that necessitate their admission to a medical facility, whereas younger alcoholics might be engaged in socially unacceptable behavior that leads to a temporary commitment or temporary institutionalization in a state or county mental hospital.

THE AGE OF ONSET OF HEAVY DRINKING

When do most elderly alcoholics begin drinking? Have they been alcoholics since their younger years or are they people who began their

[1]The general hospital's data are on discharges, while all other data are on admissions diagnoses.

heavy drinking in old age as a reaction to changing life circumstances? We know from the survey data presented in Chapter 3 that many people reduce or stop their alcohol consumption before their later years. This, however, does not indicate when the onset of heavy drinking occurred among those who can be classified as alcoholics or heavy drinkers in old age.

Because the number of elderly people who are heavy drinkers is fairly small, most studies have chosen to look at early onset as prior to age 45 or 50. Bahr (1969) surveyed 94 men residing in the Bowery area of New York City. He found that 7 percent had begun their heavy drinking after age 45. Bahr also surveyed 104 men who were residents of a custodial and rehabilitative institution near New York that specialized in serving chronic alcoholics. At this institution, 20 percent had begun their heavy drinking at age 45 and over. A similar community survey of Chicago skid row residents conducted by Bogue (1963) indicated that only 4 percent of the 339 men studied began their heavy drinking at age 45 and over. In their study of a Geneva, Switzerland, alcoholism clinic's clients, Favre and Meuron (1963) found that of their 232 men, 6.9 percent began their heavy drinking between ages 41 and 50 and that none started drinking heavily later in life.

Unfortunately, the above studies do not provide sufficient data to estimate the proportion of elderly alcoholics in the general population who began drinking heavily in their later years. The statistics indicate, however, that there is a sufficiently small onset of heavier drinking in late middle age, which at least suggests that the percentage of drinking problems that develop over age 60 is probably quite small, at least in the population studied. Gaitz and Baer (1971) studied 100 persons over age 60 admitted to a Texas psychiatric screening ward. They found that of the elderly alcoholics, 11.4 percent began their heavier drinking after age 60. This is by far the largest percentage of drinking problems intensified in old age that we have found in the literature.

Present knowledge does not allow us to speculate on the incidence of people who seek escape or solace for problems in old age by imbibing alcohol. Most studies have been interested in comparisons between the very young and the late middle-aged. Although clinical histories occasionally mention the older person whose drinking problems began with the death of a spouse in old age or as a response to the boredom of retirement, it is not known to what extent such case histories reflect a common pattern of drinking among the elderly. It is known, however, that some elderly people who were alcoholics in their younger years do survive to continue their drinking in old age.

CHARACTERISTICS OF ELDERLY PROBLEM DRINKERS

How, if at all, are older problem drinkers different from the elderly population in general? Why do older people become problem drinkers? The answers to these questions seem crucial for formulating prevention programs to avoid problem drinking in old age. One must bear in mind that most of the older problem drinkers identified in research had an onset of their drinking problems well before they reached old age. Thus the reason for starting drinking for many older problem drinkers may rest in the distant past and be difficult to apply to current drinking habits. There can be an important difference between why a person started drinking and why, years later, he or she continues to drink. The question may shift to why a person has continued an earlier pattern of drinking rather than ceasing this behavior before reaching old age.

The characteristics of elderly problem drinkers have been studied by several investigators. The authors often speculate on how the problems associated with old age lead people to drink. Unfortunately, there are few data comparing elderly people who are problem drinkers to those who drink but do not exhibit alcoholism problems, or comparing problem drinkers to those who abstain in old age. Furthermore, comparative studies have not been conducted to determine whether older people drink for different reasons than younger people.

It is also important to note that all studies have been cross-sectional in nature, sampling different age groups at one point in time. This method does not allow determination as to whether people actually change their characteristics and their reasons for drinking, nor does it allow determination of whether any differences between older and younger groups reflect patterns and changes inherent in the aging process or just differences between the *generation* of people who are younger and the generation of older people, many of whom lived under Prohibition and experienced quite a different cultural upbringing.

Are older alcoholics or older problem drinkers different from younger problem drinkers? What are older alcoholics like? Answers to these questions vary depending on where you select your sample of elderly alcoholics. Elderly skid row problem drinkers probably exhibit different characteristics in their drinking than, for example, those who seek treatment in expensive private hospitals. Rosin and Glatt (1971) studied 103 people over age 65 with drinking problems in England. Their sample included psychiatric patients or patients of alcoholism treatment centers and those in a "geriatric" unit. There was a 3:2 ratio of women to men. From this sample, they identified a group with long-standing problems who continued to drink in old age and a second group who they felt had previously indulged in "innocuous" drinking that was "exacerbated by the physical, mental, and environmental effects of aging."

Rosin and Glatt found a number of important characteristics of the problem drinker that they called "primary factors," as well as a number of life circumstances that were termed "reactive" factors. The most common primary factor, occurring in 43 of the 103 cases, was habitual, excessive, "inveterate" drinking. They identified this long-standing pattern of problem drinking as relating to psychological traits of neuroticism, self-indulgence, egocentricity, and a reliance on alcohol as a psychological support. The psychological factors were most evident in the group whose drinking was recently exacerbated by physical, mental, or environmental conditions. In 6 people, drinking had not been a problem until the onset of "dementia," which occurred with advancing age. Among the reactive factors, they cited bereavement as the most important cause precipitating excessive drinking. Other important causes of drinking problems were retirement, loneliness, and less frequently, physical infirmity and marital stress.

Rosin and Glatt also observed that the psychiatric group drank mostly distilled spirits, while the geriatric unit patients tended to be divided between beer drinkers and drinkers of distilled spirits. Six of the geriatric patients changed their beverage in their later years, usually to spirits. It is not stated whether or not this shift to hard liquors paralleled the onset of their drinking problems. They observed a wide range of problems related to excessive drinking, which they reported was similar to those that occur among younger alcoholics. Most frequent was deterioration of physical, mental, or social conditions, followed by self-neglect, falls, excessive incontinence, aggravation of confusion, paranoia, and family quarrels or estrangement.

Rosin and Glatt concluded that excessive long-standing drinking habits related most often to basic personality factors. A second group of old people, however, had not experienced any difficulty until the effects of aging directly influenced their drinking behavior. For example, depression resulting from bereavement or retirement precipitated heavy drinking in this group. They suggested preretirement courses to help people cope with this major life change, as well as general improvement in the health care and social support systems of older persons.

The often cited findings of Rosin and Glatt were supported by preliminary results reported by Wax (1975). She found that most known problem drinkers had been separated from spouses and alienated from children. Wax felt that there was a high rate of repeaters, people who were admitted over and over again for inpatient alcoholism treatment, because they returned to their previous environment in which they had no useful ways of occupying their time. She stressed the importance of social and environmental factors as precipitating and supporting alcoholism among the aged.

Bahr (1969) distinguished between early (before age 45) and late (after age 45) onset heavy drinkers in samples of residents of the New York Bowery area and a New York area treatment program for chronic alcoholics. Late-onset heavy drinkers were more likely to live with their families throughout their lives, although as people aged, the likelihood of living with families declined steadily. Late-onset drinkers also had more affiliation and more occupational stress than early-onset drinkers.

An article appearing in *Alcohol Health and Research World* ("Older Problem Drinkers," 1975/1976) suggested that current reasons for excessive drinking among the elderly, even those who had been drinking for many years, were often related to boredom, loneliness, poor health, loss of status, and lower income rather than to psychological problems. No substantive data were offered to support this conclusion.

The issue at hand is whether or not problem drinking in old age is related primarily to environment or to long-standing personality characteristics. The distinction made by Rosin and Glatt (1971) attempts to identify two different groups on the basis of life patterns. Each group is thought to be primarily influenced by a long-term personality or mental health difficulty, while the person whose alcohol problems began or became troublesome in old age is more likely to be reacting to life stresses associated with aging, such as retirement, loss of spouse, or physical declines.

Some authors tend to ignore the unique effects of aging in their recommendations about problem drinking in old age. Riccitelli (1967) studied alcoholism in the elderly but did not distinguish any special characteristics of old age that help in one's understanding of alcoholism or problem drinking in this age group.

In studies conducted in Italy, Lutterotti (1969) suggested that one of the most important factors in alcoholism in old age is the nature of the family situation. Lutterotti points out that a harmonious family situation is best for older people, but when an alcoholic is in the family, it is difficult to avoid family problems. Sometimes alcoholism is a result of abandonment by a family, resulting in a lonely life in a hospital or psychiatric hospital. On the other hand, alcoholism might result from problems in the family, such as separation or divorce, death of a spouse, or family discord. A lowering of social status, the feeling of loss of control that may accompany old age, and retirement are also cited as important precipitating factors among workers who become alcoholics.

Marital status has been studied in terms of its possible influence on alcoholism throughout the life span. In a study by Rosenblatt et al. (1971) in the age group of 35 to 44, marital status shown to be a factor in multiple hospital admissions for alcoholism. The authors suggested that younger people may not have had time to establish stable marriages, while in older age groups, marriages tend to break up through death of a spouse, so the destructive effects of separation and divorce would not be present. In a follow-up study of psychiatric hospital admissions, the data replicated their conclusion that disrupted marriages relate to multiple hospitalizations for acute alcoholic psychoses at age 45 and below but not in the older groups (Rosenblatt et al., 1971).

Schuckit (1976, 1977) and Schuckit and associates (1976, 1977) conducted a number of in-depth surveys of elderly alcoholics. In the first study (Schuckit & Miller, 1976), 113 consecutively admitted male patients aged 65 and over were studied on the acute medical wards of a California Veteran's Administration hospital. On the basis of structured interviews within 5 days of hospital admission, they determined that alcoholics who were currently "active" and those who were "inactive" (defined as having alcohol-related problems in the last 6 months) did not differ with respect to their psychiatric or medical histories or demographic characteristics, such as age, marital status, education, or occupation. Furthermore, the active and inactive alcoholics did not differ on tests of organic brain syndrome. Active alcoholics had a higher rate of health and marital difficulties related their drinking and were heavier smokers.

The alcoholics in this study were compared to elderly psychiatric and medical patients. The people with alcohol-related problems tended to be younger and were more likely to live alone and to report multiple marriages, suicide attempts, and having been in jail. The elderly alcoholics were more likely than the elderly medical patients to report a better employment record, a *decreased* rate of cardiac disease, and an increased rate of chronic lung disease. The authors suggest that a lower rate of cardiac disorder may be due to the fact that "so many alcoholics die at younger ages from accidents and suicide in addition to cancer and lung disorders, that fewer of them remain at risk for cardiac disorders." Their position represents a skeptical view of studies that may indicate the possible benefits of imbibing alcoholic beverages (see Chapter 6).

Schuckit and Pastor (1978) vividly characterized what they felt were common forces and problems among elderly alcoholics. First, they observed that depression is almost invariably present in active alcoholics "as a result of pharmacologic effects of alcohol and the social stresses generated by inactive drinking life styles" (p. 12). Since this is a transitory effect that may disappear after abstinence, it does not indicate that the alcoholic necessarily suffers from an affective disorder. Second, they observed that the clinical picture of alcoholics can mimic schizophrenia. Symptoms such as auditory hallucinations and/or delusions may appear but will clear up following a period of abstinence. Third, they depicted alcoholics, particularly the elderly, as being in a state of confusion and disorientation. Therefore, it is important to realize that a seemingly "senile" older person who has alcohol-related problems may be reflecting a transitory acute organic brain syndrome that will disappear once the alcohol difficulties are treated. Furthermore, this picture of organic brain syndrome may relate to other common problems among alcoholics, such as vitamin deficiencies (especially thiamine) and general ill health and nutrition.

Schuckit et al. (1977) compared alcohol problems in elderly men and women. Their samples consisted of 191 women admitted to a Seattle detoxification center in 1976, and 186 men admitted to the inpatient alcoholic treatment program of a Seattle Veteran's Administration hospital in 1975 and 1976. They interviewed the women, but they obtained data from the men using a self-administered written questionnaire. As the authors point out, one must keep in mind that the differences between the men and women may be the result of differences between the characteristics of the detoxification center and Veteran's Administration samples. They also caution that structured interviews and questionnaires may not reflect actual life events, since they rely on the accuracy and honesty of the participants. Overall, characteristics of elderly alcoholic men and women were found to be quite similar. Both samples tended to be more stable in "general life" as compared to younger people with alcohol problems. The picture they arrived at was one of older people who developed alcohol-related problems later in life for "unknown reasons" after a more stable early life.

A few studies have investigated age differences in personality characteristics of problem drinkers. For example, Hoffman (1970) administered the Personality Research Form (PRF) to 377 hospitalized male alcoholics in four age groups, including an elderly group from ages 56 to 72. As with our criticism of other alcohol research, it should be kept in mind that this is a cross-sectional study and so can only indicate differences between people at their present ages rather than indicating changes that may accompany aging. Furthermore, the importance of comparative studies that use detailed pencil-and-paper measures can be determined only after the results are replicated with other populations of elderly people. Hoffman found that with increasing age, the factors of "change, dominance, exhibition, impulsivity, and play" *decreased* significantly. This indicated a general tendency toward introversion with increasing age. Other scales such as "cognitive structure, order, and harm avoidance" *increased* with age, and a number of other factors were low at both the youngest and oldest age groups. Unfortunately, no comparison group of nonalcoholic individuals of the same age was obtained to establish the baseline. It is impossible to tell, without such general age norms, to what extent their findings indicate characteristics of all elders as opposed to the subgroup of elderly alcoholics.

Apfeldorf and Hunley (1975) conducted a somewhat better controlled study in which they used an established alcoholism scale based upon the Minnesota Multiphasic Personality Inventory (MMPI) to compare older people diagnosed as alcoholics with people who were not alcoholics and with people who had disciplinary problems related to drinking but were not (yet?) diagnosed as "alcoholics." They studied 243 men residing at a Veteran's Administration treatment center. Thirty-one were alcoholics, 94 were nonalcoholics with records of "offenses indicating drinking problems," and the remaining 118 had no record of such offenses. The alcoholism scale differentiated the alcoholics *and* the residents with disciplinary problems related to alcohol from the control group who had no history of alcohol-related difficulties. They suggest that perhaps the scale can be used to identify problem drinkers who have "as yet not received diagnoses of alcoholism" and may be a useful research tool to study "decline with age in symptoms or personality traits of diagnosed alcoholics" (p. 652).

Thus far, we have looked at studies where outside observers have attempted to determine the characteristics, life situation, or psychiatric evaluation of older people with drinking problems by means of observation, interview, or questionnaire. Another research strategy would be to ask older people with drinking problems and others who have contact with them what they think are the reasons for their difficulties. Williams and Mysak (1973) surveyed 100 care providers in three communities, which included 15 separate agencies having contact with older problem drinkers. They divided the agencies having contact with older problem drinkers into four groups: health, social service, old age-related, and alcoholism agencies. A high proportion of both the health (72 percent) and the social service (79 percent) agencies' workers perceived loneliness, loss of spouse, or loss of other meaningful relationships as the most frequent cause of problem drinking. The second most frequently mentioned cause was physical and mental deterioration, which was reported as a major cause by 65 percent of the respondents from health agencies and 48 percent of the respondents from social service agencies. Other responses included depression, a sense of worthlessness and rejection, marital difficulties, insecurity and anxiety, isolation, financial problems, loss of employment, or lack of adjustment to retirement. The alcohol-related and old-age agencies rated loneliness and loss as causes in 72 percent and 75 percent respectively. The alcoholism agencies rated physical and mental deterioration 68 percent as compared to the age-related agencies, 39 percent. It is interesting to note that retirement was mentioned less frequently than in the specific inpatient studies cited earlier.

The views of people who work in agencies that have contact with older problem drinkers may give an interesting perspective on the problems presented by clients. It must be kept in mind, however, that an unknown number of people with alcohol-related problems do not come to agencies for aid, and thus the agencies' interpretations of the causes of the difficulties may not be applicable to the entire population of elderly people with drinking problems.

CONCLUSIONS

Because older problem drinkers have not been studied in as great depth as younger populations, it is difficult to know if the information we have accurately describes problem drinking in old age or merely indicates the characteristics of the tip of the iceberg, with the vast majority of hidden problem drinkers having much different characteristics. Before proceeding to conduct more in-depth investigations, it will be necessary to develop special definitions of "problem drinking," since definitions and criteria used to assess alcohol problems in younger age groups often do not apply. Studies of individual agencies and institutions suggest that alcohol problems among the elderly may be much more prevalent than indicated in nationwide surveys. It is difficult to draw firm conclusions from studies conducted in one location, however, since data are not available comparing the populations being studied with the elderly population as a whole. Studies show that there exist older persons who continued to have alcohol problems as an extension of a lifelong behavior pattern, as well as older persons who begin to have alcohol-related problems as a reaction to difficulties experienced in old age. These studies, considered together, emphasize the importance of educating personnel who deal with the elderly in recognizing and anticipating alcohol problems that may be masked by what some erroneously consider to be behavior typical of old age.

REFERENCES

A paradoxical refuge. *New England Journal of Medicine*, 1951, *245*, 268–269. (Editorial.)

Apfeldorf, M., & Hunley, P. J. Application of MMPI alcoholism scales to older alcoholics and problem drinkers. *Journal of Studies on Alcoholism*, 1975, *36*, 645–653.

Bahr, H. M. Lifetime affiliation patterns of early and late-onset heavy drinkers on skid row. *Quarterly Journal of Studies on Alcoholism*, 1969, *30*, 645–656.

Bogue, D. J. *Skid row in American cities*. Chicago: University of Chicago Community and Family Center, 1963, p. 294.

Cahalan, D., Cisin, I. H., & Crossley, H. M. *American drinking practices*, New Brunswick, N.J.: Rutgers Center of Alcohol Studies, 1969.

Carruth, B. Toward a definition of problem drinking among older persons: Conceptual and methodological considerations. In E. P. Williams et al. (Eds.), *Alcohol and problem drinking among older persons*. Springfield, Va: National Technical Information Service, 1973.

Chu, G. Drinking patterns and attitudes of roominghouse Chinese in San Francisco. *Quarterly Journal of Studies on Alcoholism*, 1972, Suppl, *6*, 58–68.

Drew, L. R. H. Alcoholism as a self-limiting disease. *Quarterly Journal of Studies on Alcoholism*, 1968, *29*, 956–967.

Favre, A., & Meuron, B. De aspect psychological de l'alcoolisme du 3e age. *Praxis*, 1963, *52*, 711–716.

Gaillard, A., & Perrin, P. L'alcoolisme des personnes dgèes. (Alcoholism in aged persons.) *Review Alcoolisme*, 1969, *15*, 5–32.

Gaitz, C. M., & Baer, P. E. Characteristics of elderly patients with alcoholism. *Archives of General Psychiatry*, 1971, *24*, 372–378.

Gillis, L. S., & Keet, M. Prognostic factors and treatment results in hospitalized alcoholics. *Quarterly Journal of Studies on Alcoholism*, 1969, *30*, 426–437.

Graux, P. L'alcoolisme des vieillards. (Alcoholism of the elderly.) *Review Alcoolisme*, 1969, *15*, 46–48.

Harrington, L. G., & Price, A. C. Alcoholism in a geriatric setting. *Journal of American Geriatric Society*, 1962, *10*, 197–211.

Hoffman, H. Personality characteristics of alcoholics in relation to age. *Psychological Reports*, 1970, *27*, 167–171.

Kramer, M. Patients in state and county mental hospitals. *Public Health Service Publication No. 1921*. Chevy Chase, Md.: U.S. Department of Health Education and Welfare, NIMH, 1969.

Lennon, B. E., Rekosh, J. H., Patch, V. D., & Howe, L. P. Self-reports of drunkenness arrests. *Quarterly Journal of Studies on Alcoholism*, 1970, *31*, 90–96.

Lutterotti, A. De L'aspect social de l'alcoolisme dans la viellesse. *Revue d'Hygiene et Medecine Scolaries et Universitaires*, 1967, *15*, 751–760.

Myerson, D. J., & Mayer, J. Origins, treatment and destiny of skid row alcoholic men. *New England Journal of Medicine*, 1966, *275*, 419–426.

Older problem drinkers. *Alcohol Health Research World,* Spring 1975, pp. 12–17. (Cited in *Journal of Studies on Alcoholism,* 1976, *37,* 486).

Pequignot, H., Voisin, P., Guerre, J., Christoforov, B., & Portos, J. L. Aspects de l'alcoolisme du sujet age hospitalise dans un service de medecine generale. (Aspects of alcoholism in the aged, hospitalized on a general medical ward.) *Review Alcoholisme,* 1969, *15,* 33–45.

Riccitelli, M. L. Alcoholism in the aged—modern concepts. *Journal of the American Geriatric Society,* 1967, *15,*(2), 142–147.

Rosenblatt, S. M., Gross, M. M., & Chartoff, S. Marital status and multiple psychiatric admissions for alcoholism. *Quarterly Journal of Studies on Alcoholism,* 1969, *30,* 445–447.

Rosenblatt, S. M., Gross, M. M., Malenowski, B., Broman, M., & Lewis, E. Marital status and multiple psychiatric admissions for alcoholism: A cross-validation. *Quarterly Journal of Studies on Alcoholism,* 1971, *32,* 1092–1096.

Rosin, A., & Glatt, M. M. Alcohol excess in the elderly. *Quarterly Journal of Studies on Alcoholism,* 1971, *32,* 53–59.

Schuckit, M. A. An overview of alcohol and drug abuse problems in the elderly. Testimony before the Subcommittee of the Senate Committee on Alcoholism and Narcotics and Subcommittee on Aging of the Senate Committee on Labor and Public Welfare, Washington D.C., June 7, 1976.

Schuckit, M. A. Geriatric alcoholism and drug abuse. *Gerontologist,* 1977, *17*(2), 168–174.

Schuckit, M. A., & Miller, P. L. Alcoholism in elderly men: A survey of a general medical ward. *Annals of the New York Academy of Sciences,* 1976 *273,* 558–571.

Schuckit, M. A., Morrissey, E. R., & O'Leary, M. R. Alcohol problems in elderly men and women. Unpublished manuscript, University of Washington, Seattle, 1977.

Schuckit, M. A. & Pastor, P. A. Alcohol-related psychopathology in the aged. Unpublished manuscript. University of Washington, Seattle, Washington, 1978.

Simon, A., Epstein, L. J., & Reynolds, L. Alcoholism in the geriatric mentally ill. *Geriatrics,* 1968, *23,* 125–131.

Simon, A., & Neal, M. W. Patterns of geriatric mental illness. In C. Tibbitts & W. Donahue (Eds.), *Process of aging* (vol. 1). New York: Atherton Press, 1963, pp. 449–476. (Cited in Gaitz & Baer, 1971).

U.S. NIMH, Mental Health Statistics. *General hospital inpatient psychiatric services, 1967.* Series A, No. 4, 1969.

U.S. NIMH, Mental Health Statistics. *Private mental hospitals 1969–1970.* Series A, No. 10, 1972.

U.S. NIMH, Survey and Reports Section, Biometry Branch. *Statistical Note No. 31,* Washington D.C.: U.S. Government Printing Office, 1970.

U.S. NIMH, Survey and Reports Section, Biometry Branch. *Statistical note No. 49.* Washington D.C.: U.S. Government Printing Office, 1971.(a)

U.S. NIMH, Survey and Reports Section, Biometry Branch. *Statistical Note No. 48.* Washington D.C.: U.S. Government Printing Office, 1971.(b)

Von Mering, O. S., & Weniger, F. L. Social-cultural background of the aging individual. In Birren (Ed.), *Handbook of aging and the individual.* Chicago: University of Chicago Press, 1959, pp. 328–329.

Wax, T. Alcohol abuse among the elderly. Paper presented at the annual scientific meeting of the Gerontological Society, Louisville, Kentucky, 1975.

Williams, E. P. Alcoholism and problem drinking among older persons: Community agency study. In E. P. Williams et al. (Eds.), *Alcohol and problem drinking among older persons.* Springfield, Va.: National Technical Information Service, 1973.

Williams, E. P., Carruth, B., Hyman, M. M., et al.: *Alcohol and problem drinking among older persons.* Springfield, Va: National Technical Information Service, 1973.

Williams, E. P., & Mysak, P. Alcoholism and problem drinking among older persons. In E. P. Williams, et al. (Eds.), *Alcoholism and problem drinking among older persons.* Springfield, Va.: National Technical Information Service, 1973.

5
Treatment of Problem Drinking Among the Elderly

CAN THE ELDERLY PROBLEM DRINKER BE HELPED?

The answer to the question of whether the elderly problem drinker can be helped is directly related to the more general attitudes about treatment of the problems encountered by the aged. Within our society, it is often assumed that advanced age is a contraindication to active treatment of almost any type. This sets up a self-fulfilling prophecy. The assumption has the effect of limiting attempts to provide the help that elderly people sometimes need, and so there is little opportunity to determine if the assumption is valid.

Because of this tendency to associate advanced age with reduced treatment or rehabilitation potential in general, one might expect that the same attitude would govern the situation of the elderly problem drinker. There is, however, a divergence of opinion on this. An editorial in *The New England Journal of Medicine,* for example, emphasized the uniqueness of problems involved with treatment of elderly people. Old men and women are said to have "decreased capacity for reorganization which makes depth psychotherapy difficult to carry out, and cardiovascular impairments which are usually present and do not allow use of drugs such as antabuse and behavior modification techniques" ("A Paradoxical Refuge," 1951, p. 268). Lack of hope for the future is cited as another problem that stands in the way of treatment. According to the editorial, however, this assessment does not mean that treatment efforts should be neglected. The physician can provide something in the way of psychosocial guidance for the individual, and society can do more to decrease the life frustrations that lead some elderly people to numb their distress with alcohol. Nevertheless, it was argued that "bodily changes and personality patterns not prepared to meet the vicissitudes and stresses of old age are predisposing factors that, when combined with specific physical, psychologic and stress situations, can and do precipitate alcoholism."

On the other side is the position held by Seliger (1948), who believes that problems relating to alcoholism are essentially the same throughout the adult age range. In presenting a set of case histories, Seliger acknowledges that the older patient may be somewhat more set and less malleable in attitude than younger patients. But this can be more than compensated for by a sincere desire to break free of alcoholism and a greater stability of personality on which decisive change can be built. We are so accustomed to hearing that whatever is distinctive about old age is also somehow more pathological or distressing that this view at least has a refreshing quality. And, as we turn to the available reports on treatment outcomes, we will see that Seliger's relative optimism has some support.

Outcome Studies and Observations

In considering the prognosis of older clients, it should be kept in mind that relatively few outcome studies have directly compared elderly with younger problem drinkers. Many studies that do include a wide age range do not report or comment upon possible age differences in treatment effects. Furthermore, elderly clients constitute a relatively small proportion of the total number of clients seen by most agencies and institutions. This means that sample sizes are often rather small for the older age groups when data of this kind are reported.

As will be seen below, the available data are perhaps more encouraging than many people might have expected. Therapeutic nihilism with respect to the elderly problem drinker appears to be out of place based on the limited information presently available.

Two treatment centers in the Belfast, Ireland, area were studied by Blaney, Radford, and MacKenzie (1975). Eleven clients aged 60 and over were identified in one hospital. Nine of these elders were rated as showing favorable treatment outcomes after 6 months of follow-up. This rate was approximately the same as adults in the 30 to 49 age range and somewhat better than younger age groups. The sample at the second hospital included 15 elderly clients. Here, the elderly group had the most favorable outcome of all—a 77 percent improvement rate. The youngest clients (aged 20 to 29) showed only a 36 percent improvement rate, and there was a direct linear relationship in general between age and rate of improvement. Percentages must not be taken too seriously, of course, when such small samples are involved.

In quite a different socioenvironmental context, Ferguson (1970) examined a treatment program for Navaho alcoholics. It was noted that Navahos who "speak English poorly or not at all, who have less than 4th grade education, and who are between 30 and 55 years old are more likely to respond well to a treatment program of this kind than younger, better educated Navahos . . ." (Ferguson, 1970, p. 917).

Wilkinson's (1971) review of experiences with alcoholic patients in an Australian hospital led her to conclude that prognosis is often better for elderly patients because they are less likely to have severe psychopathology. Most of the alcoholics who came to her attention had long dependency histories, but for approximately one-third of this group, excessive drinking did not occur until late in life. Heightened use of alcohol was often precipitated by some major emotional crisis such as bereavement or retirement. Wilkinson does caution, however, that when substantial chronic brain damage is present, the prognostic outlook is markedly reduced.

Cohen (1975), among a number of other clinicians and researchers, has emphasized the difference between two groups of elderly problem drinkers. Those who have a long history of heavy drinking tend to have a guarded prognosis in old age, while those who turned to the bottle when encountering traumatic loss late in lfie have a more favorable prognosis. Although Cohen is an experienced and justly respected authority in the area of substance abuse, it is unfortunate that these impressions have not been bolstered by clear and definitive data.

A study of a rather different type has also yielded some encouraging data. Cermak and Ryback (1976) tested young and elderly Veterans Administration alcoholic inpatients before and after their participation in a psychological counseling program. Unlike most other available studies, this effort focused on an objective performance measure (a short-term memory distraction test). The performance of the older alcoholics improved over the 1-month testing period. The pattern of data for all subgroups of patients involved suggested that elderly alcoholics may suffer a *temporary*—and reversible—impairment of ability to memorize new material. This impairment did not seem to be present with the other patients in the study. It appeared to Cermak and Ryback that a systematic approach to therapeutic counseling held definite promise for improving at least some types of functioning in elderly alcoholics.

The advantage of a 25-year follow-up opportunity is a major feature of a study reported by Ciompi and Eisert (1971). A sample of 197 former alcoholics was studied at a point in time when the average age of this group was 74 and a quarter of a century had elapsed since their first psychiatric hospitalization with a diagnosis of alcoholism. The authors note that it is often assumed that drinking behavior is relatively immutable—those who drink, especially those who drink heavily, are thought to keep on drinking.

Improvement over a prolonged period of time was "amazingly frequent" in this population, however. Almost two-thirds of these people showed a significant decrease in alcohol consumption. There was also a marked decrease in previously noted psychiatric diagnoses such as depression, mania, and aggressiveness. The social situation stabilized for many of the former alcoholics. Although they continued to lead relatively dependent lives, they now experienced much less interpersonal conflict. Approximately two-fifths were judged to be in "satisfactory" or "good" condition from the psychiatric standpoint, and only one-fifth showed clear psychiatric pathology. Severe senile changes and dementia were noted in 9 percent of the sample. Although it was thought that this incidence is a little higher than might be found in a matched nonalcoholic cohort (not actually included in this study), it was also judged to be a lower percentage than might have been previously expected.

Another set of observations with moderately encouraging implications also has a point to make about the evaluation of differential treatment outcomes in older patients. Droller (1964) visited 7 elderly clients in their homes. He found that "the families were scandalized and afraid of gossip; they felt that no one should know about their mother's failings; hence they gave money and often brought drink themselves to the house." It was only when physical illness or an accident resulted that the family turned to a physician for help.

If, as Droller suggests, older alcoholics are often hidden by their families until the problem has gone so far that medical attention is urgent, then one might predict that the elderly would have an unusually low cure or rehabilitation rate because their alcoholic problems tend to be discovered and treated only when they have progressed to the point of causing obvious physical harm. Each of the 7 individuals treated by Droller recovered physically. Two had to be retained in a hospital because of increasing dementia; another 2 were discharged home without relapse (although the extent of followup is not reported), and the remaining 3 were discharged to other hands in the community, as it was judged that the unsatisfactory family situation would produce a relapse.

Droller is not alone in believing that many elderly alcoholics remain unidentified and untreated (Christmas, 1977; Mayfield, 1974). Presumably, the longer these people remain "hidden," the less favorable will be their prognosis. Yet even when identification is delayed, as in the cases studied and treated by Droller, favorable outcomes seem to occur with some frequency. This suggests that more prompt identification of elderly problem drinkers would result in an even more favorable rate and extent of improvement.

Not all studies indicate that elderly alcoholics have a more favorable prognosis than younger drinkers. Myerson and Mayer (1966) reported on the outcome of "skid row" alcoholic men in two residential treatment programs in the Boston area. Their sample ranged in age from the late 20s to the early 60s, with an overall outcome failure rate of 24 percent. No significant differences related to age were found, but there was the general observation that the younger clients tended to be more successful. The need for early intervention programs was emphasized, as many of the men in this study had been alcoholics or had suffered from alcohol-related problems since early youth. In this study, "success" was defined as maintaining a sober life, restoring meaningful family relations, and working steadily.

Part of the variance noted in all the observations summarized above can probably be attributed to differences within the population of problem drinkers. The nature of the "successful outcome" criterion may also be involved. The criterion is not always carefully specified, making it more difficult to evaluate different rates of outcome. Some attention to the nature of the criterion might be useful here, even though it cannot be applied in detail to all the studies already reported.

What the Outcome Measures Indicate

What constitutes the best measure of successful treatment remains somewhat controversial. Alcoholics Anonymous, for example, considers complete success only in terms of total abstinence from alcoholic beverages. Others, such as Faillace et al. (1972), believe that those who drink alcoholic beverages as part of their treatment do just as well, if not better, than those who are required to reach total abstinence. Still other research has indicated that people who maintain abstinence do not always improve in other important areas (Gerard, Saenger, & Wile, 1962). There are a number of studies that indicate that problem drinkers may be able to adjust to life successfully without abstaining totally (Davis, 1962; Kendall, 1965). One might then opt for at least three types of "success" criteria: (1) total abstinence; (2) abstinence with significant improvement in major domains of functioning as well; (3) significant overall improvement in functioning without giving up all use of alcoholic beverages. Apart from the question as to which of these types of criteria is most appropriate, we can see that a failure to think through or to specify which criteria are actually being invoked in a particular outcome study can lead to confusion and misinterpretation. In addition, some criteria may be less broadly applicable to elderly as compared to younger problem drinkers (e.g., return to the work force may not be possible for elderly problem drinkers even if they have the skill, endurance, and motivation because of mandatory retirement provisions and other barriers to employment for the aged). The appropriateness of these various criteria was discussed in more detail in the previous chapter.

Another factor that is associated with success criteria may also be involved in the low number of referrals of old people to treatment. As noted in a previous chapter, family problems in the usual sense are less prevalent among some subgroups of the aged because they do not have much available family left to them. This might partially explain the relatively low frequency of referral of elderly problem drinkers for treatment, since in the younger age groups, many referrals occur as a direct result of family pressure (as well as pressures related to job performance).

This could also be one of the main reasons why the medical hospital is the most common type of treatment facility for the elderly. Perhaps the major reason one would seek treatment would be for medical problems, not only because these tend to increase with advancing age anyway but also because family and job pressures are no longer relevant. One might then expect that the type of people who seek treatment when they are older might be different from those in younger age groups.

But one might apply still another criterion for "successful" treatment. Perhaps a person has improved in an important sense when he or she no longer experiences a "craving" for alcohol, when the compulsion to drink has been eliminated. This could be taken either as the sole or as a supplementary criterion. There is the practical difficulty here that the client may not choose to admit to this socially undesirable craving for drink—or that the client may not even recognize that there actually is such a craving present.

It may be worth reflecting on the value judgment that a craving for alcoholic beverages is, in and of itself, a major problem or form of pathology. An alternative view is that drinking is an adaptive effort—perhaps not the most adequate adaptive effort, but still a behavior pattern that represents some endeavor to cope with problems that have gone out of control. A number of clinicians and researchers have suggested that "burying one's woes" in alcohol is associated with the inherent loneliness and isolation of many people in their old age. According to this view, drinking might be regarded as a simple and available mechanism for those who have few other resources accessible either in themselves or in their environment. The fact that an old person drinks substantially might, in this instance, lead to no value judgment as such. The question instead might be: How adequately does this behavior pattern accomplish its objective? How deleterious are its side effects and correlates, especially when compared with other alternatives?

In this context, it might be appropriate to bear in mind that the suicide rate is at its peak in old age. It is also likely that deaths hastened by suicidal intent but not classified as suicide per se are also prevalent in old age (Kastenbaum & Mishara, 1970; Mishara & Kastenbaum, 1973; Mishara, Robertson, & Kastenbaum, 1973). As unattractive as the picture of the bottle-addicted old person may be, one might continue to ask what realistic alternatives are available in a society that so often places care and concern for the elderly near the bottom of its social priority list. While this line of reasoning is not intended as a defense for alcohol abuse in old age, it does suggest that some caution be exercised before automatically concluding that the use of alcohol in old age is itself a fundamental problem. It can be seen instead as a simplistic and less than optimal response to other problems that are much more fundamental. From the practical standpoint, the latter view might lead to more attention being paid to the identification and alleviation of the causes of alcoholism rather than the problem drinker per se.

This leads to what is perhaps the major controversy in alcoholism research: *why* do people drink? There are those who believe that alcoholism should be viewed as a disease that develops because of the chemical properties of alcohol and perhaps because of personality disorders or even some genetic predisposition. Treatment methods that derive from this "medical model" stress the need to break the chemical addictive tie between the individual and alcohol. This approach usually involves inpatient treatment. Alternative supports are provided to these individuals while an attempt is made to bring about a long-term change in their lives.

An alternative approach derives from a sociocultural framework. Here, emphasis is given to the life events that may lead to problem drinking. Intervention frequently emphasizes bolstering social support networks or helping the individual to cope in a more successful manner with losses and stresses.

Many of the actual treatment programs that exist today are eclectic rather than exclusively following either the medical or the sociocultural model. The range of services and flexibility that are often associated with an eclectic approach would appear to be valuable. From the research standpoint, however, the mix of services sometimes makes it more difficult to identify which components are the most effective or what particular configuration and phasing of services is most effective for individuals with particular backgrounds and drinking patterns. The following section explores a number of currently employed methods for the treatment of problem drinking. Research specific to older clients will be cited where available, but each approach will be discussed in terms of its potential application to the elderly as well.

TREATMENT METHODS WITH OLDER PEOPLE

Should the elderly problem drinker be treated in the same way as younger people with the same difficulties? Will similar methods yield similar results? Are there particular hazards in applying general treatment techniques to the elderly? Are there perhaps some techniques that have special value for the elderly even if not especially useful with younger adults? Unfortunately, no comparative research that focuses directly on the differential benefits or liabilities of various treatment modalities for younger and older adults has yet been done. Furthermore, there has not been adequate attention directed to individual differences *among* elderly problem drinkers. The broad distinction already noted between people with long histories of alcohol abuse and those who have started heavy drinking late in life appears reasonable and useful. There are many other differences among elderly people, however, as general research in gerontology has demonstrated. Until these differences are clearly recognized and taken into account in alcohol treatment research, we will be running the risk of drawing conclusions that apply to a fictitious "old person" when in fact there are many "kinds" of old people with many different reasons for drinking and who would respond differentially to a variety of specific treatment efforts. With these limitations of present information in mind, we will survey the major treatment modalities being practiced today.

Drug Treatment

Drug treatment approaches are based on the assumption that alcoholics suffer from dysphoric symptoms such as anxiety or depression (Kissen, Charnoff, & Rosenblatt, 1968) or will suffer symptoms of withdrawal if deprived of alcohol when physically dependent. It is further assumed that a drug that can reduce these dysphoric symptoms will also eliminate or reduce the need to seek alcohol for relief.

Some critical reviews of the literature indicate that there is no conclusive evidence for the efficacy of drugs (Verdon & Shatterly, 1971; Aharan, Ogilvie, & Partington, 1967; Ditman, 1956; Mottin, 1973). Nevertheless, drugs are widely used for this purpose and have been advocated for the elderly.

There are no reports available from controlled research on the effectiveness of drugs with elderly alcoholics. Zimberg (1974) reports on the basis of case histories that geriatric alcoholics can be treated successfully with a combination of antidepressant medication and socialization programs. He judged that his own patients responded favorable to such a regime.

At this point, a cautionary note is in order. Medications pose special problems for the elderly and require special precautions (Viamontes, 1972). The sedating effects of 12 of the 20 most commonly used medications in persons over 65 (e.g., Doriden, Librium, phenobarbitol) can exacerbate decrements in speed and coordination in old age. Some patients may react to the effects of drug treatment with fear and depression and even come to the conclusion that they are dying. Furthermore, metabolic and other changes associated with aging may result in drug effects that are prolonged or excessive. The process of detoxification may also be slowed. In addition, the possibility of iatrogenic illness must be acknowledged here. Tranquilizers and hypnotic medications are the most likely to cause brain syndromes (some of which may not be reversible), and phenothiazine poses the danger of tardive dyskinesia.

Disulfiram, Antabuse, and citrated calcium carbinide differ from the medications discussed above. Rather than influencing moods that are presumably "causes" of drinking, these drugs produce extremely unpleasant psychophysiological reactions if the patient drinks. This reaction—and the fear of having it recur—presumably keeps the person from reaching for the bottle again. Schuckit (1977) observes that older alcoholics are less likely to receive this form of treatment because they are thought to have more medical problems that would limit the use of such medications. No studies have yet been done of the possible age effects on either risks or successful outcomes with the use of these aversion-producing medications. Because of the health risks involved, one would want to be quite cautious in any use of these drugs with elderly people.

Outpatient Psychotherapies and Outreach

In general, older people are unlikely to receive outpatient psychotherapy for any type of mental health problem. This is not because the need for help is less frequent among the elderly. The deficiencies in providing service can be related instead to negative attitudes and expectations on the part of the potential therapists (Butler & Lewis, 1977) and to a reluctance on the part of the elders themselves to seek or accept treatment by this modality. There is no evidence that elders are unresponsive to psychotherapy. Many types of psychotherapy are practiced today, and it seems likely that at least some of these techniques would be successful with elderly clients (Kastenbaum, 1963, 1978). For a detailed discussion of the various forms of psychotherapy and counseling techniques in use today, readers are referred to *Consumer's Handbook of Mental Health* (Mishara & Patterson, 1977).

Behavior-oriented psychotherapy is an increasingly popular approach to treatment of alcohol abuse in the United States. Behavioral therapies assume that alcoholism is a learned behavior. This is taken to indicate that alcoholism can be unlearned as well or that alternative behaviors can be substituted by applying principles derived from laboratory studies of the learning process. In *aversive conditioning,* clients learn to associate uncomfortable feelings, such as nausea or pain, with the use of alcohol. This form of treatment has been applied less frequently with elderly than with younger clients because of the risks associated with electric shocks and with CNS depressants that cause nausea, such as apomorphine and emertine.

It would seem logical to attempt an alternative form of aversive conditioning that would not have to rely on physical stimuli to produce the effect. In *covert desensitization* procedures, the behavior modification therapist attempts to *weaken* the relationship between a psychological response and the cue that sets it off. A person who is anxious in the presence of a dog, for example, may learn to relax by a graduated series of exercises in which the therapist helps him to imagine himself coexisting with a dog in pleasant circumstances. A similar technique might be used to produce covert aversive conditioning. The elderly problem drinker might be guided to imagine herself becoming nauseous or anxious when using alcohol. Application of such a technique would at least remove the risks associated with administration of mild electric shocks or CNS-influencing medications.

Luthringer (1973) is among those who have made systematic efforts to organize outreach programs for elderly alcoholics (in this case, in the Ocean County, New Jersey, area). Locating the elderly alcoholics was a major problem. Various social service agencies in the community needed considerable education in order to become useful collaborators. This included training in the diagnosis of alcohol problems in older people and in deciding what steps to follow. Luthringer reported outstanding success with an outreach approach that did not wait for clients to come to her but instead went to the home of potential clients even when the referral was initiated by relatives or neighbors rather than by the alcoholics themselves. This is typical of reports that outreach programs can be successful with the elderly alcoholic, but people experienced with this kind of work know very well that it is a difficult enterprise to organize and carry out.

Alcoholics Anonymous

Alcoholics Anonymous (AA) has been estimated to have over 650,000 members in the United States (AA, 1972a) and to serve more alcoholics than all the "professional" services combined. AA claims that 60 percent of the alcoholics who attend their meetings achieve sobriety within a year (AA, 1972b). It is difficult to verify this claim, however, because AA is reluctant to cooperate with scientific investigations of its success rate.

AA does not offer special programs for the elderly. However, elderly alcoholics are welcomed to join AA, and some AA groups meet in areas that have high proportions of eldelry people. Trice (1959) reports that AA members tend to be socially isolated. If it is assumed that many older people turn to the bottle as a reaction to loneliness and loss, then AA might be particularly appealing to this group. However, it is also possible that because elderly alcoholics tend to be more hidden in their drinking practices, they may not be noticed and referred to AA.

Inpatient Treatment

Older alcoholics tend to receive inpatient treatment in public institutions such as state and Veterans Administration hospitals. Clinical reports suggest that older clients can benefit from institutional programs (Zimberg, 1974; Trice, 1975), although there is much to learn about the optimal matching between type of patient and type of program (Mishara, 1978). A combination of individual and group counseling and outpatient therapy has been found successful with elderly problem drinkers at the Queen Nursing Home and Treatment Center in Minneapolis. After discharge, clients were encouraged to join an AA group and were also provided with financial assistance and follow-up.

An Example of Treatment Programs Available in One City

To gain a better understanding of the treatment options available for older problem drinkers, one of the authors (B. L. M.) tried to obtain information from the various alcohol treatment agencies in Boston. Armed with a letter of introduction, a research assistant attempted to interview agency directors or their representatives.* Questions were asked about the nature of the agency, the number and percentage of clients over age 60, and how many clients came to that agency, where older people were referred, type of help given, origins of alcohol problems in their older clients, treatment effectiveness, and opinions about various treatment needs among older problem drinkers. Data were gathered from seven organizations serving problem drinkers in the community, six inpatient facilities, the state Department of Elder Affairs and Division of Alcoholism, as well as from an alcoholic information referral service and a television reporter interested in alcoholism and the elderly.

The first priority was to determine where older problem drinkers were referred for help. In Massachusetts, people may call an alcohol information service. This service in Boston receives about 6000 calls a year, of which about 10 percent concern elderly individuals (in some cases the age of the caller cannot be determined). There is a slight preponderance of males over females in the calling-in population (55 percent vs. 45 percent). This may be worth noting, because the population of old people in general, both locally

---

*We thank Kathleen Hurley for collecting the data for this inquiry.

and nationally, has more women than men, the ratio increasing with advancing age.

Where older clients were referred depended chiefly upon their living situation. People living at home were generally referred to AA or for outpatient counseling. Homeless people were generally referred to a state hospital. This is where a "catch-22" came in. Only two of the state hospitals would accept people over the age of 65. The Department of Elder Affairs (DEA) indicated that about 2 percent of their calls for information were in regard to alcohol problems. Most of these were referred to AA or to alcohol treatment programs in the community that provide service to all age groups. The DEA saw a need for programs for the elderly with alcohol-related problems. This need was reiterated by a local television reporter, who felt that alcohol problems were almost at an "epidemic level" among elderly people in this part of the country.

Community agencies varied greatly as to clientele and treatment approach. AA did not have data on the age of its members. Attendance at three meetings, however, showed that few of those present were elderly (less than 3 percent). Such limited sampling must be viewed with caution, of course. The local family service association, which provides a variety of services, saw about 500 people over age 60 in 1 month. Help for various general problems of the elderly was given. This took such forms as a widow's program, retirement counseling, individual counseling, and needs assessments. Most of the referrals for alcohol-related problems came from visiting nurses. The people referred tended to be elderly males who were living alone in low-income housing for the elderly on their social security benefits. The agency had no special alcohol-related programs but made referrals for detoxification to three such centers; one was intended for middle-class clients who could afford to pay, and the other two provided services for low-income elderly (interviews with these agencies are summarized below).

Visiting nurses were contacted, since the family services association indicated that they received some referrals from this source. A social worker employed by the Visiting Nurses Association felt that alcohol-related problems were not common in the people they saw. Most of the elderly clients under their care had serious medical problems that ruled out the use of alcohol. The alcohol problems they did encounter were handled on an individual basis. A religious charitable bureau that serves about 100 older persons a year in impoverished areas of the city indicated that most alcoholics were referred to detoxification programs because they were "too deteriorated" to benefit from AA. An alcoholism program in a community health center that served 513 clients a year included 13 percent over the age of 60. All of these clients, with but one exception, were men. This program provided a wide range of services, including individual and group counseling, Antabuse administration, halfway houses, and referrals to "detox" centers. They found that *all* ("100 percent") of their older problem drinkers had long histories of this kind. None had come to drinking for the first time as a result of aging or retirement. Once again, the importance of specifying the nature of the population in question can be seen as critical in making sense of treatment and prognosis. Most of the alcoholic men in this sample lived with families and had low incomes. The program director felt that those elderly people who were living alone and essentially isolated within the community seldom received help. It was difficult to determine what types of treatment were most common with elderly clients, although the halfway houses were reserved for those under age 60. This program claimed that 100 percent of those treated remained sober—but as it turned out, anyone who did not remain sober would not be continued in treatment but referred elsewhere.

In Boston, the Salvation Army and two other organizations provide food, shelter, and clothing for alcoholics. One of these organizations serves men, the other, women. The men's program was visited. Before the doors are locked at 10 P.M. each night, between 300 and 350 men make use of its services. These consist primarily of meals and a cot for sleeping. About 15 percent of those who use this facility are over age 60. Approximately one-third of this group consists of men who are not alcoholics but are homeless for other reasons.

The last community service visited was a pilot program for elderly alcoholics initiated by the Boston Housing Authority. This project was started after many requests for help were received by managers of housing for the elderly because of alcohol-related problems among the tenants. The program used outreach techniques and made referrals to a detoxification center when appropriate. Outreach workers continued to follow up clients who were in the detoxification center, assuring them that their property was safe and smoothing the transition home.

Visits were made to seven inpatient programs that included detoxification services. By law, "detox" services in Massachusetts cannot discriminate on the basis of age. However, in practice, admissions policies sometimes made it more difficult for older clients to gain admission. Some required in-depth medical examinations. These resulted in numerous rejections of admission because of the "increased risk" of the detoxification process. Between 5 and 35 percent of the clients were over age 60, with men outnumbering women at least 3 to 1 (a striking reversal of the male/female ratio among elders in the population in general). It was estimated that between 2 and 30 percent of the clients had started their drinking later in life, often in reaction to loss of a spouse or retirement. Most of the clients were poor and came to the programs from emergency wards, nursing homes, or other social agencies. There was one program that reported receiving approximately half of its referrals from physicians. Treatment in this one program was provided only to those with private insurance or adequate funds to pay—others were referred elsewhere. All programs offered a combination of detoxification with various forms of counseling and therapy. Some staff members felt that older people who began to drink in their later years were not being seen because their problems were more likely to have remained hidden, and they were less likely to be brought in for help by physicians. Estimates of treatment success rates ranged up to 50 percent and staff members of all these programs agreed that elderly clients had at least as good a prognosis as their younger clients. It should be kept in mind, however, that fewer older than young people may be admitted because of screening techniques or devices. The older person who actually comes for help and finds admission may be quite different from the types of younger people who seek treatment.

CONCLUSIONS AND RECOMMENDATIONS

Based upon the available information, with all its limitations, there is no reason to believe that older clients have any worse prognosis than younger clients. The pattern of observations, in fact, suggests that the prognosis may be somewhat better, at least for those whose alcohol problems developed in later life.

The population of elderly clients receiving help may represent just the tip of the iceberg. Since little effort has been made to find older problem drinkers and attract them to treatment programs, we have no way of knowing how well those who have not yet come forth might fare in treatment.

A reasonable interpretation of the available clinical and research experience, then, would be (1) that therapeutic nihilism is not justified by the facts and (2) that there is a clear need to identify and help elderly problem drinkers whose situation has not come to attention through existing traditional referral sources.

A major issue in treatment centers on whether older clients should be treated for "alcoholism" per se or whether the roots or causes of their problems should be attacked. This latter alternative can be very difficult to pursue. The problems may have been in existence for many years. The roots of these problems may have long ago been buried under a life history of bouts with drinking. For others, however, drinking began as a reaction to life circumstances in which alcohol represented an attempt to cope with isolation, loneliness, or despair newly experienced in old age. Elimination of drinking behavior does not eliminate the causes of this difficulty. Unless significant socioenvironmental improvements are made, it is probable that the drinking problem will return or that some other technique of no greater effectiveness will be sought to deal with the despair.

In a report prepared for the National Institute on Alcohol Abuse and Alcoholism (NIAAA), Parker Marden (1976) recommended that the NIAAA *not* develop special programs to provide direct treatment and rehabilitative services to the elderly problem drinker. This conclusion was based on the belief that there are relatively few problem drinkers among the aged. Furthermore, even if there are more than previously estimated, they would be hard to find. Marden's alternative recommendation was that NIAAA develop special programs *within* existing services for both alcohol abusers and the aged.

Although the cost-effectiveness of these recommendations seems sound, it would also appear that a tremendous amount of educational effort would have to be made before alcoholism programs would accept—much less reach out—to serve elderly problem drinkers. Better education about aging and the aged would have to be provided to workers in the relevant health and social service agencies. This education might also have to include substantial attention to revising attitudes and emotional orientations toward the potential of old age, as well as professional and scientific information. Geriatric service personnel, for their part, would need to learn how to recognize and help problem drinkers. These are worthy objectives. It would be self-deceptive, however, to believe they could be achieved easily and inexpensively. The culturally rooted aversion among mental and public health personnel in general toward devoting themselves to care of the aged does not yield simply and automatically to the call for action, nor should it be expected that geriatricians would readily overcome their resistances to working with alcohol-related problems.

Before extensive service delivery programs are planned, it would make sense to learn much more about elderly problem drinkers and about the effectiveness of various treatment modalities with this population. Quite simply: the basic data are not there.

The answers are less complicated if one assumes that the treatment of older clients need be no different than that used with younger adults. However, there is reason to believe that the most effective treatment may require some different characteristics because of the distinctive features of older clients. Those whose drinking problems are a continuation of earlier behaviors are distinctive, perhaps unique, in that they have not succumbed physically to any of the common medical problems associated with continued alcohol abuse. They have become accustomed to living as a problem drinker. The problems here are very different from those of younger persons who have just recently started to experience stress and loss and who have turned to drink as a possible "out."

Those people who begin their problem drinking in old age do so as a result of life circumstances that are often quite different from the circumstances of the young. Many have a long history of satisfactory adjustment behind them before they turn to drink. Many of their problems—poverty, isolation, lack of meaningful work after a forced retirement—are fostered as much by society as by any intrinsic personal characteristics. Because of these unique characteristics of the elderly population, it is imperative that more systematic research be conducted to determine the most appropriate treatment programs for the various subgroups of older problem drinkers.

REFERENCES

Aharan, C. H., Ogilvie, R. D., & Partington, J. T. Clinical indications of motivation in alcoholic patients. *Quarterly Journal of Studies on Alcoholism,* 1967, *28,* 486–492.

Alcoholics Anonymous. *The fellowship of alcoholics.* New York: Alcoholics Anonymous World Services, Inc., 1972. (a)

Alcoholics Anonymous. *Profile of an AA meeting.* New York: Alcoholics Anonymous World Services, Inc., 1972. (b)

A paradoxical refuge. *New England Journal of Medicine,* 1951, *245,* 268–269. (Editorial)

Blaney, R., Radford, I. S., & MacKenzie, G. A Belfast study of the prediction of outcome in the treatment of alcoholism. *British Journal of Addiction,* 1975, *70,* 41–50.

Butler, R. N., & Lewis, M. I. *Aging and mental health.* St. Louis: C. V. Mosby, 1977.

Cermak, L. S. & Ryback, R. S. Recovery of verbal short-term memory in alcoholics. *Journal of Studies on Alcohol,* 1976, *37,* 46–52.

Christmas, J. E. Delivery of alcoholism services: Meeting whose needs? Seminar on Alcohol Treatment in Prepaid Group Practice, Group Health, Boston, Feb. 25, 1977.

Ciompi, L., & Eisert, M. Retrospective long-term studies on the health status of alcoholics in old age. *Social Psychiatry,* 1971, *6,* 129–151.

Cohen, S. Drug abuse in the aging patient. *Journal of Studies on Alcoholism,* 1975, *37,* 1455–1460.

Davis, D. L. Normal drinking in recovered alcohol addicts. *Quarterly Journal of Studies on Alcoholism,* 1962, *23,* 94–104.

Ditman, K. S. Review and evaluation of current drug therapies in alcoholism. *Psychosomatic Medicine,* 1956, *28,* 667–677.

Droller, H. Some aspects of alcoholism in the elderly. *Lancet,* 1964, *2,* 137–139.

Faillace, L. A., Flamer, R. N., Imber, S. D., & Ward, R. F. Giving alcohol to alcoholics. *Quarterly Journal of Studies on Alcoholism*, 1972, *33*, 85–90.

Ferguson, F. N. A treatment program for Navaho alcoholics. *Quarterly Journal of Studies on Alcoholism*, 1970, *4*, 898–919.

Gerard, D. L., Saenger, G., & Wile, R. The abstinent alcoholic. *Archives of General Psychiatry*, 1962, *6*, 83–95.

Kastenbaum, R. The reluctant therapist. *Geriatrics*, 1963, *18*, 296–301.

Kastenbaum, R. Psychotherapy with the older client. In M. Storandt, I. Siegler, & M. Elias (Eds.), *Clinical psychology and aging*. New York: Academic Press, 1978, pp. 199–224.

Kastenbaum, R., & Mishara, B. Premature death and self-injurious behavior in old age. *Geriatrics*, 1970, *26*, 70–81.

Kendall, R. E. Normal drinking by former alcohol addicts. *Quarterly Journal of Studies on Alcoholism*, 1965, *26*, 247–257.

Kissen, B., Charnoff, S. M., & Rosenblatt, S. M. Drug and placebo responses in chronic alcoholics. *Psychiatric Research Reports*, 1968, *24*, 44–60.

Luthringer, R. Outreach and intervention: Problems and methods. In J. Newman (Ed.): *Alcohol and the older person*. Pittsburgh: University of Pittsburgh, 1973.

Marden, P. G. *Alcohol abuse and the aged*. Unpublished report to the National Institute on Alcohol Abuse and Alcoholism, 1976.

Mayfield, D. G. Alcohol problems in the aging parent. In *Drug issues in geropsychiatry*. Baltimore, Md: Williams & Wilkins. Co., 1974, pp. 35–40.

Mishara, B. L. Geriatric patients who improve in token economy and general milieu treatment programs: A multivariate analysis. *Journal of Consulting and Clinical Psychology*, 1978, *46*, 1340–1348.

Mishara, B., & Kastenbaum, R. Self-injurious behavior and environmental change in the institutional elderly. *International Journal of Aging and Human Development*, 1973, *4*, 133–146.

Mishara, B. L. & Patterson, R. D. *The consumer's handbook of mental health*. New York: New American Library, 1977.

Mishara, B. L., Robertson, B., & Kastenbaum, R. Self injurious behavior in the elderly. *The Gerontologist*, 1973, *13*, 311–314.

Mottin, J. L. Drug-induced attenuation of alcohol consumption. *Quarterly Journal of Studies on Alcoholism*, 1973, *34*, 444–472.

Myerson, D. J., & Mayer, J. Origins, treatment and destiny of skid row alcoholic men. *New England Journal of Medicine*, 1966, *275*, 419–426.

Schuckit, M. A. Geriatric alcoholism and drug abuse. *Gerontologist*, 1977, *17*, 168–174.

Seliger, G. W. Alcoholism in the older age group. *Geriatrics*, 1948, *3*, 166–170.

Trice, H. M. The affiliation motive and readiness to join Alcoholics Anonymous. *Quarterly Journal of Studies on Alcoholism*, 1959, *20*, 313–320.

Trice, H. M. Older problem drinkers. *Alcohol and Health Research World*, Spring 1975, pp. 12–17.

Verdon, P., & Shatterly, D. Alcoholism research and resistance to understanding the compulsive drinker. *Mental Hygiene,* 1971, *55,* 331–336.

Viamontes, J. A. Review of drug effectiveness in the treatment of alcoholism. *American Journal of Psychiatry,* 1972, *128,* 1570–1571.

Wilkinson, P. Alcoholism in the aged. *Journal of Geriatrics,* 1971, *34,* 59–64.

Zimberg, S. Two types of problem drinkers: Both can be managed. *Geriatrics,* 1974, *29,* 135–138.

6
Alcohol and Health in Old Age

We have already explored the major physiological effects of alcohol, the patterns of consumption in old age, and some of the dimensions and correlates of problem drinking. Attempts to prevent or treat problem drinking have also been considered. Still ahead are those approaches that emphasize the possible beneficial effects of alcoholic beverages for the elderly. This means that we are standing at the moment between the "abuse" and "use" polarities of alcohol effects. In this chapter we will again examine the relationship between alcohol and physical health status. That both the ethanol and congeners in alcoholic beverages have substantial physical effects is a point that was not difficult to establish (Chapter 2). It is another challenge, however, to determine how these complex effects are related to general health status. There are some who hold that *all* drinking is problem drinking, while others see alcoholic beverages as panacea for many of the physical as well as the emotional difficulties often associated with aging. The available data are neither as extensive nor as clear as one would desire, but they are certainly worth our attention.

THE ALCOHOLIC IN OLD AGE

The personal distress and social dislocation of the alcoholic adult have been documented repeatedly. The question before us now, however, concerns the physical status of old men and women who can be classified as alcoholics or problem drinkers.

Neuropsychological Functioning

Psychological testing has become an accepted technique for evaluating the status of the CNS, although this approach, like any other, has its limitations and ambiguities. Two recent studies are particularly relevant here. Williams, Ray, and Overall (1973) administered the Wechsler Adult Intelligence Scale (WAIS) to 158 male and female alcoholic patients who were consecutively admitted to a state mental hospital in Texas. The sample of patients had first been screened with the Shipley Institute of Living Scale to eliminate those who were markedly below the normal range of intelligence. The alcoholic sample was divided into four chronological age groups that corresponded to the age norms available for the WAIS in general.

These investigators were chiefly interested in the possibility that alcoholics might undergo a kind of *accelerated aging* in the mental sphere. They also considered the alternative hypothesis that alcohol abuse leads to organic brain pathology of the more familiar type. In other words, this was an attempt not only to document further the existence of CNS impairment in general with chronic problem drinkers but also to see if the damage is patterned more similarly to common forms of CNS impairment or to a form more specifically associated with age-related changes. Previous research (Overall & Gorham, 1972) had yielded differential profiles for the two types of neurophysiological impairments on WAIS subscale scores.

The alcoholics in this study showed a pattern and level of WAIS test performance that indicated more CNS impairment than the adults who comprised that norm group for the intelligence test. This was true across all age echelons, but increased with advancing age. It is important to note that this study, like most others focusing on alcoholics, does not extent through the entire old age spectrum. The oldest echelon, in fact, was the 55 to 64 decade. Despite this limitation, the study does encompass a reasonable age range (22 to 64) and can be taken as indicative of age-related trends.

The finding that has just been cited is consistent with previous observations that organic brain syndrome is more common in alcoholic than in nonalcoholic populations. And yet this finding did not rule out the alternative hypothesis. Mental aging index scores indicated "a significant acceleration in mental aging in the alcoholic sample as compared with the corresponding normative groups. The highly significant main effect for chronological age groupings provides support for validity of the previously derived index as a sensitive measure of aging in intellectual functioning" (Williams et al., 1973, p. 394). The alcoholic patients showed more test-measured signs of mental aging at every chronological age grouping, although more so in the older than in the younger adult echelons.

Williams et al. (1973) conclude that those who chronically abuse alcoholic beverages tend to show two distinct patterns of mental deterioration, one of which is consistent with general organic brain syndrome, while the other is more closely associated with aging. (Correlation between the two profiles was at the zero level, confirming their independence as first established in the Overall and Gorham study.) The finding that alcoholics tend to show both types of impairment was stronger than the trend toward greater impairment with advancing age. In other words, the alcoholic patient was "older" (in a negative sense of this term) than the nonalcoholic individual when they were matched for chronological age—but the differential between the two increases only slightly at the upper age levels. There is a methodological point worth noting. The researchers recognized that they were comparing a regional sample of alcoholics with a national sample of adults. They were able to check out some possible effects of this difference within their own sample and, at least tentatively, did not find substantial differences from the national sample that might have distorted the main results.

Results of this study suggest that the organic brain syndrome versus accelerated aging distinction might be an important one to look for, not only with elderly alcoholics, but with problem drinkers of all ages. Furthermore, it is possible that differential treatment strategies might be developed that take this distinction into account. A therapeutic procedure that is effective in alleviating or reversing changes associated with aging might be of value to the individual, even if it had little or no effect on that aspect of his functioning more closely related to generalized organic brain syndrome.

Fortunately, a well-designed follow-up study by an independent research team has already been conducted. Blusewicz et al. (1977) studied three groups of 20 men each. These consisted of alcoholic and nonalcoholic men in their early thirties, and a group of normal men with a mean age of 71. This was a somewhat different research design, then, from the one employed by Williams et al. The normal young men were slightly more educated than the alcoholics, who had more educational background than the normal elders. This is not an unusual pattern, and the differences were not large. The alcoholics were recruited from rehabilitation centers in the Salt Lake City area and had, on the average, about 13 years of problem drinking. They had a mean period of abstinence from alcohol of 37 days at the time of their participation in this study.

There was also a difference in the assessment procedures in this study. Instead of using WAIS, the most popular individually administered intelligence test, they employed a battery of objective measures that test sensory and perceptual functions. These included, for example, a spiral aftereffect test, a complex reaction time test, a memory-for-designs test, and others of this general type.

Blusewicz et al. set out to test the hypothesis that chronic alcoholism produces accelerated or premature aging of neuropsychological functions. Such findings on the behavioral test level would be suggestive of underlying CNS changes, most likely in the brain.

The general level of neuropsychological functioning was highest for the normal young adults and lowest for the normal elderly men. Within the young alcoholic group, a distinction was made between nonsevere and severe (more pronounced signs of alcohol-related symptoms in their history) subgroups. While the severe group showed a lower level of neuropsychological functioning than the nonsevere, they were still somewhat superior to the normal elderly on the tests in this battery. Another data analysis procedure distributed all participants in the study into brain-damaged and non–brain-damaged groups on the basis of an impairment index score. "Neither the young normal nor the nonsevere alcoholic group would be classified, *as a group,* in the brain damaged category while both the severe alcoholic and elderly normal groups would" (Blusewicz et al., 1977, p. 353).

The investigators clearly acknowledged the limitations of a cross-sectional design in trying to reach a conclusion in which the true effects of *aging* can be distinguished from other variables. Nevertheless, they believed that intrinsic effects of aging are likely to have been the most powerful factors contributing to the main findings. There were rather substantial indications of a general decline in neuropsychological functioning with aging and suggestions that the same is true with alcoholism. This does not mean that the effects were precisely the same in all specific domains of neuropsychological functioning. Alcoholism seemed to leave its most damaging mark on the higher mental processes such as abstract reasoning and short-term memory. Vision, audition, and sensorimotor functions were not as severely affected. "Deficits in (higher mental processes) without deficits in fundamental perceptual and motor functions suggest subtle and diffuse changes in the state of the cortex rather than severe or focal deterioration. It would be expected that problems with short term memory and abstract reasoning would be among the first to appear as a consequence of the progressive and diffuse brain changes associated with aging. To this extent, the deficits seen in the young alcoholics resemble those seen in elderly populations" (p. 353).

Despite its contributions, this study still leaves unanswered the question of whether or not alcoholics age (in the negative sense) even faster as they advance in chronological age. This question could not have been answered definitively even if the study had included a group of alcoholic elderly men for further comparisons, although such a group would have been useful.

Both of the studies described here do suggest that people who use alcoholic beverages to excess appear to run an additional risk of neuropsychological impairment beyond whatever may be "normal" with intrinsic aging. Whether or not this excess impairment should really be interpreted as accelerated or premature aging, on the one hand, or as an additional load of generalized brain damage, on the other, cannot be definitively answered at this time.

General Health Status

The neuropsychological data suggest that higher mental processes, and therefore the *integration* of physical and psychosocial realms of functioning, tend to be impaired when there is chronic abuse of alcohol. Individuals who are less able to cope with the complexities of life become more vulnerable to a variety of afflictions and deficiencies. Such persons are probably less equipped to regulate their nutritional intake, sleep properly, take effective measures against illness, and so on. Even if excessive use of alcohol had no direct effects on the body apart from its impairment of CNS processes, this could well be enough to account for other physical disorders that might develop as a consequence. It is known, however, that alcoholic beverages in excess can produce other deleterious effects (e.g., cardiotoxic effects, Chapter 2), in addition to those more directly affecting the CNS.

Mezey (1974) has surveyed many of the medical problems associated with alcoholism. Some of his conclusions are probably already known to the reader from other sources. Chronic alcoholism, for example, is often associated with malnutrition and vitamin deficiencies. Almost everything goes wrong with the nutritional process when alcohol is poured into the body in excessive amounts over a prolonged period of time. Digestion, absorption, and utilization of nutriments depart significantly from the normal. The vitamin deficiencies common among alcoholics (particularly in the B-complex vitamins and folic acid) lead to clinical conditions such as anemia and glossitis. The deficiencies may also play a role in creating or intensifying cardiac dysfunction.

Although Mezey does not discuss these problems in relation to the elderly, it is not hard to fill in the picture. Nutritional difficulties beset many old people even apart from alcohol involvement. Inadequate income, depression, loneliness and the like (nobody to cook for, nobody to eat with) often result in a diet that is not in the elderly person's best interest. Should excessive drinking become associated with a pattern of nutritional intake that is already out of balance, then vulnerability to a variety of physical problems increases even further.

One problem area mentioned in passing by Mezey may be of particular relevance for the health of the elderly problem drinker. He notes that "chronic alcoholic patients without significant liver disease have an increased tolerance to a variety of drugs when sober, but a paradoxical increased susceptibility to them when intoxicated. These changes in the susceptibility to drugs are probably due to a combination of adaptive and synergistic effects of drugs on the central nervous system as well as to changes in their rates of metabolism. . . . Administration of a number of drugs when alcohol is still present in the body results in a decrease in their metabolism, owing to competition of the ethanol and the drugs for metabolism by the microsomal mixed function oxidase system" (Mezey, 1974, p. 298).

Those familiar with the clinical management of geriatric patients recognize how difficult it can be to establish and maintain a proper dosage level and mixture of drugs when the individual is suffering from a variety of disorders. A relatively small difference in dosage can make the difference between an effective and an ineffective or even a counter-productive treatment regime. Furthermore, the elderly person, like any-one else in our society, sometimes engages in extensive self-medication. The drug-and-alcohol mix is a potentially dangerous one in general, most particularly when there is not an attentive physician on the scene. How much apparent senility and confusion or other syndromes in old age are related to an adverse drug–alcohol interaction is difficult to determine but certainly warrants concern.

The long-term heavy drinker is at particular risk for developing cirrhosis of the liver as that organ's capacity to metabolize alcohol finally is overcome by prolonged and excessive intake. Chronic as well as acute pancreatitis is another significant risk, giving rise to symptoms such as abdominal pain, weight loss, and diabetes. Perhaps less well known is the incapacitating atrophy and weakness of muscles suffered by some chronic alcoholics. In chronic alcoholic myopathy, the lower extremities may be especially affected.

The variety of alcohol-related pathologies is extensive. Red blood cells, platelets, and white blood cells all tend to decrease with excessive use of alcohol. The body's defense against infections tend to be weakened as a result of such changes. Pneumonia and pulmonary tuberculosis occur more frequently in alcoholic populations at all age levels than among normal adults. Korsakoff's psychosis is one of the more dramatically disabling conditions that has become associated with excessive drinking. The mental changes are conspicuous and include

massive loss of recent memory, confabulation, poor insight, and behavioral inertia. It often occurs in conjunction with Wernicke's disease
in which drowsiness and disorientation are accompanied by a variety of
physical disturbances such as ataxia of stance and gait, nystagmus, and
ocular palsies. Both the Korsakoff and the Wernicke syndromes have
been related to thiamine and other vitamin deficiencies, which, as
already noted, are frequent correlates of prolonged heavy drinking.

Many attempts have been made to determine the possible relationship between excessive use of alcohol and the incidence and severity of
cancer. Methodological problems (particularly in distinguishing between
alcohol effects per se and other possible etiologies such as smoking,
exposure to pollutants, and malnutrition) make it difficult to arrive at a
clear picture. Furthermore, this is an active field of research in which
findings tumble rapidly upon each other and make it hard to form a
stable view of the alcohol–cancer relationship. The particular relationship between alcohol and cancer in old age has not yet received the
attention it deserves and no doubt will receive in the future. There is
enough available evidence, however, to implicate alcohol abuse in the
development of certain cancers (especially when associated with heavy
smoking). The heavy drinking/heavy smoking constellation appears to be
especially significant in the development of cancers of the mouth,
pharynx, larynx, and esophagus. Excessive consumption of distilled
spirits in particular appears to be linked with esophageal cancer (Keller
et al., 1974). Alcohol does not appear to play an equal role in the
development of all types of cancer. A number of problems remain to be
resolved, including "the decline in the rate of cancer of the stomach in
the United States in recent years while the consumption of alcohol has
apparently increased" (Keller et al., 1974, p. 65).

A recent study of elderly cardiac patients did not find a higher rate
of alcoholism (Schuckit, 1976). They did tend to have a somewhat higher
level ol alcohol intake and more history of minor alcohol problems than
elderly veterans with other types of medical disorder. The somewhat
higher incidence of alcohol use (but not alcoholism) among elderly
cardiac patients was part of a more general picture of psychiatric
difficulty and social dislocation in this group (e.g., higher divorce rate,
greater frequency of living alone in a hotel, history of emotional problems).

Is there a relationship between excessive use of alcohol and the
individual's self-perception of health status in old age? This is one of the
questions explored by Monk, Cryns and Cabral (1976) as part of a more
general inquiry into alcohol consumption and alcoholism as a function of
adult age. The respondents were 100 men and 137 women above the age
of 60 drawn from a larger stratified sample in the western part of New

York State. On the basis of their questionnaire responses, the elders were classified into good and poor health groups. The cross-classification was in terms of extent of self-reported drinking: "never," "rarely," "moderate," and "heavy." The majority of respondents in all drinking categories thought of themselves as being in good health. The self-reported heavy drinkers were the most likely, however, to see themselves as in poor health. What makes this finding more provocative is the fact that the elders who never drank were not far behind the heavy drinkers in their reporting of relatively poor health. This means, of course, that the more moderate categories tended to report better health status than either extreme group. Monk et al. suggest that this apparent curvilinear relationship between health and drinking in old age "may point to a streak of realistic awareness among heavy drinkers: they know that their health status is poor. Unfortunately, this study does not answer the question whether their health is poor because they drink, or conversely, whether they drink heavily because they know their health to be poor. The relatively high incidence of poor health reported by 'never' drinkers or abstainers lends itself to an analogous interpretation: they may be abstaining from alcohol because of actual ill health or they are health-concerned individuals who fear the possible negative effects of alcohol" (pp. 11–12).

Another possibility, not mentioned by Monk et al., is that moderate use of alcohol may be more positively associated with favorable health status in old age, either because of direct alcohol effects or because moderate use is part of a more health conducive life-style in general. In any event, this self-report study would be a useful one to repeat with other samples of elderly men and women throughout the nation to see if the curvilinear relationship is a consistent one.

Many of the physical problems described above can be alleviated or even reversed when the elderly alcoholic or heavy drinker abstains. As Drew (1968) and others have observed, both spontaneous abstention and abstention as response to medical guidance are not at all rare occurrences among elderly people who have a history of excessive alcohol use. It would be a mistake to assume that old age somehow forecloses the possibility of substantial health improvement or relinquishing a deleterious habit.

For a general index of the alcohol–health relationship in old age, one might expect mortality data to be important. Furthermore, the expectation would be that excessive use of alcohol would be related to higher mortality. The general expectation is borne out with respect to alcoholism and mortality throughout the broad age and disease spectrum (e.g., Keller et al., 1974, pp. 79–92). Heavy drinkers tend to be more vulnerable to death from a variety of causes. Beyond this general statement, however, one must become more cautious. As Keller et al. and numerous others have pointed out, the situation for heavy drinkers and for the population at large should not be treated as identical. Some people are at much greater risk than others. Excessive drinking should be clearly distinguished from moderate consumption.

There are other reasons to proceed slowly in drawing conclusions about alcohol use and mortality, particularly in old age. It has already been mentioned here and in Chapter 3 that many heavy drinkers reduce or end their alcohol consumption as they grow older (Drew, 1968; Cahalan et al., 1969; Amark, 1951). This progressive abstention has an effect on mortality, but one that cannot be determined with certainty. .

There are at least two other effects to consider:

1. The greater vulnerability of heavy drinkers leads to higher mortality at younger adult years. The people most at risk from alcohol-related disorders are less likely to reach old age.
2. Specification of "cause of death" is not as dependable and standardized as the layman might assume. There are regional, ethnic, and sociohistorical time-trend differences in what conditions are recorded as causes of death. This is especially true when such causes are linked with emotionally sensitive concerns (suicide is a major example). It is difficult to draw firm conclusions about the incidence of alcohol-related causes when death certificates differ in the manner in which they are completed because of a variety of psychosocial reasons.

The latter point was emphasized anew in one of the most recent surveys of the alcohol–mortality data. Statisticians for Metropolitan Life Insurance Company analyzed data on the general U.S. population made available by the National Center for Health Statistics, as well as data specific to their own policyholders (Metropolitan, 1977). The national data are of interest not only for their comprehensiveness but also because they make it possible to compare mortality for two points in time (1963–1964 versus 1973–1974), broken down by age, sex, and race. These data are presented in Table 6.1 through the courtesy of Metropolitan Life.

It is obvious that mortality from alcohol-related disorders rose sharply during this 10-year period. The increase was appreciable for both whites and nonwhites,[1] but especially so for the latter. Mortality for nonwhite males doubled across all age groups, including the oldest echelons. The less precipitous increase for white males was also ex-

---

[1] Unfortunately, all nonwhite groups are still grouped in this one category, a fact that should lead to some caution in the conclusions that are drawn.

Table 6.1

Mortality from Alcoholic Disorders[a] United States, 1963–1964
and 1973–1974

| Sex and Age | Average Annual Death Rate per 100,000 | | | | Percent Increase, 1963–1964 and 1973–1974 | |
| | 1963–1964 | | 1973–1974 | | | |
	White	Nonwhite	White	Nonwhite	White	Nonwhite
Male						
20 and over	11.5	20.6	16.8	42.6	46	107
20–29	.6	4.9	1.1	7.3	83	49
30–39	4.9	23.1	7.0	39.7	43	72
40–49	15.2	33.4	22.9	70.6	51	111
50–59	25.1	29.2	34.9	76.0	39	160
60–69	25.9	24.3	40.0	48.7	54	100
70 and over	13.7	10.4	18.5	22.3	35	114
Female						
20 and over	4.2	9.5	5.7	16.2	36	71
20–29	.2	2.6	.2	2.5	—	−4
30–39	2.4	12.9	2.3	15.2	−4	18
40–49	7.5	16.0	9.2	30.5	23	91
50–59	9.2	12.5	13.4	27.7	46	122
60–69	6.0	7.0	10.4	15.5	73	121
70 and over	2.5	[b]	3.3	4.8	32	**

Note: This table is reprinted through the courtesy of Metropolitan Life Insurance
Company from its *Statistical Bulletin,* December 1977, 58, 2.

[a] Disorders include alcoholic psychosis, alcoholism and cirrhosis of liver, alcoholic as
listed in the International Classification of Diseases.

[b] Fewer than 20 deaths.

pressed at all age levels, including the oldest groups. The greatest increases
in mortality for men tended to occur in the younger adult years for
whites (the twenties were disproportionately affected) and the later adult
years for nonwhites.

Among women, clearly the most significant increases have taken
place for nonwhites from the age of 40 upward. Older nonwhites of both
sexes, then, seem to have become much more susceptible to alcohol-
related causes of death within the past decade. White females continued
to have relatively low frequencies of alcohol-related deaths in the
younger age echelons but showed a progressive increase from their
forties upward. This parallels the trend for nonwhite females, although it
starts a little later and is much less steep. Nevertheless, there is a strong

progression in alcohol-related deaths with advancing adult age from the forties to the sixties. At age 70 and over for all groups, the actual incidence of alcohol-related deaths is relatively low. Nevertheless, even here, the percentage increase for white women is moderately large. Inspection of Table 6.1 also confirms the continued higher prevalence of such deaths among men at all age levels as compared with women within the white and nonwhite subgroups.

We will not speculate here on the specific meaning of these time trends except to note that a distinction should probably be made between characteristics of the *people* who are growing up and growing older and the *situations* that confront them. It is not easy to determine how much of the differential mortality between these two recent points in time can be attributed to problems relating to the era in which people were brought up and how much to the problems encountered at a later date, for example, with age-related losses. But there is another point here that merits our attention. If alcohol-related mortality can change so much within a relatively short period of time, then it hardly seems adequate to concentrate on disease syndromes alone. One must also gain a better understanding of how life-style and social conditions interact with physical status. Those who advocate a holistic approach to health in general seem to have additional evidence for their position in these data.

In examining death claims submitted on behalf of their own policyholders, Metropolitan Life found that cirrhosis of the liver was by far the most commonly stated underlying cause. About four out of five alcohol-related deaths occurred among men, most of these in the 45 to 64 age range. Men aged 65 and above also were relatively high in proportion among the total of alcohol-related deaths, but the peak age for women was lower. And, as previously noted, the Metropolitan statisticians called for more complete and standardized recording of causes of death to provide a more accurate source of information on alcohol-related mortality.

The data we have reviewed in this section support the concern of public health officials about health effects of excessive drinking in general, although many questions remain to be answered. There may well be some new or intensified factors operating in our society at present that make this concern even more justified than usual. Among older adults, there appears to be a substantial relationship between mental and emotional problems and the abuse of alcohol (e.g., Schuckit, 1976). There are also many specific ways in which excessive drinking can impair physical functioning. On the other hand, most studies indicate that the proportion of alcoholics tends to diminish as we move from midlife to the older age groups (Drew, 1968).

Examination of the health correlates and outcomes of excessive drinking is only part of the total story. We turn now to the data (again, limited!) on the relationship between health and the moderate use of alcoholic beverages in old age.

MODERATE DRINKING AND HEALTH STATUS IN OLD AGE

Continuum or Dichotomy?

The destructive effects associated with long-term excessive drinking have been well established. Many claims have been made, however, for the positive effects of light to moderate drinking. The advocates include some clinicians, medical historians, and the consumers themselves. How are these two positions to be reconciled? The following possibilities exist:

1. Those who believe that moderate use of alcoholic beverages has health benefits for the elderly are mistaken.
2. Some people do derive benefits from the moderate use of alcoholic beverages, while others do not and may, in fact, be adversely affected by any level of intake.
3. There is a gradient or continuum of effect that is dependent on amount of alcohol used. Excessive drinking leads to major pathology, moderate drinking to lesser pathology, while the negative effects of light drinking are difficult to detect and may be obscured by a purely subjective sense of well-being.
4. The alcohol–health relationship is more accurately regarded as dichotomous. What happens to the body when it is exposed to large amounts of ethanol over a long period of time is qualitatively different from the response to light and moderate use. The two patterns are really very different, and therefore both claims—the destructive and the beneficial—can be accurate but only when their respective parameters are clearly identified and kept in mind.

The continuum versus dichotomy issue is perhaps the key one here. It has been recognized by a number of observers, but so far has not yielded itself to definitive research. As usual, when working with human beings in the midst of their complex and individual lives, one cannot easily "hold constant" all the variables that are associated with health and any particular "independent variable" (in this case, use of alcohol). Multivariate statistical techniques are of some help in this regard; even so, the conflicting positions have not yet been resolved by adequate research.

Both views seem plausible, although it is difficult to see how both could be factually correct. Light use of alcohol might serve as a minor stressing agent (in a broad sense of this term) that is rather easily handled by otherwise healthy people. The degree of impairment or hazard involved in light drinking might be well within the range of many other effects generated by an individual's total life-style. Many of us do not follow a dietary plan in general that is optimal for health. We are warned constantly these days about nutritional imbalances in the most popular foodstuffs consumed (including, e.g., high-calorie but unnourishing soft drinks). Health authorities scold us for becoming too sedentary a nation and then shake a cautionary finger at the joggers who are trying to keep themselves fit through physical activity. The implications of life-style for health extend well beyond diet and physical activity. Perhaps enough has been said, however, to indicate that light to moderate use of alcohol *could* have minor negative effects that are simply one aspect of the total life-style developed by some of us. Given this view, alcohol use might constitute a "small negative" health factor but with some redeeming characteristics that even the opponents of drinking, if knowledgeable, might have to grant. If people *enjoy* an occasional drink, if in some situations it does facilitate amiable *social interaction,* and if the consumer does *feel relaxed,* these would seem to be to the good. One could still argue that the "price" for even light use of alcoholic beverages is too high (physically, psychologically, financially) and that it is still a poisonous substance, but it would be hard to deny that pleasure, social solidarity, and relaxation are conducive to both mental and physical health.

The dichotomous view can also be presented in a reasonable light. Alcohol is a drug (although it is also more than a drug). Like other drugs, dosage level and proper use are very important. There is no completely "safe" drug—and perhaps no completely safe food either for that matter—because all can be misused. In recent years, for example, increased attention has been given to the deleterious effects of even the most familiar and supposedly innocuous drugs such as aspirin. The effects of a little ethanol at appropriate times and of large amounts at indiscriminate times are paralleled by the positive and negative effects of variations in dosage along the whole spectrum of pharmacologically active substances. From an even broader perspective, the distinction between moderate and extreme indulgence in almost anything can again be brought into focus. Is exercise good or bad? Is fasting? Is engaging in competitive activities? Is studying or working? The wisdom of the centuries suggests that how and how much we devote ourselves to certain activities may be just as important as the nature of these uses and activities themselves. On this view, it makes sense to see alcoholic beverages as potentially beneficial *or* as potentially harmful, depending on the extent and pattern of use. One does not have to concoct a special theory for the dichotomous interpretation but simply refer to our general knowledge of what happens when we do things in moderation or to excess.

Factors More Specific to Old Age

When our interest turns more specifically to the alcohol–health link in old age, there are some factors that require particular attention:

1. Elderly people do not necessarily favor the same pattern of alcoholic intake as do adults in general (Chapter 3). Furthermore, this pattern may change by cohort. A study we will be examining in more detail below, for example, finds more of a preference for wine than for other alcoholic beverages among the oldest respondents (Yano, Rhoads, & Kagan, 1978). This is a fairly typical finding, even though the sample in this particular study is different from the typical white middle-class populations (Japanese men living in Hawaii). We do not know what beverages will be preferred by younger adults in the same sample as they grow old. Will preference for wine increase for reasons associated with the aging process in some way? Or will the generational or cohort differences persist through the years? In any event, we must obviously make sure that we are taking the *type* of beverage, as well as the amount, into account when trying to understand the health-related effects of alcohol use in old age.

2. Because a general decrease in drinking with advancing adult age has been reported by most surveys (Chapter 3), this selectivity must also be considered in interpreting the health status of those who do continue to drink.

3. Tolerance for alcohol seems to vary as a function of adult age, with older people, in general, having a reduced capacity to "handle" ethanol. Another way of saying this is that a smaller amount of alcohol will have an effect similar to what formerly was produced by a larger amount. This does present the possibility that potentially beneficial effects will be missed or even turned into adverse effects because the elderly person might rapidly pass from the low-dose zone of positive effect to the zone of negative effect.

At least two additional observations should be made about the relationshop between tolerance and age. As Cicero (1978) points out, "tolerance" is best defined with respect to specific physical and behavioral effects. Although there is some utility to the concept of a generalized level of tolerance to alcohol, careful research indicates that specific realms of tolerance should also be distinguished. We would like to suggest in addition that more attention be given to individual differences in tolerance. What is true for an age echelon in general does not hold equally for all its members. Some old people have greater tolerance than others for a variety of foods and drugs other than alcohol. The clinician or anyone else concerned about the possible value of alcohol for a particular old person should not be satisfied with the generalities but seek to identify the level of use that might be appropriate for this individual.

4. Elderly people are somewhat more likely to have multiple medical problems and to be taking more than one kind of medication. This increases the possibility of alcohol–drug interactions.

This list does not exhaust the factors that are likely to be salient in the alcohol–drug relationship in old age, but it at least reminds us that there are many possible differences to study.

Appetite and Digestion

Sensory acuity tends to diminish with age. The gustatory and olfactory senses are included as part of this general decline, which probably contributes to the observed reduction of appetite in old people. It is not uncommon for elderly people to complain of food as "tasteless" even though others find it to be well seasoned. Sensory decline is not the only factor involved. Many elders have a monotonous diet because of budget limitations or the habit of eating alone. Others are restricted to bland diets; still others reside in institutions in which the fare is less than inspiring. While some reduction in appetite may be appropriate for an older person's altered needs and lower level of physical activity, the lack of interest in adequate nutrition can work against health.

Some of the earliest controlled research on alcohol effects inovlved its possible role as an appetite stimulant. The distinguished physiologist Ivan Pavlov (1910) characterized alcohol as a "psychic stomachicum," a substance that improves appetite or palatability. Over the years, particular attention has been given to wine as an appetite stimulant or "psychic stomachicum." Lucia (1970) has abstracted and annotated almost 2000 references to the effects of wine on the digestive system. These range from controlled research to opportunistic clinical observations and position statements. From the available data and from his own clinical and research experience, Lucia concludes that "one to three ounces of wine excites the appetite, two to four ounces stimulates salivary secretion. By this dual effect on appetite, as well as on secretion, wine stimulates the digestive function throughout" (p. 155). He further concludes that wine facilitates the assimilation of nitrogeneous substances and deamination by the liver.

Beyond its apparent benefits as part of a normal diet, wine sometimes is used in a specifically medicinal or quasi-medicinal way:

In Latin countries, and especially in France, wine, often medicated, is used
widely in the treatment of diseases of the digestive system, particularly anorexia,
hypochlorhydria without gastritis, and hyposthenic dyspepsia. Minor hepatic
insufficiency responds favorably to table wine, an observation rediscovered by
modern clinicians. . . . The anesthetic properties and the tannin content of wine
makes it a valuable adjunct in the treatment of colitis, spastic constipation,
diarrhea and in certain infectious diseases of the gastrointestinal tract. The nausea
and vomiting of gastric irritation is alleviated by the use of effervescent wines or
champagnes. This action is due to the anesthetic effect of carbon dioxide and the
accelerated absorption of alcohol under these circumstances. (Lucia, 1970, p.
156).

These conclusions offered by a contemporary medical researcher
recall the advice given by Avicenna a thousand years ago (Chapter 1).
Like his notable predecessor, Lucia has distinctions and counterindications to share as well. He particularly recommends moderately sweet
wines because they tend to be more palatable stimulants of digestive
function and have analgesic effects as well as calories. For geriatric
patients and other convalescents, he recommends the "light aged red
wines." Young and yeasty wines are cautioned against because they are
fermentable, and he suggests that wines that contain more than the usual
amount of ethanol should be diluted. Contraindications to wine include
diseases of the gastrointestinal tract characterized by hyperacidity, pep-
tic ulcer, cancer of the stomach, gastritis, and pyloric stenosis. Any
indications of potential hemorrhage should also be taken as counterindications for wine, according to Lucia. Acute inflammatory diseases of the
pancreas and dysfunctions of the gallblader and biliary tract are other
conditions in which use of wine is likely to be unwise.

Lucia's discussion of the advantages and disadvantages of wine as
part of a treatment regime for conditions related to digestion is set within
a context that assumes adequate diagnosis and monitoring by a careful
physician and the use of a moderate dosage level. Similar needs for
balance and caution are expressed by others who see value in the
inclusion of wine for people with problems related to appetite, nutrition,
or digestion. White (1973), for example, reviews in some detail the
nutritional components of wines (there are differences between table and
dessert wines that need to be taken into account). Intelligent management of wine in the total diet is seen as making the critical difference as
to whether this beverage will be helpful or deleterious. It can be used,
for example, to help control obesity, but unrestrained use can lead to the
opposite effect. White corrects the long-standing assumption that port
wine is particularly effective in treating iron deficiency anemia. Actually,

ordinary white and red table wines generally contain more iron than does port (the red wines more reliably so, since the ferrous content of white wines is sometimes decreased deliberately in order to prevent clouding). In a particularly careful review of the claimed appetite-stimulant effects of wine, Powers (1973), a leading researcher in this area, points to many questions that have yet to be satisfactorily resolved. This is largely because wine is now recognized to be an exceptionally complex substance from a biochemical standpoint, and many of its constituents have barely been identified let alone studied definitively. He does conclude, however, that there is a sound basis in general for the belief that wine does have stimulant effects on the appetite.

Professionals working in the field of geriatrics tend to comment favorably on the use of wine in this as well as in other spheres of functioning. Huffman (1972), a dietician, is among those who recommend wine for elderly patients to serve as part of their nutritional intake as well as for purposes of tranquilization and sedation. She points out that the value of wine for all of these purposes is not as well known to physicians of today as was the case a few decades ago and further back over the centuries. "Wine often lacked the dramatic effect of aspirin, barbitals, vitamins, hormones, antibiotics, tranquilizers, and sedatives, so the use of wine fell into disuse to make room for the new. With the advent of temperance and prohibition in the United States, wine was removed from the pharmacopoeias. The United States now has a generation of physicians who generally are not aware of the therapeutic values of wine" (Huffman, 1972, p. 3). Among slightly unusual uses for wine, she suggests its use as a flavoring of food for diabetics through cooking in which the alcohol evaporates, leaving only the flavor. Like some other dieticians and physicians, she also suggests the use of dry wine for diabetic patients, since it can serve as a source of energy because of its rapid metabolism without using insulin.

Balboni (1963) asked elderly men in both Italy and the United States why they drank wine regularly. The Italian elders specified its value as a digestive, although not in a distinctively medical sense. Instead, they were inclined to feel that a meal was not really a meal without wine. Neither the Italians nor the Americans emphasized the nutrient value of wine. The beverage helped to complete a meal, in its social and gustatory aspects, and was pleasurable in its general effects. The elders in this study were healthy individuals who generally took their wine with meals and recognized that possibly intoxicating effects were minimized by this practice. Although some of these people also made use of other alcoholic beverages, they were aware of the differences between "strong drink" and the more moderate effects associated with the use of wine at mealtime.

Among the stronger ethanol-containing beverages, vodka has received more favorable comment than whisky (Demrau & Liddy, 1960, 1960). They found that some geriatric patients may be adversely affected by the congeners in whisky, which produce prolonged aftereffects because they slow the rate of oxidation. Hangover symptoms were rare among those who used vodka instead (2 oz. of either drink were used). The investigators also note that some people have whisky allergies related to the grains from which the whisky is derived. With specific reference to digestion, vodka was recommended by Demrau and Liddy because it is less likely to produce gastric irritation. They also note that vodka is a relatively pure and uniform beverage as contrasted with whisky, which contains variable and uncertain mixtures of congeners.

Cardiovascular Functioning

The relationship between alcohol and cardiovascular functioning in general has already been touched upon (Chapter 2). This is obviously a significant area to consider in old age. As Kennedy (1974) and many others point out, cardiac disease is among the leading causes of disability and mortality in the aged. People may bring cardiovascular difficulties with them into old age as well as incur such problems for the first time in their later years. Any socioeconomic or attitudinal factors that lead to less frequent or careful medical attention can also contribute to failure to diagnose and treatment cardiovascular conditions in the aged. Even under the best circumstances, some diagnoses may be difficult to make, as in the case of endocarditis. The fact that there is still so much to learn—and to put into practice—in the detection and treatment of cardiovascular problems in old age has implications for the linkage with alcohol. Until the disorders and their etiologies are well understood, it is also hard to assess the possible role of alcoholic beverages in these respects as well. Degenerative calcification, for example, is one pathway to damage of the mitral valve in the aged, especially in women (Pomerance, 1965). Whether or not use of alcoholic beverages has any bearing on this specific life-threatening condition does not appear to have been studied, nor does it even appear to be ripe for study until more is learned about the basic condition itself.

The important topic of cardiovascular functioning and its relationship to alcohol use in old age—among nonalcoholic individuals—must be approached, then, at a time when much still remains to be learned about the fundamental physiologic changes associated with aging of the heart and the entire cardiovascular system. Research on this topic is becoming more abundant, and clinicians have both more information and more treatment resources available to them, and yet it is still difficult to specify the role of any one particular influence, such as alcohol, on the total picture.

When the stakes are high, as in cardiovascular status, and the information available less than definitive, it is not surprising that there is spirited controversy. Those who oppose the use of alcohol in general can and do point to the cardiotoxic potentialities of this substance at any age level. There would be no risk of a toxic reaction to alcohol in old age if one simply eschewed this substance. Others believe either that moderate use of alcohol is not dangerous except where specific counterindications exist or even that alcohol may in some way protect against coronary failure. The data are far from conclusive. Nussenfeld (1974) and colleagues, for example, reviewed 118 consecutive cases of sudden cardiac death in the Miami area in light of previous claims that alcohol might be of benefit to geriatric patients, particularly in reducing the chances of myocardial infarction. Autopsies were performed on all the deceased, who were classified as substantial to heavy alcohol users or as those with little or no history of drinking. These groups were compared for presence of chronic coronary artery stenosis and acute heart vessel or muscle damage. These investigators concluded that neither protective nor harmful effects on heart tissue could be ascribed to alcohol from this study.

A different approach was taken recently by Yano, Rhoads, and Kagan (1977), who were interested in the risk of coronary heart disease as related both to alcohol and to coffee use. The study was part of a larger epidemiological investigation (the Honolulu Heart Study) involving 7705 men of Japanese ancestry born in the years 1900 to 1919. The risk of coronary heart disease during a 6-year follow-up period was related to baseline examination data. New cases were found on reexamination and by surveillance of morbidity and mortality data on hospital records, death certificates, and autopsy reports. When the 294 new cases of coronary heart disease (CHD) were examined, there was at first a positive relationship seen between coffee intake and risk. This association was reduced below statistical significance, however, when cigarette smoking was taken into account. In regard to the relationship with use of alcohol, beer was the most frequently used alcoholic beverage in this population and proved to be the only one with a significant relationship to incidence of morbidity and mortality (although parallel trends were noted for wine and hard liquor). The *direction* of the trend was the finding to make one pause: Those who did *not* drink had a higher rate of CHD. This applied both to CHD with fatal and nonfatal (at that time) outcomes. A further analysis indicated that the higher incidence of CHD in nondrinkers could not be attributed to the possible existence of latent coronary disease in this group.

The basic data are summarized in Table 6.2. When a multivariate logistic analysis was conducted to determine if these findings were confounded by other risk factors, it was learned that the relationship

Table 6.2

Age-adjusted Six-Year Incidence Rate of CHD According to
Alcohol Consumption

Alcohol Consumption[a] (ml/day)	Men at Risk	Incidence Rate per 1,000				
		Total CHD	CHD Death	Nonfatal Myocardial Infarction	Acute Coronary Insufficiency	Angina Pectoris
0	3,565	46.0	6.8	21.2	2.8	15.2
1–6	1,034	41.2	6.3	22.0	3.2	9.7
7–15	962	30.7	4.2	14.0	3.1	9.4
16–39	1,024	26.7	4.0	15.6	3.0	4.1
40+	1,006	21.2	3.0	4.2	6.6	7.4
Significance test for trend		$P<.001$	NS	$P<.001$	NS	NS

Note: Reprinted with the permission of the *New England Journal of Medicine,* August 1977, *297,* (8), 407.

[a] Sum of absolute alcohol contained in wine, beer, and hard liquor usually consumed per day, with conversion rates of .10, .037, and .38, respectively.

actually became stronger when factors such as cigarette smoking were taken into account. (People who used alcohol also tended to make more use of cigarettes; the latter practice was independently established as an added risk for CHD rather than a factor in prevention.)

Yano et al. recognized the difficulties involved in trying to draw conclusions from any one study as well as in trying to reconcile the variety of studies and observations that had previously been made in this area. They note that *excessive* drinking has often been found to be related to *increased* CHD risk (e.g., Tibblin, Wilhelmsen & Werko, 1975). In their own study, the decreased risk correlation was found in the range of moderate rather than excessive consumption; therefore their findings are not necessarily inconsistent with the others—amount of alcohol used is a critical variable. Yano et al. also point out that their research was prospective in design and *did* take into account the interaction with other major risk factors.

Some previous observers suggested that cirrhosis of the liver—itself a pathological developmental—might be the primary mechanism for prevention or reduction of atherosclerosis (Hirst, Hadley, & Gore, 1965). This did not seem to be a likely explanation for the new data, however. The level of alcohol use in the Honolulu sample was low in comparison with worldwide survey data. As Yano et al. (1977) report: "Nearly half the drinkers consumed less than 15 ml of absolute alcohol (roughly equivalent to 1 bottle of beer or 1 drink of whisky) daily, and only 3 per cent of them consumed 90 ml or more per day. Thus, it is unlikely that the lower risk of CHD among drinkers in this population can be attributed to gross hepatic dysfunction resulting from excessive intake of alcohol'' (pp. 408–409). Autopsy data substantiated the same relationship between myocardial infarction and alcohol use even when all deaths closely related to excessive alcohol consumption were excluded. The most promising clues to the mechanism by which alcohol use might possibly protect against CHD seemed to be in the relationship with cholesterol level. This suggested linkage needs to be pursued in further research.

Editorial comment from an eminent researcher appeared in the same issue of the *New England Journal of Medicine* as did the Yano et al. article. William B. Kannel, of the Heart Disease Epidemiology Study in Framingham, Massachusetts, indicated that the findings were not at all unique to Hawaii and its particular population of elderly men. Kannel noted that the present data were ''solid,'' while previous data suggesting harmful effects of moderate use of alcohol were ''weak indeed.'' Referring to the research literature in this area, Kannel declared that ''although heavy use of alcohol is clearly toxic to the heart muscle, this fact does not preclude a beneficial effect of moderate use on the coronary vessels. This finding is certainly worth further prospective investigation, taking into account the type of alcoholic beverage, the amount, the pattern of drinking and the associated risk factors—including triglyceride, high-density lipoprotein and blood pressure. The relation of alcohol to cardiovascular disease appears to be different in different cultures, and its varying effects must be sorted out.'' Kannel adds a comment that we have not been able to avoid repeating several times already: ''In all such studies, it is important to distinguish alcohol abuse from alcohol use in moderation'' (Kannel, 1977, p. 444).

Kannel is of the opinion that excessive alcohol use certainly should be discouraged for reasons of general health as well as for social and psychologic reasons. He is not convinced, however, that alcohol in moderate amounts is to be blamed for the development of CHD. ''Physicians, interested in protecting patients against atherosclerotic cardiovascular disease, have no good reason to restrict social drinking in moderation. Although one does not want to make too much of the apparent benefits, what data there are show, if anything, a lower incidence in those who drink a little.'' Those who enjoy coffee and alcoholic beverages in moderation do not seem to be placing themselves at risk for CHD.

What we have here, however, is not likely to be the end of the story regarding alcohol and cardiovascular functioning in general or in old age in particular. There is still much to be learned, and it is possible that present conclusions may be revised appreciably in the future. At the moment, it would seem premature to urge the addition of alcohol to the diet of elderly people with the intention of protecting against CHD, but it is also unnecessary to inveigh against its use in moderation. As always, knowledge of the particular individual and his or her distinctive life circumstances is of major importance.

THE DESERT OF IGNORANCE

The evidence and learned opinion reviewed in this chapter represent a few cases of knowledge within a larger desert of ignorance. There is little solid information available about the effects of alcoholic beverages, used in moderation, on either the processes most closely associated with aging per se or on old people. Among the major gaps, we would call particular attention to the possible effects of ethanol on processes that regulate the body as a whole. Researchers who are attempting to understand the fundamental nature of aging are often inclined to view this process as a progressive failure of regulatory mechanisms. Some theoreticians hold that the failure of regulatory mechanisms is programmed genetically. Much of the growing edge of biogerontology consists of data and controversy on this point. A variant of this position would emphasize "aging" as a series of commonly incurred misfortunes, disease, impairments, and "accidents" that occur on the journey through life. Regulatory mechanisms may fail on this view as well, but the assumption that such failure is programmed and "required" is not deemed necessary. The possible role of alcohol in either variant of the progressive failure of regulatory mechanisms with age is simply not known today.

There would be little value in continuing to emphasize what is not known. An exception or two to this statement will be made in Chapter 8 in the context of new research directed toward hypothesis testing in the interface between biological and psychosocial realms.

REFERENCES

Amark, C. A study in alcoholism. *Acta Psychiatrica Scandinavia,* 1951, Suppl., *70,* 273–278.

Balboni, C. Alcohol in relation to dietary patterns. In S. P. Lucia (Ed.), *Alcohol and civilization.* New York: McGraw-Hill, 1963, pp. 61–74.

Blusewicz, M. J. Dustman, R. E., Schenkenberg, T., & Beck, E. C. Neuropsychological correlates of chronic alcoholism and aging. *Journal of Nervous and Mental Disease,* 1977, *165,* 348–355.

Cahalan, D., Cisin, I. H., & Crossley, H. M. *American drinking practices.* New Brunswick, N.J.: Rutgers Center of Alcohol Studies, 1969.

Cicero, T. J. Tolerance to and physical dependence on alcohol: Behavioral and neurobiological mechanisms. In M. A. Lipton, A. DiMascio, & K. F. Killam (Eds.), *Psychopharmacology: A generation of progress.* New York: Raven Press, 1978, pp. 1603–1618.

Damrau, F., & Liddy, E. Hangover and whisky congeners, comparison of whisky with vodka. *Journal of Natural Medicine,* 1960, *52,* 262–266.

Damrau, F., & Liddy, E. The whisky congeners, comparison of whisky with vodka as to toxic effects. *Current Therapy Research,* 1960, *1,* 453–455.

Drew. L. R. H. Alcohol as a self-limiting disease. *Quarterly Journal of Studies on Alcoholism,* 1968, *29,* 956–967.

Hirst, A. E., Hadley, G. G., & Gore, I. The effect of chronic alcoholism and cirrhosis of the liver on atherosclerosis. *American Journal of Medical Science,* 1965, *249,* 143–149.

Huffman, M. K. Wine in geriatrics: Pros and cons. *Western Care,* 1970, *15,* 2–7.

Kannel, W. B. Coffee, cocktails and coronary candidates. *New England Journal of Medicine,* 1977, *297,* 443–444.

Keller, M., Promisel, D. M., Spiegler, D., Light, L., & Davis, M. N. (Eds.), *Alcohol and health.* Rockville, Md: Alcohol, Drug Abuse & Mental Health Administration, 1974.

Kennedy, R. D. Recent advances in cardiology. In W. F. Anderson & T. G. Judge (Eds.), *Geriatric medicine.* New York: Academic Press, 1974, pp. 213–224.

Lucia, S. P. *Wine and the digestive system.* San Francisco: Fortune House, 1970.

Metropolitan Life. Mortality from alcoholism. *Statistical Bulletin,* 1977, *58,* 2–5.

Mezey, E. Medical problems associated with alcoholism. *Primary Care,* 1974, *1,* 293–316.

Monk, A., Cryns, A. G., & Cabral, R. Alcohol consumption and alcoholism as a function of adult age. Presented at 30th Annual Scientific Meetings of the Gerontological Society, San Francisco, Calif., November 1977.

Nussenfeld, S. R., Davis, J. H., Nagel, E. L., & Hirschman, J. C. Alcohol benefit for the geriatric patient. *Journal of the American Medical Association,* 1974, *227,* 439–440.

Overall, J. E., & Gorham, D. R. Organicity versus old age in objective and projective test performance. *Journal of Consulting and Clinical Psychology,* 1972, *39,* 98–105.

Pavlov, I. P. *The work of the digestive glands.* London: Charles Griffin, 1910.

Pomerance, C. Senile cardiac amyloidosis. *British Heart Journal,* 1967, *27,* 711–714.

Powers, J. J. Appetite stimulation: Possible support to dietary function. In S. P. Lucia & T. Berland (Eds.), *The medical importance of wine.* San Francisco: Fortune House, 1973, pp. 87–96.

Ribblin, G., Wilhelmsen, L., & Werko, L. Risk factors for myocardiac infarction and death due to ischemic heart disease and other causes. *American Journal of Cardiology,* 1976, *35,* 514–522.

Schuckit, M. A. The high rate of psychiatric disorders in elderly cardiac patients. Presented at 22nd Annual Meeting, American College of Angiology, Palm Springs, Calif., Janaury 1976.

White, P. M. The nutritional value of wine. In S. P. Lucia & T. Berland (Eds.), *The medical importance of wine*. San Francisco: Fortune House, 1973, pp. 81–86.

Williams, J. D., Ray, G. G., Overall, J. E. Mental aging and organicity in an alcoholic population. *Journal of Consulting and Clinical Psychology,* 1973, *41,* 392–396.

Yano, K., Rhoads, G. G., & Kagan A. Coffee, alcohol, and risk of coronary heart disease among Japanese men living in Hawaii. *New England Journal of Medicine,* 1977, *297,* 405–409.

7

Experimental Study of Possible Benefits of Alcoholic Beverages for the Elderly

Research over the past 15 years suggests that the moderate use of alcoholic beverages for institutionalized elders has beneficial psychosocial effects and rarely produces physical difficulties. This chapter critically reviews these studies.

Perhaps the earliest research interest by psychologists in alcoholic beverages began with the Russian scientist Ivan Pavlov. Based upon observations from his own use, as well as from experimental physiology, Pavlov (1910) characterized alcohol as a "psychic stomachicum," a substance that improves appetite or palatability. The appetite-stimulating effects of alcoholic beverages later proved to be more complex than first reported by Pavlov, although it is only recently that apparent contradictions have approached resolution through more differentiated types of research (Irvin, Ahokas, & Goetzl, 1950).

Since the beginning of the twentieth century, there have been studies on the effects of alcohol upon a variety of somatic ailments. Perhaps the first such controlled investigation was by Benedict and Torok (1906). They examined the effects of alcohol on diabetes. Working with a small clinical sample in Budapest, they reported that cognac, beer, and wine all had favorable effects when included in the diet of diabetic patients.

More recently, there have been a series of controlled investigations into the possible benefits of alcoholic beverages in institutionalized elders. Before considering these research studies in detail, let us consider some general characteristics of the research.

GENERAL CHARACTERISTICS OF THE RESEARCH

A number of generalizations can be made about the nature of the research in this area (see Table 7.1 and 7.2):

1. Most of the studies involved elderly men and women who were institutionalized, often in relatively deprived environments.
2. There has been a fairly broad spectrum of mental functioning and general health represented among the institutional samples, however. Occasional attempts have been made to study effects of alcoholic beverages with elders of markedly distinct functional status within the same institution, as in the Cushing Hospital and Bensenville Home Studies (described in more detail below).
3. The typical study has been conducted by personnel of the institution itself, as distinguished from teams of externally based researchers.
4. The typical study has concerned itself with sociobehavioral outcome measures such as attitude, morale, and interpersonal interaction.
5. The methods of data gathering, analysis, and reporting are quite variable. Few studies are directly comparable.
6. Subjective methods of evaluation have predominated over the objective. Typically, the participant reports on his or her own state of mind. These responses are either treated on a qualitative level by the investigator or quantified by means of a simple scale. Objective measures (e.g., the frequency of observed conversations with another person) have been less frequently employed.
7. Relatively few data have been collected in the medical/physiological realm.
8. Individual differences, whether in the sense of presituational variables or differential outcomes, received scant attention.
9. Theory and process have also received relatively little attention. Most studies have acknowledged the historic tradition of alcohol use as a "license" for the investigation and have pointed to the need to explore a wide variety of therapeutic or comfort-giving modalities to improve the well-being of the elderly. With the exceptions to be noted below, however, theoretical models have not been offered, nor has the process or mechanism of action been elucidated.
10. A number of studies of the use of alcoholic beverages have been accompanied by other concurrent milieu modifications that make it difficult to interpret alcohol-engendered effects per se.

Although the above generalizations can be made, some of the research, for example the extensive study sponsored by the National Institute on Alcohol and Alcoholism conducted by Mishara et al. (1975), employed a fairly sophisticated research methodology and confirmed many of the general findings reported in previous, less detailed studies.

THE CUSHING HOSPITAL STUDIES

The first series of investigations into possible benefits of alcoholic beverages for the institutionalized elderly was conducted at Cushing Hospital (Framingham, Massachusetts) from 1963 through 1968. Cushing Hospital, a state-operated medical facility, is devoted exclusively to the inpatient care of elderly men and women. There, approximately 650 patients with an average age of over 80 received a variety of medical and paramedical service. But despite the active treatment program, it was also "a place to live till you die" for most of its residents. The experimentation with alcoholic beverages represented one of the hospital's attempts to improve the quality of life for those who, most probably, will end their days within the institutional environment.

It is worth recalling the rationale for the first study. Psychotropic drugs had been in clinical use at Cushing Hospital and other geriatric facilities. Both clinical experience and controlled studies at Cushing Hospital (Kastenbaum, Slater, & Aisenberg, 1964; Slater & Kastenbaum, 1966) had established that psychotropic drugs were a useful but far from miraculous component of treatment. The effects were limited, sometimes paradoxical, and seldom if ever appeared to encompass the patients' sociophysical environment. In other words, even when an individual's mood had been efficiently "tuned up" or "tuned down," he or she still resided in a minimally interactive environment with little sense of community.

The possibility of introducing alcoholic beverages was then explored. It was hypothesized by Kastenbaum and Slater (1972) that wine

might contribute to the well-being of the geriatric patients by its double action— for both physiological and psychological routes. The connotations of wine as an accompaniment of social conviviality and, more remotely, as the "blood of the grape" that imparts bigger and new life, were recommendations for its use. Red wine appeared to be a particularly good symbol through which "society" (the hospital staff) could communicate its sanguine wishes to the patient. Red port wine was the final choice, taking into account its likelihood of being reasonably familiar to most of the participating patients, its reputed value as an appetite stimulant, and the fact that it could be served appropriately without refrigeration. The effort, then, was to evaluate red port wine as an agent which might possibly promote the social interaction of geriatric patients. Enhanced social interaction would be expected to have a favorable influence on self-esteem, mood, independence, and other aspects of the patients' general psychological functioning. (p. 193).

The participants in the first study were 40 male patients, 20 each from adjoining wards, with a mean age of 76. These patients were among the most alert and independent in the hospital; nevertheless, social interaction had been minimal. Solitary "sitting around" and "walking around" were the characteristic activities. The research sequence was as follows:

1. The medical director of the hospital personally examined all the prospective participants and alerted them to the fact that a study was being planned.
2. Psychological interviews were then conducted to evaluate mental status and obtain relevant biographical information.
3. Concurrent with the patient interviews, other staff members obtained sociometric data from ward personnel.
4. An observer began to check food consumption and mealtime interaction of the participating patients in the hospital cafeteria, while other observers made spot checks of activity on both wards, especially in mid-afternoon on the whereabouts and doings of those who would be participating in study.
5. Two rooms (solaria) were set aside for purposes of the experiment at 3 P.M. every weekday. Participants in Group A were invited to go to the northside solarium where they would find port wine and a participant observer. Those assigned to Group B were invited to the south-side solarium where grape juice and another participant observer (PO) awaited them. For the first 3-week period, this arrangement was maintained. Each patient was offered a 1½ ounce serving of his beverage, with one refill available upon request. The beverages were served in small, attractive glasses, (distinct from the usual plastic "glasses" generally used in the hospital), and trays of crackers were provided.

   The PO was responsible for beverage serving; preparing quantitative and qualitative reports of each session; functioning as host and intermediary between the patients and the hospital staff; and being a "good companion" without attempting to be a therapist. The participants were free to accept or decline the beverage, and to remain in the social area, or leave. Sociometric interviewing, appetite checks, and behavior sampling continued throughout both this and the following phase of the study.
6. A crossover period of equal length was then introduced in which the

beverages were reversed for Groups A and B (but other conditions maintained constant).

7. As the seventh experimental week began, participants in both groups were given the opportunity to choose their beverages freely (critical free-choice period).

8. Follow-up observations continued to be made through an extended free-choice period. In other words, a PO and the beverages would be available if the patients decided to make use of them after the "official" study itself ended.

The basic findings included clear-cut preference for wine as compared with grape juice, during both the critical and the extended free-choice periods. Data were reported for 6 weeks beyond the basic research period (6 weeks plus 1 day). The differential effect of wine was evidenced during the sessions themselves. Wine sessions had a longer average duration than juice sessions. A Group Involvement Score revealed significantly more involvement during wine than juice sessions. This score included items such as regularity of attendance, verbal and nonverbal participation, and formation of new relationships. The data came from daily observations by the POs, but were subject to analysis by a pair of judges not otherwise involved in the study. However, sociometric reports failed to indicate any systematic change in behavior outside of the sessions themselves. Several reasons were suggested for this lack of positive finding, but the absence of demonstrable out-of-session change remains as a fact.

The daily social gatherings continued for more than a year past the "official" termination of the study. The simple beverage-administration situation had become elaborated into something of a social club, the first that had been evidenced at this institution, and one that showed considerable staying power. There were numerous flashes of what later came to be termed "adult mutual gratification" between patients, and between patients and staff, but not much apparent carry-over on the ward.

Institutional acceptance of alcoholic beverages was reflected in the fact that other hospital units requested clinical studies. The second study was then designed and conducted on the rehabilitation ward, a relatively new facility at that time. Most of the patients on this unit (both males and females) were becoming involved in programs of intensive treatment for such purposes as rehabilitation of mobility, manual dexterity, and speech. Initial level of interaction was higher on this unit than the all-male wards involved in the first study, but there was also a greater sense of tension and pressure. Fear of unsuccessful rehabilitation and fear of success (leading to an ambivalently viewed return to the community) aroused strong competing sentiments.

Goals of the second project included the involvement of nursing personnel as key participants; broadening the participation of patients (female as well as male, including many with marked physical impairments); and diversifying the setting (intensive treatment on a bustling ward to add to the previous experience on a relatively quiet ward). This time, three groups of patients were established: all-female, all-male, and coed. Two members of the ward nursing staff accepted assignments as POs, with the third PO provided by the research unit. Training and supervision for the POs was provided by a social group worker also affiliated with the research unit.

Red port wine was served in appropriate stemware by the PO in each group; as before, the groups met every weekday afternoon. Juice could be requested in place of wine. This study continued for 10 weeks (50 sessions). Analyses were made of direct observations from the group sessions, follow-up interviews with the participants, and ratings made by the nurses on the rehabilitation unit before and after the project. The major results were as follows:

1. The all-male group showed the most rapid rate of development. It became the most cohesive and mutually gratifying group. The enhanced social interaction and self-esteem did seem to carry over outside of the beverage situation itself.
2. The all-female group was the least cohesive and least mutually gratifying. The women also consumed appreciably less wine than did the men.
3. The coed group did not develop as smoothly as the all-male group but provided highly functional experiences, especially in supporting group members through the stress and frustrations encountered in the physical rehabilitation program.

Several points should be noted about this study. On the practical or technical side, once again many of the ratings made by ward personnel proved to be of limited value. There was the impression that a need to present the situation in the best possible light prior to the experimental intervention—coupled with reticence to report certain types of observation—created a data baseline that was unrealistically high. By contrast with the first study, many of the favorable transactions in the beverage situation appeared to carry over into life on the ward. Both studies proved feasible to maintain over the required time periods, although they necessitated a variety of scheduling and other adjustments on the part of ward personnel. And neither study led to negative side effects in the physiological realm (which would have been picked up quickly in this closely monitored situation).

A rather different use of alcoholic beverages was next explored. Attention was given to the intensive care unit. This ward provided special diagnostic services, postsurgical care, and treatment for those who had become gravely ill. Known *subrosa* as "Death Valley" among the patients (Kastenbaum, 1967), this was, in fact, the place where most deaths occurred. The psychology service and its associated research unit was concerned about the well-being not only of those who lived in their final weeks and days on this ward but also of those who recovered sufficiently to return to their "home wards" but seemed to have become depleted and regressed. A program of broadened and more sensitive and individualized care was gradually developed and introduced in collaboration with ward staff. When it was judged that the time was ripe, beer was introduced on the ward. Along with personal discussion of the aims and methods of these innovations, a fact sheet was prepared and distributed, which included the following statements (Kastenbaum, 1972a):

1. Beer is of medical value to some elderly people who do not have enough fluids in their body. Drinking beer, then, is one of the most pleasant ways of battling against dehydration.
2. Beer is of social value to those elderly people who enjoy it:
    a. It is an adult form of pleasure and so encourages the patients to continue to feel and behave as responsible adults.
    b. It relaxes tensions and so increases the sense of comfort and makes it easier for the body to carry out its natural healing functions.
3. Beer is of particular value on an intensive care unit such as Ward X.
    a. Some patients feel they have come "to the end of the road" when they go the "sick ward."
    b. Some other patients feel that they must just grimly endure their period of illness and lessened activity while on the "sick ward."
    c. Friends from the "home ward" are sometimes reluctant to visit their friends on the "sick ward" because they are afraid of becoming depressed and discouraged themselves. (p. 381)

For reasons such as those stated above, it was thought that serving of beer on the intensive care unit would provide a visible symbol that life was not necessarily in suspended animation while a person was receiving intensive treatment. Hopefully, at least some patients would take the serving of beer as a clue that they were still expected to think, feel, and behave as responsible adults who could both give and receive pleasure. This attitude might attract more visits from other patients and perhaps more staff and family visitors as well, reducing some of the complaints and demands made to the ward staff and relieving apathy and depression.

Beer was served every afternoon (Sundays excluded). A genteel pub-like atmosphere became established through spontaneous actions of all concerned. Within 3 weeks, it was evident that the ward had a new look. The beer hour itself attracted an influx of visitors from all spheres (staff, family, other patients), but the enlivening effect was more general as well. Male and female patients regularly sat together during the afternoon "socials" (an unheard-of practice before), conversing quietly or singing melodies remembered from years past. Staff members found the time to mingle with the patients on a social basis, and this seemed to strengthen their relationships in general.

The amount of beer consumed was moderate, as had been the case with wine in the two preceding studies. Seldom did a patient desire more than a single stein. No instances of inebriated behavior were noted. No correlation could be established between amount of alcoholic beverage consumed and amount or type of behavioral change. Several of the individual patients who seemed to derive the most benefit actually consumed very little beer themselves; these were mostly old women who enjoyed the congenial atmosphere and just "wet their lips" with the brew.

While more formal types of data were being obtained in addition to the rich clinical observations, a new development in the "psychopolitics" of the hospital emerged. A person important in the institutional hierarchy (not a member of the ward staff) took strong exception to the practice of serving beer on the intensive care unit. A crisis atmosphere developed. The situation was brought to the attention of the director of the hospital. Examining the evidence and conducting his own investigation, he concluded that the beer experiment was being conducted in a responsible and proper manner. He found no evidence for harm to patients in any way, nor had feared attacks in the "public relations" domain materialized. Accordingly, the director extended his approval for the study to continue (proposing a few minor adjustments by way of concession and staff harmony). Nevertheless, the tension engendered among ward staff members—being caught between two institutional forces—remained high. The research unit decided it was in the best interests of the patients to let the beer phase of the study fade out, even though the study had been reaffirmed by the top administration.

This research experience seemed to yield two major implications. First, it was, in fact, possible to introduce beer (and perhaps other alcoholic beverages) with favorable effect in "Death Valley." The aged patients perked up and appeared more comfortable and more interested in their surroundings and each other. Second, the general dynamics of the environment emphasized themselves forcefully. As Ruth Bennett (1970) was to document some years later, social context is an extremely important and usually neglected variable in gerontological research. In the case of this particular study, opposition within the institution (even though a minority opposition) was sufficient to dismantle a clinical project that appeared to be on its way to a signal success. The beer experiment "worked" on its own terms but failed the environmental test.

One final study was conducted in the Cushing Hospital series (Volpe & Kastenbaum, 1967). Attention was again given to a different and extreme subpopulation of the geriatric patients. In this instance, the participants were all severely incapacitated male patients who were grossly disoriented, could not control their bodily functions, and required total care 24 hours a day. From the institutional standpoint, this ward made constant demands on personnel and offered few rewards in return. It represented a seemingly "hopeless" situation in which reasonably efficient custodial care was the only realistic goal.

The study developed in collaboration with the intention on the part of one nurse to make something better out of this ward. All 34 severely impaired patients were transferred to a larger ward area which was then provided with materials ordinarily reserved for patients known to be relatively less impaired: bulletin board, games, cards, checkers, puzzles, phonograph, and the like. Six afternoons a week, the patients were served beer, with crackers and cheese on the side. Results were clearly favorable. Because of their very low level of baseline functioning (over periods ranging beyond 5 years in some instances), it was possible to document change with simple measures. Incontinence, for example, decreased from 76 to 50 percent by the end of the first month and was down to 27 percent a month later. Jacket restraint and the administration of psychotropic drugs (especially Thorazine) also showed marked and permanent decline. The use of Thorazine, in fact, completely stopped after 2 months because patient behavior was no longer uncontrolled.

The decrease in "negative" behaviors was matched by an increase in "desirable" behaviors such as ambulating, individual and group activity, and off-ward social activities. Conversation among patients and between patients and staff no longer was a rarity. Men who had a long history of being "totally confused and disoriented" were playing checkers and cards, making their own beds, helping to decorate the ward, and so on.

As noted by Kastenbaum (1972a) in a retrospective on the study:

Perhaps the best illustration of the changes observed in the "Us/Them" relationship was a spontaneous action on the part of the ward staff. Ordinarily the half-hour lunch break is a most welcome opportunity for the personnel to get away from the patients they are "servicing" all day. This is especially the case when the patients are as impaired as those on Ward Z. But the Ward Z personnel decided to take their lunch breaks right on the ward, eating side by side with the patients. This action seemed to make a profound impression on the men. One scarcely could have planned a more effective or authentic way of conveying the sentiment that these forgotten old men were still part of the human race. Yet it is important to remember that this action was not required or asked of the staff; it just developed naturally with the new interpersonal climate. (p. 389).

The Cushing Hospital series thus explored effects of wine and beer with four types of elderly institutionalized people: (1) alert but not interacting, (2) disabled receiving active treatment, (3) seriously ill, and (4) chronically debilitated and mentally impaired. The time spans involved ranged from the aborted beer study on the acute care ward through the full-year follow-up in the first study. Taking basic research time spans only, the studies were conducted for periods of 6 weeks (Study 1), 10 weeks (Study 2), three weeks (Study 3), and 6 months (Study 4, although data for the first 2 months only were included in the publication). Results observed after each study had established itself continued throughout the duration of the study, although the later observations have to be taken against the background of the increasing vulnerability of geriatric patients to debility and mortality as time goes on regardless of environmental or therapeutic influences.

Three other points about the Cushing Hospital studies are worth mention. The institution itself became an active partner in the research after the first study. Subsequent research developed in the interaction between research and perceived clinical needs of the institution. Second, this research series actually had a generative base in developmental field theory (Kastenbaum, 1972b; Sherwood, 1972) and has been cited by a sociologist as one of the few examples of applied research emerging from a conceptual framework in gerontology (Sherwood, 1972). Finally, the fact that the Cushing Hospital research experience was, on the whole, encouraging led a number of other geriatric facilities to introduce or strengthen their programs of alcohol availability. Only a few of these facilities attempted (or reported) evaluation studies, and these will be considered next.

OTHER STUDIES

Several facilities in the Chicago area started to use alcoholic beverages to improve the well-being of their elderly residents. A clinical evaluation of the effects was conducted at the Wrightwood Extended Care Facility, a 90-bed unit (Sarley & Stepto, 1969). Residents who were considered senile or assigned custodial care only were excluded from this study. The aim was to study the effects of alcohol on the elders who represented true extended care or continuation hospital-type patients. Medical permission was required in each case (as had been true of the Cushing Hospital studies). Participants ranged in age from 65 to 95, with a mean age of 77.8 (slightly younger than the Cushing Hospital mean age). The beverage used in this study was table wine, both red and white. It should be noted that standard table wine, as used in the Wrightwood study, contains approximately 12 percent alcohol, while port wine is approximately 18 percent alcohol. Individuals with histories of excessive alcohol use were excluded.

The 90-day evaluation period involved 61 residents who signed up for wine (given in 2-oz. servings with dinner), and a nonwine sample of 140. A "gripe sheet" questionnaire was the basic data-gathering instrument, administered at the end of the 90-day period. Both wine and nonwine patients had many gripes about some aspects of institutional life, especially orientation, communication, and scheduling problems. However, there were differences between the groups in other realms of adjustment to institutional life. The wine drinkers had fewer gripes in general. They were more likely to feel they were receiving adequate nursing care, for example, and to be satisfied with the food service. More wine drinkers considered their beds to be comfortable, for example, and fewer were disturbed by hospital smells.

There were no negative side effects observed in association with wine use, nor did intoxication occur. A small number of patients (about 3 percent) refused wine because they had never used this beverage, and some (number not specified) declined wine after the program began, with comments such as "I never did like wine" or "Giving me wine is a waste of money."

Several points are brought out by the Wrightwood study. The positive findings are of the sort that are likely to be welcomed by institutional administrators: fewer gripes when wine is served. In addition, it was demonstrated that table wine, with its lower alcohol content, can be set alongside port as an effective beverage. And, once again, the research program was sufficiently convincing to the institution that alcohol availability became a permanent feature of the comfort and treatment program.

The study has significant limitations. No behavioral measures were reported to back up the questionnaire results. The questionnaire itself apparently was given only at the end of the treatment period. Because participants apparently were added and dropped throughout the 90-day period, it would be useful to have more substantial information of a statistical nature. From the data reported, it cannot be determined how many residents participated for how long a period of time, nor can any relationship be established between duration of participation and the outcome measure. Perhaps most critically, no data are reported on possible preexperimental differences between the wine and nonwine participants. It is possible that, in view of this flawed and inadequately reported design, the obtained differences could also have been obtained before wine administration.

By the time this study had been completed and reported, at least 10 other Chicago-area geriatric facilities were serving wine (and possibly other alcoholic beverages as well) to their residents. More than 30 California facilities were said to be providing alcoholic beverages to their elders, with a few other such programs noted in other states (Stepto, 1969). It was evident that more evaluation studies would be useful.

The director of the Wrightwood facility and study then collaborated with the director of another Chicago area facility, the Church Home, which is connected with the local Episcopal Diocese. Participants were healthy residents of this home for the aged, ambulatory men and women over the age of 65. After those with alcoholic histories or certain medical conditions were excluded, 60 of the 70 residents remained. The spectrum of wines was broadened to include the fortified 18 percent type as well as standard table varieties. An aperitif hour was offered before dinner in a parlor setting with conversational chair arrangements, a piano, and a television set. Residents entered the room, ordered the type of wine they desired (or juice instead), and received 2 oz. in a glass. This was another 90-day study. Participants served as their own controls, filling out questionnaires at the beginning, midpoint, and conclusion. There was also a 30-day follow-up questionnaire after wine had been discontinued.

Data were limited to responses to six questions. Sarley and Tyndall (1971) concluded that ". . . wine affects a person's attitudes toward his creature comforts. It is also evident that this attitude change is, in the long run, very positive, but that there is an adjustment period of a month or so before the attitude stabilizes." The authors appear to have made anecdotal observations that convinced them of substantial and enduring positive effects. Inspection of the data actually reported, however, does not appear entirely convincing to the reader. Four of the six items received approximately 90 percent agreement in the positive (no-complaint) direction *before* wine was served; this means, of course, that there was little "statistical space" for positive change to manifest itself. One of the other items was also highly skewed in the positive direction before wine serving (82.4 percent who reported sleeping well). As might be expected under these baseline limitations, the absolute amount of change was fairly small. No tests of statistical significance were reported. It is doubtful that more than 1 of the 12 basic change-scores would prove to be significant at customary statistical levels, and it is highly improbable (as best as can be judged from the data reported) that an overall index of change would be significant.

Positive changes in attitude and behavior may, in fact, have occurred after the wine-serving program became established. it is difficult to see how the reported data document this change, however. But the design does have a feature that adds a little to previous knowledge. The slight reductions in "gripes" reported during the wine phase were reversed in several instances when wine was eliminated. This shows some indication of covariation of attitude change with wine, although the data are limited. As in the case of previously cited studies, the institution was sufficiently convinced of the value of alcohol availability that it became a permanent feature of the program (after the 30-day experimental elimination).

Another Chicago-area study was conducted at the Bensenville

Home, a church-related residence that houses about 130 elderly residents (Webster, 1972). This study was intended to replicate the previous Cushing Hospital and Chicago studies but with some variations. A careful survey was made of the attitudes of institutional personnel before going ahead with the study, thereby increasing the likelihood of support for the project. The residents were next asked for their attitudes on wine. Of those who were polled, 66 expressed no objections, while 15 did object and 12 gave no opinion.

A complete study was conducted with 22 mentally alert residents who resided in a physically distinct unit known as the Castle. Over a 3-month period, these participants were served 3 oz. of wine (Rhine, rose, or dry sherry) at dinner. They were compared with nonwine drinkers during this period (number not reported) on four types of measure: a self-rating Depression Scale (the Zung); the Nurses Observation Scale for Inpatient Evaluation; a questionnaire on residents' evaluation of wine effects on appetite, well-being, sleep pattern, and taste of the meal; and blood pressure. The clearest results (in our reading of the manuscript) were the relatively greater positive changes noted by the nurses in their evaluations of wine as compared with nonwine drinkers. The residents themselves did report lifting of depressive symptoms more often in the wine group (by an almost 3:1 ratio), but we were struck by the fact that over the 90-day period, more people in both groups became increasingly depressed as contrasted with those who reported reduction in depression. The nurses' evaluation instrument also showed an appreciable number of negative changes for participants in both groups. This general depressive shift over time for many participants, apart from wine effects, is not discussed by the investigators. The wine patients reported many upward shifts in self-evaluation of sleep, appetite, and so on, but this measure was not given to the control participants, so firm conclusions should not be drawn.

The blood pressure findings may be of particular interest, partially because data of this type had not previously been reported in connection with a clinical evaluation of wine effects on the elderly. It was found that frequency of decreased blood pressure over the 90-day period was almost identical for both groups. Increases in blood pressure were only half as frequent among the wine users, however. Another and even more striking difference between the groups was the report that "fluctuating" blood pressure was found with 31 percent of the wine users but with none of the controls.

Attempts were made to conduct systematic clinical evaluations with two other subpopulations at Bensenville, but each of these fell short of completion and will not be further described here, except for the fact that opposition to wine use among several women was described as having "effectively sabotaged the program." This is one of the few references to peer-group pressure against use of alcoholic beverages by the elderly that has been cited in literature, although the phenomenon itself may not be uncommon.

The Bensenville Home study adds some provocative information about blood pressure that should be followed up. Unfortunately, the available report from this study is very limited with respect to amount and type of data reported. The research design is flawed, as we have seen. Once again, however, the administrators were convinced enough to install alcohol availability as a continuing program for those residents who cared to take advantage of it.

The studies described above were limited entirely to elderly participants. Funk and Prescott (1967) obtained information on the attitudinal effects of wine usage with medical patients whose ages ranged through much of the full adult spectrum. A choice of red or white wine in 4-oz. servings was offered to medical, surgical, and obstetrical patients in two California community hospitals. Individuals known or suspected to be suffering from liver disease, pancreatitis, gastric or duodenal ulcer, or any kind of drinking problem were excluded. All participation was voluntary and required specific approval from the physician. The period of wine usage was approximately 60 days. The wine group consisted of 333 men and women ranging in age from 21 upward. Another 129 patients made up the control group. Both groups were given "gripe sheets" to complete, these being 26-item questionnaires eliciting reaction to general hospital routines, food service, and room conditions. A question specific to wine was added for those in the wine group.

The authors emphasize that "no undesirable side-effects of any kind were reported. There were no instances of intoxication or even mild inebriation, nor any exacerbation of any pathological conditions. In no case was it found necessary on clinical grounds to eliminate the use of wine, although a few patients—less than 2 percent—claimed that the particular beverage offered was 'too sour' or 'too sweet,' and they themselves declined to participate" (Funk & Prescott, 1967, p. 182).

Funk and Prescott report that the use of wine lowered the overall number of patient complaints by 22 percent. Unfortunately, the authors do not tell us precisely how many older men and women were in this sample. We have only their conclusion that "for men and women in their 50's, 60's, and 70's, the use of wine was associated with a reduction of complaints by approximately 30 percent, 35 percent, and 48 percent, respectively. For elderly men and women, it would therefore appear that inclusion of wine in the hospital diet may be most clearly indicated" (p. 183).

It was also concluded that inclusion of small amounts of wine in hospital diets resulted in a general relaxation of uneasiness and tension that underlies reactions to illness and hospitalization among those adults of all ages who approved of wine usage. Results were most evident for people who were accustomed to using wine or other alcoholic beverages at home.

In examining the item-by-item results, we do not find any single item or combination that appears especially salient. One is impressed more by the small but consistent pattern of complaint differential for wine and nonwine patients. No statistical tests of the differences were reported by the authors. It is our impression that a nonparametric test of differences based upon the directional pattern would yield significant differences, but not tests based upon item-by-item responses as such. This study is somewhat limited in the reporting and may also be flawed in the basic design. Although the text implies prewine and postwine follow-up measures, with parallel measurement of attitudes for the controls, data are given for only one measure in each group. This means that variables not directly related to wine use might account for the obtained differences, a serious design flaw when no compensatory information or statistical operations (such as covariance analysis) are available.

Other studies have involved more attention to the specific milieu in which the beverages are provided. Black (1969) selected 34 residents of a 90-bed nursing home in Seattle, Washington, whose ages ranged from 38 through 94, a sample "selected as typical of the universe in most any nursing home population" (p. 453). Permission was obtained from family and physician. Participants were rated by the nursing staff on 75 behavioral characteristics categorized under headings of social competence, social interest, cooperation, personal neatness, physical condition and activity tolerance, and irritability (scored in the negative direction). Composite scores were used to represent the patient's general status before introduction of the beverage. The ratings were repeated at four additional 2-week intervals.

The experimental beverage in this study was beer. Fruit juice was employed as a control beverage. The patients were divided into two groups, both of which received their beverages under identical conditions. "They assembled in the occupational therapy room, which had been decorated as for a party, and some members of the staff were present with each group. The same records were used on the phonograph. Pretzels, crackers, or popcorn were served with the beverage. Cards, checkers, and puzzles were available for use as desired" (Black, 1969, p. 454). After a 4-week period, the juice drinkers were switched to beer.

Although both groups responded favorably to the social milieu, the progress shown by the beer drinkers was clearly superior. The investigator was particularly impressed by their reduced need for medications.

Use of sedatives dropped 36 percent, tranquilizers 57 percent, and diuretics 75 percent for the beer drinkers, while none of the juice drinkers showed sufficient improvement to warrant reduction in drugs. However, drug usage was reduced for the juice drinkers after they were switched to beer.

The improvement in functional status was clear not only in the composite scores but also in all the subscores as well. It is interesting to note that "physical condition" was the category rated as showing the greatest improvement with the use of beer; "social interest" and "neatness and grooming" followed not far behind. In addition, the extent of improvement was evident enough to be appreciated by the nursing home staff apart from the formal ratings. The beer drinkers soon began to exhibit a friendlier attitude toward other patients outside of the party hour and seemed generally much more relaxed and socially active.

Two events outside the research design per se also contributed to evaluation of this study. The beer initially had been supplied without cost by an outside agency. When this supply ended, the social gatherings were cut back from five to three a week. "Deterioration soon became apparent. The nurses reported that regression had occurred in all categories. Several patients required increase in medication; neatness and grooming were obviously less, and irritability increased" (Black, 1969, p. 455).

The other event was the response of the nursing home's owner-director. He promptly installed a draft beer dispensing unit. In his judgment, the patients were happier on a daily ration of beer and required less staff time. The expenditure, therefore, would more or less pay for itself.

THE BOSTON STATE HOSPITAL STUDIES

A pair of social milieu studies were subsequently conducted at Boston State Hospital by a psychiatric team under the leadership of Ching-piao Chien. These studies, like the one conducted by Black, were extensions of the Cushing Hospital series. The first study at Boston State Hospital involved the establishment of a publike setting in the geriatric ward (Chien, 1971). An area was modified to include a bar counter, chairs, tables covered with checkered tablecloths, poster-decorated walls, chianti bottles, and recorded music. Beer was the alcoholic beverage. Control beverages were fruit punch and fruit punch laced with thioridazine. These three beverage conditions all were located in the pub milieu. In addition, the punch-thioridazine condition was also instituted for some patients in their customary ward environs (nonpub milieu). Assessment instruments used were the Zung Depression Scale and the NOSIE (a nurse's evaluation form), as well as two behavioral rating scales. The Zung was used only for baseline data because patients resisted its use subsequently.

It was found that most improvement in general occurred in the beer group. The fruit punch participants showed the least improvement, although they were also exposed to the pub milieu, while the thioridazine recipients were in between in their response, with no differential effect for milieu. Chien concluded that the overall efficacy of beer therapy probably resulted, not from the social effect alone, but rather from the total interaction of the pharmacological properties of alcohol and the cultural expectations and experiences associated with drinking beer in a publike group setting.

This study was one of the most adequately controlled and reported experiment of its kind. It also involved a close comparison between alcoholic beverages and a psychotropic agent, with some attempt to compare the effect of the situational context. A second study by this group moved outside the mental hospital to two nearby nursing homes whose residents came from a wide spectrum of socioeconomic and ethnic groups (Chien, Stotsky, & Cole, in press). Pubs were established at each of these facilities, and a total of 64 participants were classified into three groups on the basis of medical staff judgments: (1) depressed persons who were administered a drug known as Doxepin; (2) persons suffering from a variety of psychiatric complaints who were on drugs and dosages established by their private physicians, the "doctor's choice group" composed of 30 patients; and (3) a "no medication" group of 21 residents who were not considered to require any psychotropic medication by their physicians. Surprisingly, perhaps, these groups proved *not* to differ significantly in amount of psychopathology according to the baseline data obtained (same measures as in this group's previous study). There were differences, however, on other variables, such as age and carrying a primary organic diagnosis (the "no medication" group was older and more "organic" than the others).

The first phase of the study was a nonalcohol period during which participants in each of the three groups received the particular medication (or no medication) recommended by their physicians. During the second phase, each of the three groups was randomly divided into two subgroups. Each subgroup received alcohol but under different conditions. All participants received either a can of beer (12 oz.) or a glass of wine (3 oz.) each weekday afternoon, but one set of subgroups stayed on the ward, while the other was in the pub. (The previous medication or no-medication schedule for each patient continued during this phase.)

Limiting our attention only to the most relevant findings, we learn that more positive changes were observed during the on-alcohol phase. Differences among the three drug medication/no-medication groups were slight, with the Doxepin group showing a little more improvement than the others (members of this group had showed no change during the baseline period). Those who imbibed their alcohol in the pub surroundings showed a tendency for greater improvement. Almost all differences favored the pub atmosphere, although not all were statistically significant. One of the strongest findings was increased social activity during the drinking situation itself in the pub as contrasted with the ward setting. At the conclusion of the study proper, most of the patients (about 80 percent) expressed the desire for the continuation of the program. Over the duration of the study, beer was preferred about two to one over wine, although, as the investigators note, the experiment was conducted in the summer, and this possibly could have influenced selection. Once again, no adverse side effects were noted. This freedom from side effects is perhaps especially meaningful in a study that combined alcohol with several types of psychotropic drugs. Chien and his colleagues concluded that while the pub atmosphere did maximize alcohol effects in some spheres, it did not show a clear superiority in sustained behavioral effects outside the pub situation. This interpretation appears consistent with findings from the earlier Cushing Hospital studies. In general, however, this research team concluded with the recommendation that a publike setting be instituted to derive the greatest benefit from alcohol use by the elderly.

OTHER STUDIES OF ELDERLY PSYCHIATRIC PATIENTS

Following these two well-controlled and useful studies, another Boston-area team conducted a clinical evaluation that can only be characterized as a disappointment (Burrill, McCourt, & Cutter, 1972). From a potential sample of 126 psychiatric patients in a Veterans Administration hospital, only 37 males received medical clearance to participate; reasons for this unusually high exclusion rate were not given. The final sample of participants was 30 males ranging in age from 36 to 85; therefore, it was not entirely a geriatric sample. Mean age of the sample was not given. From the investigators' description, it appears that most or all of the participants had physical infirmities in addition to a variety of psychiatric problems.

The setting employed was a recreation lounge in which tables were arranged and beer served in mugs to approximate a pub. Beer was alternated with soft drinks for six sessions, after which time a music therapist came in to play old songs on the piano and an "attractive volunteer" served as hostesss for another seven sessions. The investigators write of having both an experimental and a control group, although apparently both groups received beer and soft drinks in the same alternating pattern, with only the days of serving counterbalanced.

The most puzzling and disappointing aspect of this study is that (1) the basic data-gathering procedure, a social responsiveness rating scale, excluded both the first 15 minutes and the last 10 minutes of the hour-long session, and (2) the results they chose to report were based upon just 1 of the 13 sessions ("a session in Phase 1 for which there were reliable and complete ratings"). Neither social interaction nor beer consumption was greater for the "experimental" as compared with the "control" group. The investigators conclude with the impression that beer was enjoyed by the patients and deserves to be continued despite the lack of positive findings.

It is difficult to see, however, how this study could either prove or disprove anything about effects of alcoholic beverages on psychiatrically and physically impaired geriatric patients. A well-controlled, well-reported study that finds no effects of alcohol would deserve our close attention; it is unfortunate that this study leaves so much to be desired methodologically.

Becker and Cesar (1973) explored the use of beer in 32 elderly psychiatric patients (average age 69). The first group was given an average of 12 oz. of beer daily during 1-hour meetings held 5 days a week over 11 weeks; the other group was given fruit juice over the same period of time. Music, games, potato chips, and pretzels were provided with the beverage during all group sessions, and patients were free to drink and socialize as they pleased. Each participant was rated by three staff members (a psychiatrist and two psychiatric aides from the patients' wards) for orientation, self-care, mood, ward adjustment, and social activity on the ward before and after the 11 weeks of group sessions. In addition, two college-student assistants rated patients on the level of social interaction during the group sessions in the first and eleventh weeks. The results indicated that both groups showed a similar low level of social interaction during the first week, but after 11 weeks' participation in the groups, those receiving beer showed an increase in social activity, while the fruit juice group remained unchanged. They reported no significant improvements in ward behavior outside of the group sessions, however. They found no decrease in the use of psychotropic medications, as was found by Volpe and Kastenbaum (1967). But they observed that "patients who were given beer and reduced dosages of psychotropic medications showed improved ward behavior. The present data suggests that providing beer in a social setting perhaps in combination with some reduction in medication may be related to behavioral improvement rather than providing beer alone."

WINE AND BEHAVIOR MODIFICATION

Another study on the effects of wine was conducted in a large state-operated mental hospital in the Detroit, Michigan, area. Mishara and Kastenbaum (1974) compared wine palatability under different circumstances. The study focused upon chronic patients who had been characterized as failures after past rehabilitation attempts. In this study, the relationships between the patient's own actions and his or her access to wine was varied experimentally; that is, for one group of patients, wine was freely available regardless of how the patient behaved. For a second group, only patients who had earned the privilege by engaging in desirable behaviors had access to wine as part of a behavior modification program. This study involved observation of continuous use of wine on the same patients for 21 months in order to assess whether the effects of wine are retained after prolonged use. Participants were 80 patients with a mean age of 68.8 years and a current length of hospitalization amounting to an average of 21.4 years. Males and females were equally represented, and approximately half of the sample was at least moderately intact and communicative, while half was composed of the most isolated or regressed patients (a distinction that should be considered within the context that *all* participants were treatment "failures").

Wine was one of a spectrum of "enrichments" made available to the participants either through their own instrumental actions (in the token economy) or on an unrestricted basis (in the free enrichment condition). The other enrichments included extra food, coffee, better personal clothing, special trips, and various environmental changes. On the behavior modification/token economy unit, tokens earned by engaging in desirable behaviors could purchase these extra items and privileges. It is important to note that wine was not included as an enrichment until the basic program had been well established after 2 months. Five types of wine were available, including light sherry, port, and table varieties. Observations were made at the time of wine serving, supplemented by individual interviews, reports of sleeping habits, and systematic collection of anecdotal records. Results were reported from intensive 10-week observation, as well as a 6-month follow-up after wine availability had begun.

In both units, use of wine was associated with a reduction of sleeping problems and a decreased need for chloral hydrate, a medication given to induce sleep (see Table 7.1). These were persistent effects throughout the study period. The investigators recommended that "wine be tried in lieu of tranquilizing medication when sleeping problems and agitated behavior are encountered in the elderly. The stimulating properties of wine were evident in the increase in participation in ward activities and interpersonal communication observed in a number of subjects when wine was served." On the unit where the enrichments were provided "free," more wine was consumed and results tended to be more pronounced. As the investigators note, however, "the experience of earning one's wine was obviously significant and positive for some patients on the token economy ward. It was under these circumstances, in fact, that individual differences most clearly emerged. The opportunity to earn wine privileges by

Table 7.1
Wine Studies: Summary Chart[a]

Reference	Setting	Participants	Duration	Design Features	Major Findings
Kastenbaum and Slater (1972)	Geriatric hospital	40 M mean age 76	6 wk 6 mo follow-up 1 yr follow-up	1. Cross over after 3 wk 2. Group interaction and free choice measures	Wine preferred to juice Heightened group interaction Sustained group relationships Carryover to ward behavior not shown
Kastenbaum (1965)	Geriatric hospital	36 M and F mean age 77	10 wk	1. 3 group formats: M, F, coed 2. Nursing staff used as participant-observers	All M group: greatest development and most gratifying All F group: drank less and showed slight benefits Coed group: more ups and downs but useful mutual help
Sarley and Stepto (1969)	Extended care facility	61 M and F mean age 78	3 mo	"Gripe sheet" measure	Wine drinkers fewer gripes about life
Sarley and Tyndall (1971)	Home for aged	60 M and F aged 65+	3 mo	1. Questionnaire pre and post 2. Served before dinner 3. 1 mo experimental withholding of wine	Claim very positive social results after first month (note: data do not clearly support this claim) Taking wine away led to more grips and poorer morale (wine then restored permanently)
Webster (1972)	Home for aged	22 M and F aged 65+	3 mo	1. Used standard rating scales 2. Blood pressure taken	Self-reported better sleep and appetite Depressive symptoms self-report) lifted most frequently for drinkers (but group had overall shift toward depression) Elevated blood pressure less frequent for drinkers

Table 7.1 (continued)

Reference	Setting	Participants	Duration	Design Features	Major Findings
Funk and Prescott (1967)	General hospitals	333 M and F 2129 controls ages 21+	2 mo	"Gripe sheet" measure	Wine use lowered gripes by 22%
Mishara and Kastenbaum (1974)	Mental hospital	80 M and F mean aged 68	21 mo (10-wk intensive period)	1. Milieu enrichments 2. Compare token economy and "free" wine and other items 3. "Halo" effect precluded by research design 4. Large variety of direct and indirect measures	Decreased need for sleeping medication (chloral hydrate) Agitated behavior reduced Staff morale improved "Free" condition greater effects than token ward but earned wine associated with improvements for some who welcomed chance to earn wine
Kastenbaum (1973)	Community	32 M and F	1 month	1. Daily self reports on sleep, dream, energy, and mood 2. Detailed sleep-energy over total life	Heightened well-being with wine taken at bedtime Reduction in nocturnal awakenings Elevated sleep satisfaction ratings No effect on self-reported mental functioning

This table reprinted courtesy of Mishara et al., 1975.
[a] In chronological sequence.

behavior in a mature, responsible manner had strikingly favorable effects for some men and women in addition to other effects that could be attributed to the consumption of wine *per se*." An increase in staff morale was also observed during the course of this study, apparently linked to the animation that occurred among the patients.

THE NATIONAL INSTITUTE ON ALCOHOL USE AND ALCOHOLISM STUDY

Although the studies described up to now point to the benefits of moderate use of alcoholic beverages by elders in institutions, a number of pitfalls are evident. Most studies failed to include a control group to see if the alcoholic beverages facilitated the beneficial outcomes more than the general "Hawthorne" (novelty) effect of adding some treatment in a relatively deprived environmental situation. Most studies limited themselves to one type of alcoholic beverage, the serving situations varied from a "medicine-passing" style to the establishment of a fairly elaborate publike environment (a difference investigated only by the Chien group (1971, in press)). Furthermore, most studies were planned, conducted, analyzed, and reported by "insiders," that is, the institution's own staff. Staff expectations regarding the benefit of the programs cannot be ruled out as subtle influences in these studies.

To help clarify the extent of benefits of the availability of moderate amounts of alcoholic beverages in institutions for the elderly and further determine if there are negative medical side effects, the National Institute on Alcohol Use and Alcoholism funded a major study in 1973 to investigate the possible benefits experimentally. That study attempted to eliminate as many of the pitfalls and limitations of previous studies as possible. Even so, the investigators recognize that they could not encompass all the relevant variables and pursue all the experimental variations that might be desired. Still, the study had many advantages:

1. The study was conducted by an *independent outside organization,* Socio-Technical Systems Associates. This offered the advantage of being somewhat less biased in the observations of experimental outcome, since a variety of outside evaluators and observers were used, some of whom provided assessments while being blind to the experimental conditions of the participants and specific hypotheses being tested.
2. A *full-range of alcoholic beverages* was available instead of studying only one beverage, such as beer or wine. In this manner, individual preferences for drinks could be expressed. However, this did add the complicating factor of whether or not the effects observed were due

to certain alcoholic beverages and not others or to the more general effect of drinking anything alcoholic.

3. Participants were selected from *two very different residential settings*. This provided for separate evaluations at each institution and allowed comparison of samples that were of a high and a low functional status.

4. *Previous and present history of alcohol consumption* was gathered on all participants prior to the program, data that had not been reported in earlier studies and that might have an effect upon consumption patterns.

5. Evaluations of outcomes included a *greater variety of assessment tools* than utilized in previous studies.

6. *Detailed medical information,* including electrocardiograms and blood tests, was obtained for all who consented to those examinations. Basic physical measures of pulse, weight, and blood pressure were taken of all participants. In previous studies, positive or negative effects would have been reported as a result of routine physical care. Here, the specific use of three special in-depth medical examinations allowed for a more systematic evaluation of the possible physical effects of alcohol availability and consumption. Furthermore, the more sophisticated design of having physical data gathered by individuals who were blind to the experimental conditions of participants and their consumption rates was used.

7. Previous studies of alcohol availability often confounded the interpretation of their results by including the alcohol as part of a general social milieu or social hour. This study made it possible to *distinguish the effects due to the social milieu alone and the effects of alcohol availability and consumption* by including a control group situation. In the control group, a similar group of residents of the same institution had only nonalcoholic beverages available under the same social conditions as the experimental group, which had alcoholic beverages available.

8. Effects of alcoholic beverages were *observed over an 18-week period,* which is considerably longer than the observation period for most previous reports.

Participants in this study were residents of two institutions devoted to the care of the elderly, a *residence* and a *nursing home.* The residence provided room and board, and people living there were free to come and go as they pleased. The nursing home provided round-the-clock nursing care and met the medical standards regulating nursing homes. The mean age of the total sample was 75.35 years, and the ages were approximately the same at the nursing home and the residence. The nursing home sample consisted of 22 men and 39 women, and the residence sample comprised 19 men and 65 women.

The basic difference between residence and nursing home was in the functional status of the participants. People who lived at the residence were not in need of much supervision and were considered, by virtue of their admission requirements, to be capable of fairly independent living. On the other hand, people residing in the nursing home were assumed to be in need of 24-hour supervisory nursing care and were thus of a much lower functional status. On a random basis, two independent groups were assigned in each institution. The research design is shown in Table 7.2

Alcoholic beverages included all the major varieties of wines, four types of beer, brandy, various liqueurs, vodka, gin, rum, and the whiskies. An assortment of mixers and other accoutrements were made available, as well as cheese and crackers. Participants in the alcohol-available condition were allowed up to two drinks, each containing approximately 0.4 oz. of alcohol. Social hours occurred 5 days a week.

For the pretest and two posttest follow-up evaluations the following data were gathered:

1. *Physical health status,* determined for all elders who consented to a physical examination, including detailed blood chemistry tests and electrocardiogram. Measures of liver function and cardiovascular status were among those aspects of physical status that were given particular consideration.
2. *Functional status,* referring to the elderly person's ability to perform a variety of normal self-care behavior.
3. *Mental status,* assessed using the VIRO scale, the Babcock story-recall test, the face-hand test, as well as questions about general orientation.
4. *Socioemotional status* was assessed by observations of interactions with other people recorded by project interviewers, the morale scale developed by Lawton, and a variety of additional questions.
5. *Previous drinking history* was assessed by questionnaires developed in the previous community survey study.
6. *Sleep patterns* were observed by ward personnel and explored in conversations with participants.

Physical examinations revealed a greater prevalence of difficulties in ambulation and organically determined mental impairment at the nursing home, but other physical problems such as arteriosclerotic heart disease were highly prevalent in both facilities. Other results are summarized in Tables 7.3, 7.4, and 7.5. As shown in Table 7.3, alcohol consumption in the total sample was reported as relatively low in the past and quite infrequent during the month before the start of the study.

During the first 9 weeks of Phase I in the nursing home (NH), participants were passive at the beginning whether in the alcoholic or

Table 7.2
Beer Studies: Summary Chart

Reference	Research Setting	Participants	Duration	Design Features	Major Findings
Kastenbaum (1972)	Geriatric hospital: intensive care unit	18 ill M and F mean age: 81	3 weeks	1. Enahnced milieu 2. "Pub" atmosphere	1. Heightened social interest and interaction 2. Heightened mental alertness 3. Program discontinued because of intrastaff conflict
Volpe and Kastenbaum (1967)	Geriatric hospital: "regressed ward"	34 very regressed and impaired M; mean age: 78	6 months	1. Enhanced milieu	1. Decrease in need for psychotropic drugs 2. Decreased incontinence 3. Increased social competence and activity 4. Favorable results sustained over full 6 months
Black (1969)	Nursing home	34 M and F, range 38–94 yrs	8 weeks	1. Publike 2. Crossover after 4 wks 3. Ratings made 6 times	1. Decrease in need for psychotropic drugs 3. Heightened sociability and self-care
Chein (1971)	State hospital: geriatric unit	36 M and F chronic patients; mean ae: 74	8 weeks	1. Publike 2. Compare with drug effect (thioradazine)	1. Beer + pub atmosphere produced largest and most favorable changes in rated behavior on ward and symptoms

Study	Setting	Sample	Duration	Objectives	Results
Chien, et al. (in press)[b]	Two nursing homes	64 M and F; mean age: 69	8 weeks	1. 3 types of residents 2. Compare with drug effect (Doxepin) 3. Pub vs. nonpub	1. Tendency for + pub to be best condition for favorable behavior change 2. Drinking activity clearly greater in pub 3. Sustained behavioral effects between pub and ward drinking were not significantly different, regarding behavior outside pub per se
Burrill et al. (1972)	VA hospital: psychiatric-medical unit	30 M, age range 36–85	13 days	1. Publike 2. Alternate beer with soft drinks	1. No significant beer effects found. Note: reported data based upon 30 interaction objectives during a single session
Becker and Cesar (1973)	Psychiatric hospital	32 M and F; mean age: 69	11 weeks	1. Separate beer and fruit groups	1. Beer group: significant increase in social interactions 2. Juice group: unchanged 3. No improved behavior outside the group 4. No reduction in medications

This table reprinted courtesy of Mishara et al., 1975.

[a] In chronological sequence

[b] Participants also had opportunity to drink wine; beer was more popular (conducted during summer); results do not distinguish between beer and wine effects.

Table 7.3
Experimental Designs

			Experimental Phase I	Posttest I	Experimental Phase II	Posttest II
Set A	Group 1	Pretest	9 weeks alcoholic beverages available	Posttest I	9 more weeks alcoholic beverages available	Posttest II
More adequate functional status (*Residence*)	Treatment/ Treatment					
	Group 2	Pretest	9 weeks nonalcoholic beverages available	Posttest I	9 weeks alcoholic beverages available	Posttest II
	Control/ Treatment					
Set B	Group 1	Prestest	9 weeks alcoholic beverages available	Posttest I	9 more weeks alcoholic beverages available	Posttest II
Less adequate functional status (*Nursing Home*)	Treatment/ Treatment					
	Group 2	Pretest	9 weeks alcoholic beverages available	Posttest I	9 weeks alcoholic beverages available	Posttest II
	Control/ Treatment					

This table reprinted courtesy of Mishara et al., 1975.

Table 7.4
Summary of Changes Between Pretest and End of Phase II

Variable	Setting	Comparison	Finding
Face-hand test	Nursing home	*Within* experimental group	Decreased errors ($p < 0.051$)
	Nursing home	*Between* control and experimental groups	*Difference* in changes marginally significant ($p < 0.066$)
	Residence	*Within* people drinking 2 or less, or no alcoholic drinks	Tendency toward decrease errors ($p < 0.091$)
VIRO Interaction Score	Nursing home	*Within* experimental group	Tendency toward increase (more positive) ratings ($p < 0.069$)
	Residence	*Within* control group	Decrease (more negative) ratings ($p < 0.052$)
	Residence	*Within* people drinking 2 or less or no alcoholic drinks	Decrease (more negative ratings ($p < 0.029$)
VIRO Presentation Score	Residence	*Within* control group	Decreased (more negative) ratings ($p < 0.011$)
	Residence	*Within* people drinking 2 or less or no alcoholic drinks	Decreased (more negative ratings) ($p < 0.020$)
	Residence	*Between* control and experimental groups	Difference i changes significant ($p < 0.048$)
General attitude toward self (interviewer rating)	Nursing home	*Within* experimental group	Increased (more accepting, less depreciating) ($p < 0.039$)

Table 7.4 (continued)

Variable	Setting	Comparison	Findings
Powell Lawton Morale Scale	Residence	*Between* control and experimental groups	Difference in changes significant ($p < 0.047$) (Control decrease in morale. Experimental increased)
Worrying (self-reports)	Nursing home	*Within* control group	Tendency toward decrease ($p < 0.104$)
	Nursing home	*Within* experimental group	Tendency toward decrease ($p < 0.104$)
	Nursing home	*Within* people drinking more than 2 drinks	Tendency toward decrease ($p < 0.097$)
	Nursing home	*Within* people drinking 2 or less or no alcoholic drinks	Tendency toward decrease ($p < 0.079$)
	Residence	*Within* control group	Tendency toward decrease ($p < 0.083$)
	Residence	*Within* experimental group	Decrease ($p < 0.040$)
	Residence	*Within* people drinking more than 2 drinks	Tendency toward decrease ($p < 0.082$)
	Residence	*Within* people drinking 2 or less or no alcoholic drinks	Decrease ($p < 0.042$)
Troubling falling asleep	Nursing home	*Between* Drinkers (72 and Non-Drinkers	Difference in changes significant ($p < 0.019$) (Drinkers decreased in trouble, non-drinkers increased)

This table reprinted courtesy of Mishara et al., 1975.

Table 7.5
Summary of Changes Between End of Phase I and End of Phase II

Variable	Setting	Comparison	Findings
10-Minute recall on Babcock Story Recall Test	Nursing home NH	*Within* people drinking more than 2 drinks *Within* control group	Tendency toward decreased recall ($p < 0.062$) Tendency toward decreased recall ($p < 0.086$)
Perceived happiness	NH NH NH	*Within* control Group *Within* experimental group *Between* control and experimental group	Increased happiness ($p < 0.037$) Decreased happiness ($p < 0.017$) *Difference* in changes significant ($p < 0.002$)
General attitude toward self (interviewer rating)	NH	*Within* people drinking more than 2 drinks	Increase (more accepting, less depreciating) ($p < 0.058$)
Incidence of reported worrying	NH NH NH	*Within* control group *Within* experimental group *Within* people drinking more than 2 drinks	Tendency toward decrease ($p < 0.082$) Decrease ($p < 0.039$) Decrease ($p < 0.019$)
Trouble falling asleep	NH	*Within* experimental group	Tendency toward decreased trouble ($p < 0.083$)
Perceived health	NH NH	*Within* experimental group *Between* control and experimental groups	Increased (improved) ratings ($p < 0.027$) Difference in changes significant ($p < 0.031$) (Experimental more improved)

This table reprinted courtesy of Mishara et al., 1975.

nonalcoholic (control) social hour group. Among the imbibers, wine was slightly more popular than blended whiskey. No behavioral or management problems resulted from the use of alcoholic beverages, which relieved some of the apprehension of the NH staff. Total consumption during this stage was minimal. There were few regular drinkers among this phase, and only 8 individuals had 10 or more drinks, although these 8 people were truly regular in that they attended almost every social hour. At the residential home (RH), whiskey was the preferred alcoholic beverage among those who indulged. Overall, between the beginning of the investigation and the end of Phase I, no negative effects of the social hours or of consumption of alcoholic beverages could be observed at either facility. At that point, however, significant general beneficial effects of the program were also generally lacking. The best and only predictor of who consumed alcoholic beverages during this phase is the amount of reported preinstitutional consumption. At the RH, there were significant differences between experimental and control groups in that the experimental group reported a decrease in trouble falling asleep as compared to the control group, which showed no change.

During Phase II, consumption of all alcoholic beverages in the NH and the RH increased. Observations indicated increased communication, initiative, activity level, and socialization at the NH that was more pronounced than in Phase I. Overall, the general atmosphere became one of greater familiarity and intimacy.

The overall pattern of changes in the interview-obtained data is difficult to summarize because of the variety of sources of comparison. These data are summarized in Tables 7.4 and 7.5. In general, by the end of Phase II, no significant negative effects could be attributed either to the exposure to the availability of alcoholic beverages or to actual consumption. As the tables indicate, most of the changes were of a favorable nature (such as decrease in worrying, increased morale, less difficulty in falling asleep). There appeared to be an interaction between functional level, as determined either by living in the NH or the RH and the type of benefits gained. Positive significant findings were more frequent for the experimental as opposed to the control group and for the drinkers as opposed to the nondrinkers. The majority of significant effects occurred across the whole duration of the study, as opposed to across either Phase I or Phase II independently.

No systematic changes in physical status could be related to possible alcohol effects at either institution, although there were instances of both improvement and deterioration among some participants in each facility. Comparison of physical data before and after Phase II revealed only one significant change. When all participants (control and experimental at both institutions) were combined, there was a significant association between drinking and pulse rate. Drinking was associated with reduced pulse rate, which possibly reflects better cardiac function. The reduction of pulse rate among drinkers was not associated with any occurrence of pathologically slow pulse rate due to cardiac conduction defects. This change is not attributable to the immediate effects of alcohol ingestion, since blood pressures and pulses were not measured on the same day that alcohol was consumed.

The authors concluded that the total pattern of results tended to confirm and extend findings of previous investigations: Moderate use of alcoholic beverages appears to have benefit for those elders who choose to partake (although not necessarily the same benefits for every type of individual) and relatively few drawbacks. They cautioned, however, that their conclusions can be generalized only to situations in which adequate medical clearance and follow-up is assured. In their study, all participants had proper medical clearance and gave their voluntary written consent. Although physician approval rates were high, some elders with current alcoholism problems and a few physical contraindications were not allowed to participate. Furthermore, adverse reactions may also have been avoided by self-selection, since at least some of the elders who declined to participate may have done so in anticipation of negative effects. Some explicit comments were made to this effect.

In these social hours, the drinks were free, there was as complete a variety of alcoholic beverages as one would find in most any bar, and the social setting was quite convivial, and yet consumption of alcoholic beverages was extremely low. Also, at the RH, where mobility of participants was great, there was no indication either that participants resumed a previously high rate of consumption outside the social hour at neighboring bars or continued consumption in their own rooms with purchases made outside. One of the administrators asked before the start of the project "Will this make my people alcoholics?" The answer seems to be clearly "No, it will not."

A Tentative Explanation of the Effects

The authors suggested that there may be an interrelated sequence of changes that occurs when alcoholic beverages are available in a social setting over an 18-week period. A possible mechanism they suggest for this improvement might be the enriched sensory and interpersonal input experienced during the social hours. The elderly man or woman is exposed to a variety and density of input that is likely to exceed what has been experienced during preceding weeks or months of semi-isolation.

Sensory and cognitive abilities are stimulated and challenged by this input. The individual may experience increased "cognitive tone," which shows itself in behavioral measures such as the face-hand test. Such improvements as increased functioning on the face-hand test, which was found in the experimental group in the NH and was marginally significant among the alcohol drinkers at the RH, are contrary to the usual expectation that over time, elderly people should decline in their abilities. These cognitive task improvements are perhaps the most impressive results from the "hard-nosed" scientific standpoint. One would not expect cognitive improvement with people of this age group unless a fairly significant force was at work.

The increased behavioral-cognitive competence described above would, in turn, facilitate improved interpersonal interactions. The latter were observed in improvements in VIRO-interaction and presentation scores. The improved success in interpersonal relationships could then result in overall improvements in well-being. This end result of overall improvement was exemplified by findings showing an increase in morale at residences and a more accepting (less depreciating) general attitude toward self at nursing homes.

As with other projects, after the study was completed the administrators of both institutions initiated a regular social hour for the benefit of their patients.

GENERAL CONCLUSIONS

On the whole, it would appear that the use of alcoholic beverages with elderly men and women has some advantages, especially when served in socially conducive settings. Still, there are many sources of resistance toward the use of alcoholic beverages among both elders themselves and those who are in the position to influence treatment in comfort-giving programs. From personal experience associated with clinical and research activity, we have the impression that a number of administrators and care-givers have personal rather than evidential reasons for opposing the use of alcoholic beverages by elders. The nature and extent of this possible source of difficulty has not yet been determined and is barely hinted at in published articles. On the other hand, some of the acceptance that has been given to the alcoholic beverages program in geriatric settings may also have reflected personal rather than evidential factors. Although it is possible that future research may indicate contradictory results, the research studies to date summarized in Tables 7.1 and 7.2, coupled with the findings from the more extensive Mishara et al.

(1975) study, indicate that alcohol availability for this age group does have its advantages.

In summary, let us quote the implications reported by Mishara et al. (1975):

> Use of alcoholic beverages in moderation by both high- and low-functional status institutionalized elderly people is not contraindicated under the circumstances where participation is voluntary and physician's approval is obtained. There is evidence that participants may accrue benefits from the availability and consumption of alcoholic beverages, but for some people the alcohol may be minimally important compared to the social setting itself. There are indications that prolonged (18-week) exposure to a situation with alcoholic beverages or prolonged moderate consumption has beneficial effects.

There is a need for future studies to be conducted with considerably longer durations of time, perhaps years, to see if beneficial effects observed in these relatively short investigations continue. Such studies should consider the functional status of the participants and might attempt to distinguish differences between various types of alcoholic beverages such as wine, beer, and hard liquor.

REFERENCES

Becker, P. W., & Cesar, J. A. Use of beer in geriatric psychiatric patient groups. *Psychological Reports*, 1973, *33*, 182.

Benedict, H., & Torok, B. Der Alkohol in der Ernahrung der Zuckerkranken. *Zeitschrift fur Klinische Medizinische*, 1906, *60*, 329ff.

Bennet, R. Social context—a neglected variable in research on aging. *Aging and Human Development*, 1970, *1*, 97–116.

Black, A. L. Altering behavior of geriatric patients with beer. *Northwest Medicine*, 1969, *68*, 453–456.

Burrill, R. H., McCourt, J. F., & Cutter, H. S. G. Beer: A social facilitator for PMI patients. Unpublished paper, Brockton Veterans Administration Hospital, Brockton, Mass., 1972.

Chien, C. P. Psychiatric treatment for geriatric patients: "Pub" or drug? *American Journal of Psychiatry*, 1971, *127*, 110–115.

Chien, C. P., Stotsky, B., & Cole, J. O. Psychiatric treatment for nursing home patients: Drug, alcohol, and milieu. *American Journal of Psychiatry*, in press.

Funk, L. P., & Prescott, J. H. Study shows wine patient attitudes. *Modern Hospital*, 1967, *108*, 182–184.

Irvin, D. L., Ahokas, A. J., & Goetzl, F. Z. The influence of ethyl alcohol in low concentrations upon olfactory acuity and the sensation complex of appetite and satiety. *Permanente Foundation Medical Bulletin*, 1950, *8*, 97–101.

Kastenbaum, R. Multiple perspectives on a geriatric "Death Valley." *Community Mental Health Journal,* 1967, *3,* 21–29.

Kastenbaum, R. Beer, wine, and mutual gratification in the gerontopolis. In D. P. Kent, S. Sherwood, & R. Kastenbaum (Eds.), *Research, action, and planning for the elderly.* New York: Behavioral Publications, 1972, pp. 365–394. (a)

Kastenbaum, R. A developmental-field approach to aging and its implications for practice. In D. P. Kent, R. Kastenbaum, & S. Sherwood (Eds.), *Research, action, and planning for the elderly.* New York: Behavioral Publications, 1972, pp. 37–49. (b)

Kastenbaum, R., & Slater, P. E. Effects of wine on the interpersonal behavior of geriatric patients: An exploratory study. In R. Kastenbaum (Ed.), *New thoughts on old age.* New York: Springer, 1972, pp. 191–204.

Kastenbaum, R. Slater, P. E., & Aisenberg, R. G. Toward a conceptual model of geriatric psychopharmacology: An experiment with thioridazine and dextroamphetamine. *Gerontologist,* 1964, *4,* 68–71.

Mishara, B. L., & Kastenbaum, R. Wine in the treatment of long-term geriatric patients in mental institutions. *Journal of the American Geriatrics Society,* 1974, *22,* 88–94.

Mishara, B. L., Kastenbaum, R., Baker, F., & Patterson, R. Alcohol effects in old age: An experimental investigation. *Social Science and Medicine,* 1975, *9,* 535–547.

Pavlov, I. P. *The work of the digestive glands.* London: Charles Griffin, 1910.

Sarley, V. C., & Stepto, R. C. Use of wine in extended care facilities. In S. P. Lucia (Ed.), *Wine and health.* Menlo Park, Calif.: Pacific Coast, 1969, pp. 28–32.

Sarley, V. C., & Tyndall, F. W. Wine is beneficial to geriatric nonpatients, too. *Nursing Homes,* July 1971, pp. 73–75.

Sherwood, S. Social science and action research. In D. P. Kent, R. Kastenbaum, & S. Sherwood (Eds.), *Research, action, and planning for the elderly.* New York: Behavioral Publications, 1972, pp. 70–98.

Slater, P. E., & Kastenbaum, R. Paradoxical effects of drugs: Some Personality and ethnic correlates. *Journal of the American Geriatrics Association,* 1966, *14,* 1016–1034.

Stepto, R. C. *Journal of Practical Nursing,* April, 1969, 17–20

Volpe, A., & Kastenbaum, R. Beer and "TLC" in a geriatric hospital. *American Journal of Nursing,* 1967, *67,* 100–103.

Webster, D. H. Wine in "the castle." Unpublished manuscript, Bensonville Home, Chicago, 1972.

8

The Effects of Wine on Elderly People Who Are Self-Sufficient: A Theory and Its Research Findings

This chapter differs from the previous ones in several ways that should be made explicit in the beginning:

1. We are concerned here chiefly with elderly men and women who remain in control of their own lives. These are people who live in the community and report themselves to be in fair to excellent health. They are able to continue their accustomed style of life, although often under reduced financial circumstances. Although they confront many of the problems associated with growing old in today's urban society, in general, these people are "making a go of it" with their own resources and those available to them in their social networks.

2. The basic material on which this chapter is based come from a research project whose findings have not previously been reported to a general readership. The research reported in this chapter was conducted by one of the authors, Robert Kastenbaum.

3. The data were derived from a series of small studies that attempted to test a theory specifically concerned with the nature of a particular alcoholic beverage—wine—and the nature of the aging process.

4. Nevertheless, the data can be considered apart from the particular theoretical orientation that is developed and applied here. The reader might be interested in the effort to develop and test a theory or only in the empirical findings per se. These data do not appear to be available from other sources at this time, and they therefore supplement information contained in other sections of the book.

5. The data are mostly behavioral and psychosocial, even though the

theory eventually will require physiological and perhaps biochemical levels of investigation for complete evaluation. What is offered here is only a series of empirical explorations in the service of a theory that has a long way to go before its possible value can be fully determined.

THE BASIS OF THE THEORY

Previous research by Kastenbaum and his colleagues in institutional settings had emphasized a *mutual gratification* model of wine effects. The essential point was that moderate use of wine within a conducive environment helps to restore the older person's sense of continuity with his earlier life, reinstates a sense of personal worth and competence, and makes him a more appealing and interesting individual in the eyes of others.[1] The elderly person again becomes capable of both giving and receiving mature adult gratifications. Wine is seen as bolstering the forces of self and social solidarity against the erosive threats of alienation, social isolation, and powerlessness. Although the effects of ethanol and the congeners of wine are not neglected in this view, the biochemical and physiological effects tend to be seen as secondary to the psychosocial. This theory applies when the amount of ethanol consumed is minimal. It is not to be applied to those who consume substantial amounts of ethanol. With problem drinkers the ethanol effects are of primary importance to an understanding of the implications of drinking behavior.

The mutual gratification model itself, however, is just one component of *developmental-field theory*.[2] As the term suggests, developmental field theory emphasizes both the immediate situation and the life history and maturational level the individual brings to it. It represents an attempt, perhaps overly ambitious, to conceptualize vectors from several realms within one frame of reference. In applying this approach to gerontology, one is led to question the inevitability and universality of these phenomena that are commonly thought to compose "old age" per se. One might ask, for example, "what are those behaviors and personality characteristics we associate with being old—what are the so-called old behaviors?" A partial list of such behaviors was used as the basis for a symposium of the American Psychological Association that focused on possible theories that might serve as alternatives or supplements to strictly biological models of aging. These characteristics included deficits in learning, memory, and attention; lack of available free energy; somatic preoccupation; dysphoria; irritability; and aversion to novel problems and situations.[3] The author proposed a developmental field approach that would lead to efforts to create or at least simulate "old behavior" and then to modify or reverse it—all through psychosocial modalities. Simulation studies, if successful, would be followed up by experiments conducted in complex "real-life" settings.

A truly experimental approach to psychosocial gerontology was envisioned to see how much of what is usually regarded as inevitable age-related change is, in fact, learned or developed. Although this approach runs counter to some deeply ingrained assumptions (chiefly that aging is almost entirely biological and therefore cannot be modified), such assumptions need to be reviewed carefully.[4]

One series of pilot studies that followed from this framework was concerned entirely with psychosocial interventions. Attempts were made to provide young adults with a foretaste of old age through manipulating such variables as environmental tempo, experience with a task, and role in the power structure.[5] These preliminary research experiences suggested that behaviors commonly associated with old age could be increased among chronologically young adults through experimental manipulations of the type sketched above. Our interest here, however, is in another branch of developmental-field theory research, one that led to the concern with sleep and wine.

It was noted that many, if not all, the behaviors often taken as hallmarks of being old are also fairly typical of people who suffer from a fatigue state, whatever their chronological age.[6] Perhaps, then, at least some of what passes for characteristics of "bad old age" might instead be manifestations of a chronic fatigue state. At the time the research series was planned, there was little information available on changes in sleep with advancing age. The available data did suggest, however, that sleeping behavior does change with advancing adult age.[7] Superficially, it would appear that these changes are for the worse. In particular, the delta phase of the sleep cycle, in which one is in a state of deep sleep as indexed by slow electrical activity in the brain, appeared to diminish considerably. An older person might spend as much time in bed, or even as much time asleep, as in previous years, but will receive less benefit. Complaints about not sleeping well or not feeling well rested had also been expressed to the author many times in his clinical work with old people. Such complaints seem to be familiar to other clinicians who work with elderly people as well. As part of our working assumptions, we interpreted the pattern of sleep changes with advancing age as negative in the sense of impairing the individual's ability to cope with the challenges of waking life. It was recognized, however, that a case might be made for the reduction of sleep in old age as itself reflecting some kind of adaptive response that we are not yet in a position to understand. More will be said about the possible relationships between sleep and adaptation in old age in the discussion section at the end of this chapter.

Prior to this study, there was already some sensitivity to a possible link between wine and sleep in old age. As we have seen earlier in this book, over the centuries, wine has enjoyed a certain reputation for facilitating easeful sleep, especially for the old person. A more specific link now came to our attention. Wine normally contains gamma-amino-butyric acid

(GABA). This is not found in other alcoholic beverages. There is some evidence that GABA and its metabolic products and successors may play a role in the human sleep arousal system. The link was speculative, in the absence of the necessary physiological research to test this hypothesis. The hypothesis, however, seemed consistent with expert opinion on the significance of nonalcoholic constituents of wine[8] and with studies of mechanisms that influence cyclical behavior.[9]

It was proposed, then, that nightly ingestion of wine might halt, slow down, or even reverse the dropout of delta sleep during the later years of life. This outcome on the physiological level (if, indeed, this proved to be the outcome) should then become manifest behaviorally and phenomenologically. The "old age" syndrome should diminish much in the way that a younger adult would regain his or her verve and competence after recovering from a period of sleep deprivation. No longer suffering from excessive fatigue, the old person should be able to function more adequately in the mental and emotional spheres, with more free energy available for the positive enjoyment of life.

It was recognized that even if this view should turn out to be correct, the actual magnitude of the effects could be relatively great or relatively small. To imagine that competent functioning and a sense of well-being could be a simple function of improved rest that is, in turn, related directly to ingestion of a particular substance (GABA) seemed naive. Yet one did not really have to be this naive in order to proceed with the study. Even a fairly modest improvement in sleep might make enough difference in performance and attitude to enable individuals to draw more successfully upon their total resources. Furthermore, improvement in any sphere of functioning of any discernible magnitude might help the person to be more motivated and more responsive to other types of supportive efforts. An exercise program, psychotherapy, or efforts to make new friends are examples of ventures that might be more successful if the old person felt less fatigued, more energetic. Wine might, then, be regarded as a potential *change agent* to alter the particular developmental-field situation in which "old behavior" had become an apparently fixed configuration. Changes that begin on a physiological level within the individual's inner environment might make it possible for him or her to alter the overall relationship with the outer environment—at least enough to shake partially free of those dysphoric attitudinal states and unadaptive behaviors we tend to associate with "bad old age."

This rather focused and simplistic theory also appears to neglect the possible effects on sleep that might be associated with anything aside from the GABA in wine. This is not really the case, but it was not considered useful to dwell on all the possible factors until there were some relevant data in hand. Should the use of wine fail to show any association with these outcome measures, there would not seem to be much value in examining the full array of factors contributing to a "nonresult."

CORE HYPOTHESES AND GENERAL RESEARCH PLAN

Core Hypotheses

The hypotheses guiding this research series can be stated as follows:

1. Some of the undesirable behaviors and experiences associated with old age can be regarded as "excess deficits" attributable to a chronic fatigue state.
2. The moderate but systematic use of wine might lead to more adequate sleep—because of GABA and possibly other natural components—which, in turn, might lead to amelioration of at least some of these excess deficits.

General Research Plan

The general research plan was to observe a relevant range of psychological functioning in elderly people prior to their use of wine, with continued and repeated observations after introduction of wine. The study was conducted in six phases. Each year, a new sample of elderly people was recruited. The major research question asked in the preceding phase was retested with the new sample, and some new dimensions or questions were also examined. Each phase beyond the first, then, served as a replicability check of earlier results and also brought into focus additional factors that were relevant to the core hypotheses. With one exception to be noted later, the design was limited to before–after comparisons. The limitations of this or any other single type of design were appreciated from the beginning. It was decided, however, that this was the most direct and effective way to determine if "something might be happening" that could be related to wine effects. Since the research was to be conducted in the real world with very real restrictions on time and energy available, this type of design seemed likely to yield the most relevant information for the effort expended.

The specific method and procedures used in each phase of the study are presented in the appendix to this chapter. Here we will briefly describe the basic features of the typical phase, along with summary information on the series as a whole.

A TYPICAL PHASE

1. Elderly men and women living in the community who consented to participate in the study were interviewed to obtain information about their health and life-style. Those who were already using wine regularly or who were opposed to the use of alcoholic beverages were not included in the final sample.
2. The participants were provided with forms on which to report on their

own daily sleep/energy/mood status. The "Snooze News" was completed prior to retiring each evening; the "Early Bird Report" was completed soon after awaking each morning. Each day these forms were mailed back to the investigator in the stamped, addressed envelopes that were provided. The participants' monitoring of their sleep/energy/mood started with their introduction to the study and continued throughout both the prewine and on-wine periods. These, then, were *continuous* sources of data.

3. · A battery of psychological measures was administered on an individual basis to each participant. The particular procedures used and the size of the battery varied somewhat from phase to phsae.

4. After a baseline (prewine) period, the participants were provided with wine and stemware glasses. The participants were given the opportunity to make their selections from a variety of red, white, and rosé wines.

5. The psychological measures were repeated after the participants had made regular use of wine for a specified period of time. This period was 10 days in Phase 1 and was subsequently lengthened to 15 and 20 days.

In the typical phase, then, participants provided *one-time* background information on their life-styles and *continuous* information on their sleep/energy/mood patterns, and they were *retested* on a battery of psychological measures after becoming established on the regular use of wine.

Participants were requested to use either one or two servings of wine each evening. A serving contained approximately 3 ounces of wine. The choice of one or two servings was left to each participant, who was also free to vary between a single and a repeated serving as desired. Of the total sample ($N = 213$), 84 percent typically limited themselves to a single daily serving of approximately 3 ounces. No participants reported using more than two servings per day. Although this flexibility (both of one vs. two servings and specific wine) surrendered a certain degree of experimental control, it made participation in the project more congenial and seemed to be appreciated.

PARTICIPANTS

Basic characteristics of the sample for all six phases are summarized in Table 8-1.

Additional information regarding the participants is given in the appendix.

MEASURES

Participants in all phases provided life-style information and daily continuous monitoring of sleep/energy/mood. The other measures are described at the point of their introduction into the study in the appendix. As an overview and guide, Table 8-2 indicates the measures used in each

Table 8.1
Participants by Phase

Phase	Men N	Men Mean Age	Women N	Women Mean Age	Total Age Range	Total Number of Participants
I	16	64.2	16	61.0	54–78	32
II	11	64.9	29	69.3	60–84	40
III*	24	74.4	24	73.9	67–82	48
IV	14	73.5	16	77.2	67–84	30
V†	9	72.9	18	79.1	66–86	27
VI†	15	72.0	21	74.3	67–82	36
						N = 213

*Composed of two equal-sized independent samples varying in functional level.
†Residents of congregate living facilities.

Table 8.2
Measures by Phases

Measure	I	II	III	IV	V	VI
Snooze News	x	x	x	x	x	x
Early Bird Report	x	x	x	x	x	x
Earliest memory		x	x			
Tempo Variability Test		x	x	x	x	x
Digit span		x	x	x	x	
Similarities		x	x	x	x	
What are they thinking?		x				
Recall test		x				
Free recall		x		x		
Memory card test		x	x			
Story completion		x	x			
Sorting task		x	x			
Inquiry strategy task		x				
(20 questions)		x				
Incidental observations		x	x			
Life gestalt		x				
Maze test		x				
Dart throwing		x	x			
Lawton Morale Scale			x	x	x	
Rehearsal-recall procedure				x		
Beck Hope Scale			x	x		
Disassembly test				x		
Turning test				x		
Personal Age Scale				x		
Weschler Adult Intelligence Scale						x

phase. Information about a specific measure can be found by consulting the method section for the phase in which it was first used, as given in the appendix. Thus, for example, the Tempo Variability Test is described in the method section for Phase II and the Lawton Morale Scale in the section for Phase III.

As might be inferred from this table, Phase II provided the occasion for the most thorough exploration of a wide variety of procedures. This battery was too large to continue throughout the entire study, and only those measures that appeared most useful for the particular purposes of this study were retained, although other measures were introduced at subsequent points as appropriate.

MAJOR FINDINGS

Sleep Quality

The strongest and most consistent finding throughout the course of this study was improvement of sleep quality. It should be kept in mind that the relevant data here come from the participants' continuous, daily self-reports. Whether or not a similar pattern would have been revealed by EEG tracings using a sleep laboratory technique is a question that cannot be answered on the basis of these data. The self-report data appear to be adequate on their own terms, however. The sleep quality scores were not obtained simply by asking people retrospectively to make global ratings. Instead, the participants answered specific questions about a particular night's sleep and its effects and immediately sent these observations to the research director via stamped, addressed envelopes. This procedure was thought to minimize bias and habit and to maximize the likelihood that the person would be reporting accurately on a particular night's sleep. The composite sleep quality score itself was also analyzed according to its item components.

The general improvement took the form of reduced lag time between going to bed and falling asleep, fewer nocturnal awakenings, and enhanced sense of satisfaction with a particular night's sleep.* The typical participant reported sleep quality as being between "fair" and "fair-to-good" before the use of wine. "Good" became the most typical report during the on-wine period. Shifts toward improved sleep quality were noted most often during the second half of the on-wine period. Extension of both the baseline and on-wine periods from 10 to 15 and then to 20 days each throughout the course of the study helped to make this trend more apparent.

---

*Results reported as significant in this section reached at least the $p<.05$ level of confidence (two-tailed test).

Many of the participants continued to awaken once or twice during the night while on wine, but the number of people who were "up and down all night" (multiple awakenings) significantly decreased. There was no difference between baseline and on-wine periods with respect to degree of fatigue reported at the time of retiring for sleep in the evening. There was a fairly consistent but statistically insignificant tendency for women to show more improvement in sleep quality with the use of wine than men. Individual differences appeared more dominant than sex differences per se.

There was no indication that the use of wine was associated with more awakenings, more difficulty in falling asleep, or lower sleep quality in general. Participants reported either improved sleep or substantially no change.

Energy and Accomplishment

The data available regarding energy and accomplishment were also drawn from the continuous self-report measures and have the same strengths and limitations. Although energy and accomplishment were reported as separate items, it soon became clear that the results were usually given in tandem, and so these item scores were combined for analysis.

The results here are a little more difficult to summarize. Individuals who on baseline reported energy/accomplishment states that were close to either extreme (low or high) generally showed little change during the on-wine period. The lack of upward movement for those who were already reporting high energy levels could be explained either as an artifact of the reporting instrument (the top categories had already been utilized in the baseline phase, so there was no way to indicate further improvement) or simply as a representation of a sense of completely adequate energy level that did not need to be and could not be improved. The lack of upward movement for those with very low energy levels appears to be a rather different matter. The most obvious implication here is that use of wine did not help them in this regard. When both extreme groups of energy level at baseline are set aside, however, there is a consistent trend for reported energy level to increase with the use of wine. The improvement in energy level was significant for three of the independent samples ($p<.05$) but not significant for the total number. While the trend is for a raised energy/accomplishment level, the magnitude of this change, as well as the number of individuals showing the change, is not as pronounced as with the sleep quality index, which consistently showed changes significant at or beyond the $p<.05$ level.

Sleep and energy/accomplishment data on each individual were also combined for one set of analyses. Each person was classified according to functional level on the basis of both sets of data at baseline. These data were then examined to determine the frequency and direction of shifts from one functional level to another during the on-wine period. The level shifts were predominantly in a positive direction and occurred throughout the entire range of levels ($p < .05$). While at baseline approximately half of the participants had been classified at the two lowest sleep/energy/accomplishment levels, the number of these levels declined to approximately 20 percent during the on-wine periods. Nevertheless, it seemed reasonably clear that improvements in the sleep component made more of a contribution to these shifts than in the energy/accomplishment items. It might be noted in passing that it appeared easier to ask and obtain more specific information on sleeping behavior than on energy and accomplishment; possibly the better specificity and clarity of the sleep items had something to do with the obtained findings.

Mood and Morale

The participants' sense of well-being was ascertained in the initial interview and then continuously as part of the daily self-report forms. In later phases of the study, the Lawton Morale Scale and Beck Hope Scale were introduced at both baseline and on-wine points of assessment. In addition, information regarding the participants' view of their current life situation could be gleaned through other measures that were used in one or more phases. The elderly participants who lived independently in the community (not in any form of age-congregate housing) consistently described themselves as being in a moderate-to-good state of mind at the point of entry into the study and during the baseline period. The Phase I sample nevertheless showed a heightened sense of well-being with use of wine, taking into account both direction and magnitude of change in daily mood scores (significant beyond the .01 level as determined by the rank-order sign test). This finding was not replicated in Phase II. Daily ratings of mood and of "the kind of day it was" were even higher for this sample than for the Phase I sample during the baseline period.

The Phase III participants generally described their life situation and sense of well-being in less favorable terms than had the earlier participants. The objective facts regarding their life circumstances appeared to be in keeping with this less sanguine subjective state. Significant improvement in mood and related measures was found with this sample during the on-wine period. In addition to the daily mood measures, it was also possible to examine changes in morale scale scores and in emotional quality scores reliably derived from the earliest memory inquiry. These latter scores were for general emotional quality of the reported earliest memory and for the presence of danger–loss themes in the memory recalled. The shift in the morale/well-being domain was rather striking for this sample. Almost all of those shifting in morale scores from pretest to on-wine periods were in a positive direction (25 positive, 4 negative, $p < .01$). Shifts in general emotional quality of the earliest memory were even more marked (22 positive, 1 negative, $p < .01$), and no participants introduced danger–loss themes for the first time during the on-wine period, while 15 who had previously reported such themes did not do so. There was a nonsignificant tendency for women to show more marked improvement, a tendency that could have been related to their relatively less favorable expressions of mood and morale at the outset. In general, the mood/morale shift noted in Phase III was one of the clearest areas of improvement found in any domain throughout the entire course of the study.

Phase IV emphasized the exploration of possible individual differences in response tó wine. Most benefit seemed to be derived by those female participants who initially had expressed relatively low morale, hope, and self-esteem. These measures were independent of their sleep quality and initial level of cognition at point of entry into the study. Significant improvement ($p < .05$) was also shown by participants of both sexes who had shown low morale and poor sleep quality on baseline but who functioned on a high or moderately high cognitive level at the start of the study. Two other subgroups of participants were identified during this phase: those who had been functioning well in the spheres of sleep, morale, and cognition at baseline, and those who had been functioning poorly in all these spheres. The *direction* of change was positive for all these subgroups on the mood/morale indices. The first two subgroups noted above showed more frequent and larger shifts, however, and the four subgroups differed in other respects in the baseline/on-wine comparisons (see below).

Phases V and VI provided additional support for the pattern of improved mood and morale or hopefulness whenever individual changes in these respects could be detected. The most relevant new finding was the stability of the improved mood status over a somewhat longer period of time than could be observed in the preceding phases.

In general (cutting across differences in specific samples and in slightly varied research designs), it would be fair to say that significant positive changes in mood/morale/hopefulness were common and negative changes uncommon. There were some individuals who did not show much change one way or the other on the measures employed. If the study could be "retrofitted," it would have been wise to introduce both the morale scale and earliest memory procedure at the very beginning and use them for all phases, as well as perhaps to include an adjective checklist or more behaviorally oriented technique for a more complete and systematic examination of mood/morale effects.

Cognitive and Behavioral Variables

Starting with Phase II, a variety of measures were introduced to examine possible changes in cognitive performance, as well as a few measures that provided the opportunity to observe and quantify integrated behaviors within the interview-testing sessions (see Table 8-2 for the measure-by-phase guide). The Tempo Variability Test and the dart-throwing exercise exemplify perhaps the most straightforward behavioral measures utilized in this study. (It is always somewhat arbitrary to separate cognitive from behavioral measures; the distinction is made here only to suggest slightly different emphases.)

The overall cognitive–behavioral status of the elderly participants in this study prior to their use of wine can be assessed most adequately from the results obtained in Phase II when our assessment battery was most extensive. Mental performance as assessed by the standard tasks in the battery (e.g., digit span and similarities) was well within the normal range for people of this age. The more experimental-type procedures, however, indicated more deficits. On the Tempo Variability Test (TVT), for example, only a few participants could exercise the degree of control necessary to slow down spontaneous writing tempo to any appreciable degree. Free recall and incidental observations tasks also indicated impairments or limitations in learning, memory, and attention. (The data base for comparison on these variables is not as neatly arrayed as in the case with IQ-type tasks, but there are sufficient data available on younger adults to suggest strongly that the participants in the present study had more difficulty with these tasks than do adults in general.) The overall impression was that the typical participant appeared reasonably intact when given relatively familiar tasks but had problems in mental functioning that came to light when asked to cope with new situations and to think freshly. This impression is consistent with R. B. Cattell's research that distinguishes between so-called crystallized and fluid forms of intelligence[10] and also with distinctions between "hold" and "don't hold" components of intellectual functioning as recognized by many psychologists who work with IQ-type instruments. While it appears appropriate to acknowledge the consistency of the present data with the empirical findings and theoretical constructions of other investigators, it also appears wise to caution that all *explanations* of these data should be regarded as tentative, given our current state of knowledge.

Possible wine-related effects are also best examined by concentrating first on Phase II, with its sample of intact, independent-living elders, a large test battery, and a very straightforward research design. Results can be grouped into the specific areas of functioning assessed. In the area of *memory,* the free recall technique indicated significant improvement

($p<.05$) from baseline to on-wine performances. There were favorable but less than significant trends on the digit span and recall tasks, both immediate and delayed. The type of memory function assessed by the Free Recall Test, then, seemed to improve with use of wine, but comparable change on the other measures was not found. Particular individuals did improve on the other measures, especially the recall of story elements, but this was not true for the group in general. *Concentration, control, and coordination of thought* were assessed by measurements such as the TVT, mazes, and dart throwing, Previous research with the TVT[11] indicated that elderly people have considerable difficulty in slowing down their spontaneous tempo and often cannot exercise an inhibitory influence over their own manual behavior, even with repeated efforts. Tempo *variability* increased significantly ($p<.01$) during the on-wine period. The participants also adopted a faster spontaneous tempo ($p<.05$). There was a nonsignificant tendency toward a faster accelerated tempo as well. But the most substantial change was in what might be described as the inhibition process, as indexed by a slower performance when given the instruction, "Write the same phrase as slowly as you can while still keeping your pencil moving." The combination of slightly accelerated tempo with the "write-as-quickly-as-you-can" instructions with an appreciably prolonged slowed tempo resulted in a significantly broader range of total tempo flexibility. During the on-wine condition, then, the elderly participants exercised a greater range of control over the tempo of this form of behavior. No changes were found with the maze test. Significant improvement was found in the flinging of darts at a standard bull's-eye target ($p<.05$). This improvement appeared to be attributable mostly to more "zip" in the throws, which resulted in more darts lodging in the target, although there was also a tendency toward improvement in accuracy as well.

On measures of *verbal intelligence and reasoning,* there were no significant changes in performance. Similarities scores seemed particularly immune to change. Interestingly, the range into the past and future that participants took their story inventions on the Story Completions task did change during the on-wine condition. The typical shift was toward utilization of a broader psychological time field in creating their story productions ($p<.05$). A provocative finding was noted in one aspect of the *problem-solving* tasks. Some participants arrived at the correct solution to the inquiry strategy task with its "20 questions" format more rapidly during the on-wine condition. This did not seem to involve a different search strategy than what they had applied during the prewine performance. Instead, it appeared to represent a more efficient and goal-oriented use of the same strategy they had previously employed, to the extent that the nature of this strategy could be determined in the first place. Performances also showed a tendency toward improvement on the sorting task, particularly among those who had already shown better than average (for this sample) performance at baseline. This tendency approached but did not reach significance. We were not able to distinguish the possibility of improved cognitive functioning as such from heightened persistence and motivation (the desire and expectation to do the task as thoroughly as possible).

Measures of *personal and social insight, judgment, and reflection* in general did not show clear evidence of change from baseline to on-wine periods. Exceptions were two measures of the emotional quality of earliest memory (EM), which has already been noted in the morale/mood section above. More memories with pleasant affect and fewer with danger–loss themes were given during the on-wine condition ($p<.05$). Because it is known from previous research[12] that questions such as the EM often are answered differently depending on the respondent's current life situation, this finding suggests that our participants gave a more positive "reading" of their own past than they had before entering the on-wine period of the study. At least one other finding—in this case, more of an impression based on fairly complex data that are difficult to summarize—might be noted here. The life gestalt procedure is a sort of interview-within-an-interview that is organized around a constructed graphic representation of the participant's total life experience—past, present, and future. The most salient impression was that the *individual* qualities of each participant's life view emerged more clearly during the on-wine period. The specifics of the life views that emerged were so individual and distinctive that it would do them an injustice to attempt a cut-and-dried summary. The overall impression here was that the elderly men and women in this study seemed more able to more inclined to express their own distinctive view of their own lives than to come across as a stereotyped "old person" after they had been using wine regularly.

Information added (and subtracted) by the other phases includes the following:

1. Deficits in memory were the most commonly reported type of cognitive–behavioral problem by participants prior to the on-wine phase. In other words, of all the psychological and functional difficulties an elderly man or woman might experience or report, it was memory (as distinguished from, say, concentration, ability to pay attention, learn new information, etc.) that the elders themselves reported.

2. There was consistent improvement associated with use of wine on the abilities required to inhibit and modify one's own behavior on the TVT. This appears, then, to be a rather solid finding.

3. Equally solid as a "nonfinding" or a finding of no change were per-

formances on the similarities task. Performances were so stable on this measure of verbal reasoning that it could also be used as a classification variable to divide some of the later samples into levels of cognitive functioning. More generally, throughout the various measures used in the various phases, there was no indication that the ability to think abstractly (at least in the verbal sphere) had improved significantly.

4. Fairly consistent and positive findings on several other measures appeared to be related to an increased sense of zest or confidence. The heightened zest, confidence, motivation, or whatever one chooses to call this affirmative mode of being was more directly evident than any possible changes in underlying psychological functions. A good example is the sorting task performances of those Phase II participants who were classified at a relatively higher functional level than their peers during the baseline period. They showed significant improvement ($p < .05$) in a task that certainly involves some cognitive components. Yet it was easier to observe the altered spirit with which they approached and carried through the challenge of the task than to be certain that cognitive functioning as such had improved. There was a similar impression with the story completion task with the same participants, although in this instance the positive changes did not reach statistical significance.

5. We do not know precisely what functional abilities are involved to what degree in throwing darts at a target. It does appear, however, to be an activity that involves concentration, goal orientation, and the coordination of sensorimotor systems. Dart throwing might, then, represent a much larger range of actions that require mental and physical coordination in a real-life situation and that are also dependent to some degree on the individual's mood, motivation, expectations, and the like. The fact that almost all changes in dart-throwing performances throughout the study were in a positive direction at least suggests that the moderate, regular use of wine might have beneficial effects in a broad range of life activities. Practice effects provide another possible explanation (see below). Obviously, it would be useful in any further research to include more situations that require "total action" of the individual, in addition to measures that are in the "taking a test" mold.

6. Phase V involved both a variation in research design and the introduction of two assessment procedures not previously included in this study. For the first time in this research series, a comparison group was established that received a nonalcoholic beverage in place of wine for the postbaseline period. The new procedures of particular relevance here were components of the well-known General Aptitude

Test Battery (GATB), the disassembly and the turning tests. Positive changes on these test performances were observed during the post-baseline period for the wine but not for the comparison group. The controls actually showed a slight nonsignificant decline in both tasks. This indicated the lack of even an ordinary "practice effect" for the controls. The most conservative interpretation for the experimental (on-wine) participants would be that they were at least able to achieve the practice effect that unimpaired young adults might be expected to manifest on retesting. In fact, however, the improvements seemed to go beyond what would be expected for just practice effect on these particular measures, although this could not be made a firm conclusion.

7. In the later phases of the research series, several attempts were made to classify participants according to functional level at point of entry or during the baseline period and then to examine the possibility of differential response to wine. The overall pattern was for those participants with relatively better cognitive–behavioral functioning at the outset of the study to show somewhat more improvement on cognitive—behavioral measures during the on-wine period. The clearest instances involved the flexibility measure of the Tempo Variability Test and the temporal range of thought measure for story completions (both $p < .05$). Differential responses were not always found but, when present, generally favored those who had been at the higher functional level at the outset. In fact, those with better functional status at the outset tended to show more improvement throughout the total range of our measures (including sleep patterns), but this was not the case in every instance. But there was the general impression that when differences do occur, it was the more intellectually able or intact elderly person who gained the most benefit from the use of wine in the cognitive domain.

8. The particular design and sample employed in Phase IV led to one constellation of findings that is at odds with the general pattern obtained for the series as a whole. As mentioned earlier, one of the four clusters of participants identified during this phase were those who had been functioning poorly in sleeping patterns, self-reported morale, and objectively scored cognition at baseline. These people did show some of the typical positive changes noted for other participants throughout the study (significantly improved morale and hope, sleeping, and TVT performance). However, they declined somewhat in measures of memory and concentration (digit span and free recall, $p < .05$). This finding—decline in cognitive performance—deviates from data obtained earlier and later in the series and from other participants during the same phase. There may

well have been individuals with this pattern in other samples, but only the methodology used in this phase brought this phenomenon clearly to the surface.

A clinical hypothesis for this differential effect will be suggested at this point, where it is most relevant, although technically it would be more appropriate in the discussion section. We had the impression that people who were low in mood and morale, not sleeping well, and not coping well with cognitive tasks at the outset of the study experienced a heightened sense of self-awareness, as well as increased awareness, during the on-wine period. This experience seemed to be fairly consistent with that of other participants. These particular participants, however, may have been more likely to develop *expectations* for improved performance that were not realistic. The person, feeling better, thought he or she could or would do better in many areas of functioning. This made the testing situation appear more important and, therefore, more anxiety-arousing than it had been previously when the same individual expected little—and perhaps was better shielded from the negative feedback of a poor performance. The more motivated and anxious (albeit more rested and energetic) old person of this type would therefore be trying harder and would come up short of his or her own expectations. This is admittedly a speculative interpretation based on observations made in the present study and also on the investigator's experience with the response of participants in a psychotropic drug study to changes in their own condition.

In general, the findings suggested that moderate use of wine may have the effect of reducing some "excess deficits" for elders who retain reasonably intact cognitive functioning. Their morale, hopefulness, mood, and energy levels tend to rise, allowing them to use their remaining abilities more fully. People with more pronounced limitations in cognitive functioning, however, may still be as limited in objective performance or even experience more difficulties because of a possible motivation-anxiety interaction, even though they also feel better subjectively.

9. The possibility that findings associated with use of wine might instead be explained in terms of practice effect was examined most directly in Phase VI (see appendix for design summary). This phase also provided the best opportunity to examine relatively long-term effects (although still reckoned in weeks). Within the considerable limits of this small sample phase, there was no indication that observed improvements were inclined to disappear after their first appearance. On noncognitive measures such as sleep quality, most participants were still reporting better rest at the last point of measurement than they had

been at baseline, for example. There was no evidence to indicate that a "practice effect" explanation should be invoked instead of one that links the observed changes to the use of wine. Unlike the other phases in this research series, however, this small study has not been subjected to a replication effort at this time and, in any event, represents only a first effort to distinguish carefully between wine-relevant and other possible explanations of the observed effects, apart from the simple before—after design considerations built into the previous phases.

DISCUSSION

What has been learned from this series of small studies? It appears reasonable to conclude that the moderate and regular use of wine can be shown to have favorable effects on the elderly people dwelling in the community as well as those who have become institutional residents. Changes associated with use of wine are generally in a positive direction, whether reported by the elders themselves or detected through psychological assessment procedures.

Even if the wine effects were all psychological, this would have been an encouraging outcome. The mind, after all, is where we live. Improved subjective status was noted frequently with the relatively intact elderly people in this study, just as it was noted with many less intact elders who have participated in wine therapy programs in institutional settings. The present data do go somewhat beyond the subjective, however. There seems to have been enough significant changes on standard and experimental testing procedures to indicate that at least some of the effects associated with wine can take an objective form as well. Other types of change are on the borderline between subjective and objective. Sleeping patterns, for example, are in the subjective modality here because of our reliance on the participants' own reports. These reports, however, did provide specific information on items such as time of retiring, time of awakening, and the like. Such items are more objective in character, although the reports are perhaps subjective and not verified by other means in this research series. Self-reports of sleeping patterns could be augmented by behavioral and physiological observations in future studies. It would perhaps be most useful to retain the self-reports when other measures are used, both for comparability with the present research and to continue to do justice to the individual's own experience of sleep and its effects.

There have been indications that the individual's level of functioning prior to the use of wine has some relationship to the type and extent of benefits received. In the present research series, elders with relatively better functioning tended to show more improvement in performance and behaviors that have strong cognitive components. There was less difference noted in the sleep/energy/mood/morale sphere in relationship to baseline level. Most of the research on favorable effects associated with alcohol use in institutionalized populations has focused on the subjective and interpersonal spheres rather than on the cognitive. It is clear from these studies (Chapter 5) that difficulties in cognitive functioning did not preclude participants from deriving benefit from moderate use of alcoholic beverages (usually wine and beer).

The simplest explanation for both the previous studies and the present series might be that the regular and moderate use of alcoholic beverages helps elderly individuals to make better use of whatever level of functional abilities they possess. The mediational process could be reduction in chronic fatigue, such as our hypothesis here has suggested, or in anxiety-depression level. The phenomena of anxiety, depression, and inadequate sleep often appear together in clinical symptoms (not limited to elders). It is often difficult to determine which comes first or which is the most dominant. Various treatments have been addressed chiefly to one or another of these evidences of difficulty. Even when treatment appears to be successful, it is not easy to specify whether the main effect was on anxiety, depression, or sleep disturbance. Ordinarily, one would not claim that the treatment wrought a fundamental change in the individual's ability to think well. It would be more reasonable to suggest that with more serenity and vigor, the person would not have to contend with the disrupting effects of anxiety, depression, or fatigue on mental performance. This general interpretation is probably the one that is most appropriate for the new findings reported here.

But the age factor should be considered more carefully. It is usually assumed that there is "something wrong" when a young adult is not coping well with life. If we observe constriction in thought and behavior and memory deficits, then we look for specific explanations for these problems and seek means of alleviating them. The problems are seen as deviations from the expected norm of competent thought and behavior. This interpretation encourages careful assessment and active treatment. Often, however, our interpretation of the status of elderly people is quite different. Both the general public and many professionals hold a pessimistic view of aging.

The elderly person is *supposed* to be slipping. Changes are expected to be in a negative direction. Furthermore, observed difficulties are often assumed to be both irreversible and progressive. This attitude (sometimes known as "therapeutic nihilism") is often associated with inadequate assessment of the individual's actual problems and remedial efforts that are half-hearted if, indeed, any such efforts are made at all. The same behavioral or cognitive problem shown by both a young and an old adult is likely to be interpreted differently and to receive different degrees of attention. The broad field of gerontology and geriatrics has made strides in recent years to challenge this negative outlook. Those who have actually attempted to prevent or alleviate problems associated with advanced age have had enough success to continue their efforts and to spread a more hopeful message to those who are inclined to listen.

The data from the present research series, then, are either surprising or not surprising, depending on one's frame of reference. Those who assume that it is somehow "normal" for elderly people to show a variety of behavioral and cognitive deficits might want to rethink their position. "Normal impairments" associated with advanced age proved amenable to positive change, just as one might have expected with a younger population receiving care for their difficulties. Those who have been less ready to dismiss problems of the elderly as beyond successful treatment might simply add the benefits associated with wine use to a growing set of concepts and procedures that seem useful in helping people of advanced years to function well. One of the major implications here is that problems often assumed to be characteristic of old age might prove to be as amenable to treatment—and perhaps prevention—as those that afflict younger people. Restoration of serenity and vigor to help the individual function well is a commonplace goal with young adults; perhaps in the future, it will be seen as quite a reasonable and achievable goal for elderly adults also.

The Sleep-Wine Hypothesis

What can be said about the status of the specific hypothesis that guided this research series? The data indicate that "something happened." Significant benefits were derived by many of the participants. Many of the findings were replicated with independent samples. Alternative explanations such as "practice effects," while not entirely ruled out, do not appear to be as reasonable on the basis of the available information as does the tentative conclusion that the use of wine was an important factor in the observed changes.

Nevertheless, the data are a long way from providing direct information on the validity of the starting hypothesis itself. Some of the missing links can be listed briefly:

1. There are no data on possible physiological changes in sleep pattern between no-wine and on-wine conditions. If the hypothesis is correct, we might expect to find an increase in delta sleep (absolute and proportional) when wine is used and perhaps an increase in REM sleep as well. This question remains to be studied.

2. There are no data that directly test the hypothesis that it is the GABA component of wine that makes the difference. It is possible that other wine components have as much effect or more. A thorough test of the GABA hypothesis would require determination of the amount of this substance present in the particular wine used by a particular participant, but it would also require more information than is currently available on the absorption and utilization of GABA.
3. There is not sufficient informaiton to test the hypothesis that improved sleep rather than some other type of change is the factor most reponsible for the favorable changes that have been observed.

Research into the areas noted above would bring us appreciably closer to direct and thorough evaluation of the guiding hypothesis. At the same time, one would need to continue to explore and refine behavioral–cognitive–interpersonal measures of possible wine benefit. In addition, it would be valuable to include in the equation the socioenvironmental variables that influence the individual. The effect of "social climate" should not be underestimated. Is the elderly person living alone? In a supportive family context? In a large, rather impersonal institutional setting? What are the social expectations and pressures of everyday life for this person? How much of the individual's life is in his or her own hands, and how much of it is controlled by others? These are among the considerations that could be translated into specific variables to be studied along with the components of wine, their action on the body, and the observed changes in thought, feeling, and actions.

It should be noted that other investigators have been productive over the past few years on topics that bear upon the hypothesis of this study. The role of GABA, for example, has received much more experimental attention than had been the case when the guiding hypothesis was first developed.[13] The available findings do not answer the questions raised here but do suggest that GABA is a rather more important substance than had previously been thought. A series of studies by Webb and his colleagues[14-16] has contributed to our knowledge of the tranquilizing effects of wine. Webb has also been willing to speculate that the brain might contain amino transferases that could catalyze the conversion of gamma-aminobutyric acid into gamma-hydroxybutyric acid and vice versa.* This could be one of the links that need to discovered in the complex physiological side of the "sleep arousal system." Certainly, there has been a substantial increase of interest and provocative findings in regard to brain receptors and hormones in recent years,[17] and research is now beginning on humans in relation to alcohol and central serotonin metabolism.[18] As already indicated, the data from this realm neither confirm nor undermine the sleep/wine/excess deficit hypothesis, but it is encouraging to see the more

*A. D. Webb, personal communication, Oct. 3, 1977.

active cultivation of research topics that are both significant in themselves and eventually will prove relevant to the aims of the present study.

The literature on sleeping patterns of elderly people was sparse at the time the present research series began. While still not very extensive, the topic has benefited from continued exploration. The basic findings available to us several years ago have been confirmed and extended. Kupfer et al. for example, found very little delta sleep and a general fragmentation of sleep in a population of depressed elderly people.[19] Other useful studies include those by Prinz[20] and Feinberg.[21] The data still appear to be compatible with the guiding hypothesis, but this, of course, does not constitute proof.

There is an unusual perspective that one might take with respect to sleep and the elderly. Although this view has not actually been advanced, to the best of this writer's knowledge, it might be germane to our discussion. Researchers employing the sleep laboratory technique with all-night monitoring of EEG and other physiological functions have found differences between younger and older adults. These differences appear to be in the negative direction; that is, older adults receive less adequate sleep. One could say that older people *need* less sleep. There are opinions on this topic but no hard data one way or another. A more extreme position might be developed, however. Perhaps the changes are not negative at all. Perhaps, instead, there is a new psychophysiological "strategy" of sleep in old age. The apparent diminution of sleep might somehow serve as a protective device. "Normal" sleep (taking the earlier adult years as a model) might be too much for the aged person. If there were, indeed, some kind of survival function served by the observed changes in sleeping patterns, then whatever was done to "improve" sleep might paradoxically prove harmful. This would be not only an extreme but also a highly speculative position to advocate. The general body of clinical and research evidence runs to the other position: that a good night's sleep provides one of the most solid foundations for well-being at any age. The fact that this extreme position appears so out of keeping with established views, however, should not lead to its hasty dismissal but rather to a willingness to keep our observations fresh and as unbiased as possible.

Two methodological points that bear on almost all the existing sleep—age research should be made before closing: (1) the studies tend to be cross-sectional, so we know little about changes in sleep patterns for the same individual over time, and (2) the physical and psychological health status of the participants has not always been examined and reported in detail. How much of the obtained findings should be explained on the basis of age per se and how much on the basis of particular illnesses and impairments is difficult to determine (a problem found in many other types of age-comparative research as well).

Whether or not the sleep/wine/excess deficit hypothesis is supported by subsequent research remains to be seen. Perhaps enough has been done to suggest that it may not be premature to formulate theories in this area and at least try to put them to empirical test. Furthermore, the value of wine (or "something about wine") for elderly people appears to be supported, even though a precise and comprehensive explanation is not yet available.

REFERENCES

1. Kastenbaum, R. Beer, wine and mutual gratification in the gerontopolis. In D. P. Kent, R. Kastenbaum, and S. Sherwood (Eds.), *Research, planning and action for the elderly.* New York: Behavioral Publications, 1972, pp. 365–394.
2. Kastenbaum, R. Theories of human aging—the search for a conceptual framework. *Journal of Social Issues,* 1965, *21,* 13–36.
3. Kastenbaum, R. Perspectives on the development and modification of behavior in the aged: A developmental perspective. *The Gerontologist,* 1968, *8,* 280–284.
4. Kastenbaum, R. What happens to the man who is inside the aging body? An inquiry into the developmental psychology of later life. In F. C. Jeffers (Ed.), *Duke University Council on Aging and Human Development. Proceedings of Seminars, 1965–1969.* Durham, N.C.: Duke University Press, 1969, pp. 99–112.
5. Kastenbaum, R. Getting there ahead of time. *Psychology Today,* December 1971.
6. Luce, G. G., & Segal, J. *Sleep.* New York: Lancer Books, 1966.
7. Kleitman, N. *Sleep and wakefulness.* Chicago: University of Chicago Press, 1963.
8. Doull, J. *The pharmacology of the non-alcoholic constituents of wine.* San Francisco: Wine Advisory Board, 1970.
9. Luce, G. G. *Biological rhythms in psychiatry and medicine.* Chevy Chase, Md.: National Institute of Mental Health, 1970.
10. Cattell, R. B. Theory of fluid and crystallized intelligence: A critical experiment. *Journal Educational Psychology,* 1963, *54,* 1–22.
11. Pollock, R., & Kastenbaum, R. Delay of gratification in later life: An experimental analog. In R. Kastenbaum (Ed.), *New thoughts on old age.* New York: Springer, 1964, pp. 281–290.
12. Tobin, S. S. Earliest memory as data for research in aging. In D. P. Kent, R. Kastenbaum, and S. S. Sherwood (Eds.), *Research, planning and action for the elderly.* New York: Behavioral Publications, 1972, pp. 252–278.
13. Mao, C. C., & Costa, E. Biochemical pharmacology of GABA transmission. In M. A. Lipton, A. DiMascio, and K. F. Killam (Eds.), *Psychopharmacology: A generation of progress.* New York: Raven Press, 1978, pp. 307–318.

14. Webb, A. D., & Muller, C. J. A project to determine the physiological effect of the tranquilizing substances in wine. *Quarterly Technical Report*. Davis: Department of Viticulture and Enology, University of California, 1971.
15. Webb, A. D., & Muller, C. J. A project to determine the physiological effect of the tranquilizing substances in wine. *Quarterly Technical Report*. Davis: Department of Viticulture and Enology, University of California, 1973.
16. Muller, C. J., Kepner, R. E., & Webb, A. D. Lactones in wine—a review. *American Journal of Enology and Viticulture*, 1976, *27*, 1–14.
17. Snyder, S. H. The opiate receptor and morphine-like peptides in the brain. *American Journal of Psychiatry*, 1978, *135*, 645–652.
18. Ballenger, J. C., Goodwin, F. K., Major, L. F., & Brown, G. L. Alcohol and central serotonin metabolism in man. *Archives General Psychiatry*, 1979, *36*, 224–227.
19. Kupfer, D. J., Spiker, D. G., Coble, P. A., & Shaw, D. H. Electroencephalographic sleep recordings and depression in the elderly. *Journal of the American Geriatrics Society*, 1978, *26*, 53–57.
20. Prinz. P. N. Sleep patterns in the healthy aged: Relationship with intellectual functions. *Journal of Gerontology*, 1977, *32*, 179–184.
21. Feinberg, I. Changes in sleep cycle patterns with age. *Journal of Psychiatric Research*, 1974, *10*, 283–306.

Appendix: Research Methodology by Phase

Participants

Participants in the first phase of this study were 16 men and 16 women, ranging in age from 54 to 78. These people resided in their own houses or apartments in either the greater Detroit or greater Boston area. (All participants in subsequent phases were drawn from the Boston area.) None of the participants were debilitated, immobile, or suffering from physical conditions that interfered with a moderately active life-style. The sample as a whole could be characterized as a set of men and women who had been well integrated into society and who continued to exhibit stable "middle-class life patterns." As a group, they were on the threshold of entry into the culturally stereotyped realm of old age (total sample: mean age 62.6; women, 62.6; men 64.2) but were not to be counted among the very aged, fragile, dependent, or impoverished.

Although most of the women described themselves as housewives, mothers, and grandmothers, the sample also included several with active business or professional careers. The men included self-employed businessmen, a few professionals, and a number of salaried employees or retirees of business and industry. The economic status of the participants was judged to range from "squeezed" to "comfortable." All had financial concerns to some degree, but all claimed to be "managing."

Research Design

A before–after design was used to evaluate the possible effects of wine intake on sleeping behavior, daily activity, and sense of well-being. Wine, the independent variable, was introduced after a 10-day baseline period during which time data on the dependent variables (sleeping, activity, well-being) were collected. Another 10-day period followed during which time the participants drank wine near their bedtime and continued to provide data on the dependent variables. Participants served themselves one or two glasses of wine every evening during the experimental phase in their own homes. Selections were made by the participants from a representative sampling of domestic table wines.

Procedure

INFORMING AND ORIENTING THE PARTICIPANT

It was considered important to provide potential participants with clear and adequate information about the nature of this study. This was done by the interviewer during the first face-to-face contact and also by means of a standard fact sheet. The latter was formulated as follows:

A Research Memo

To: Men and women of fifty years and more
From: Robert Kastenbaum, Ph.D., Professor of Psychology, Wayne State University (Detroit, Mich.)
Subject: "A good night's sleep"

Would you be willing to snooze for science?

Everybody knows that a good night's sleep is important for our sense of well-being. But precisely what is a "good night's sleep"? It is not the same for everybody; we know that much. We also know that sleeping patterns change from infancy to childhood—and change again from childhood to adulthood.

What we don't know much about

How do sleeping patterns change from early through later adulthood?

How does a person's energy level relate to the amount and kind of sleep he gets?

Do men and women of your age and older get enough sleep? Do they get enough sleep of the "right kind"? (Recent studies show that there are several kinds of sleep.)

Are there any simple, safe, and inexpensive ways to help men and women with sleep insufficiencies to rest more soundly—and would this also help them feel more energetic and alert during the day?

What we are up to

We are asking a small number of mature men and women to participate in a pilot or exploratory study of sleep patterns. You may have read about studies in which people snooze over night in special laboratories with interesting kinds of scientific equipment keeping them company. This is *not* what this particular study is about (the sleep laboratory phase may come later, depending upon what we learn this time around).

As a participant in this study, this is all that would happen:

1. You would be interviewed on your sleep patterns, your energy patterns and stuff like that by myself or one of my colleagues.

2. Each day, for 10 days, you would fill out an *Early Bird's Report,* and the *Snooze News.* These are records of your sleeping and energy patterns for the day. You return the EBR & SN to us in stamped, self-addressed envelopes, fresh each day. (Where are you sleeping? In your own home, of course; you are the only reporter of your own activity.)

3. At the end of this 10-day period we talk about your sleeping and energy patterns. Depending upon your own patterns, we may or may not have suggestions to make that could possibly help you sleep better. (But we are not looking just for problem sleepers—we want to learn about as many patterns of sleeping as we can.)

If you are interested in participating, we will be happy to explain the details to you. We think this research will eventually help us to foster the health and well-being of adults throughout their lifespan. Nothing that happens in this study will be threatening or embarrassing to any of us. And the information you provide will be held in confidence. Our reports will not make it possible to identify individual participants.

This fact sheet also included a brief statement of the principal investigator's credentials. A few details were modified later to reflect the investigator's relocation at the University of Massachusetts-Boston. While this fact sheet covered many of the essential considerations related to the study, it did not mention the use of wine because of the possibility that this piece of information might introduce an unmeasurable effect upon expectations and baseline reports. The emphasis was to be upon sleep and sense of well-being, the dependent variables.

BASELINE INFORMATION

All men and women who consented to participate were then given a *Sleep Survey* (SS) questionnaire to complete. This instrument was a modification of a questionnaire developed by the author and his former colleagues for clinical research in a geriatric hospital. The SS was completed in the presence of the interviewer, who clarified questions when necessary. The SS used a fixed-choice and short-answer format with responses to both types of questions coded objectively and contained six sections: (1) background information; (2) preparing for sleep; (3) sleeping; (4)

dreaming; (5) during the day; (6) your general situation. The items are given below (response categories omitted to save space here).

1. *Background information*
Birth date, age, sex, marital status, residence

2. *Preparing for sleep*
Do you go to bed at about the same time every night?

What time do you usually go to bed?

How long until you fall asleep (usually?)

Do you take any kind of medication to help you sleep?

If yes, how often?

If yes, do you know what kind of medication it is? Please describe.

If yes, does the medication help?

Do you eat or drink anything to help you sleep?

If yes, please describe (for beverage, indicate whether warm or cold, amount taken, and exact type, and how often).

Does what you eat or drink help you to sleep?

Do you do anything else to get ready for a good night's sleep? (Include also anything you might avoid doing, for the same purpose).

If yes, please describe (e.g., warm bath, taking a walk, reading poetry, etc).

When you go to bed, how tired are you (usually)?

How often do you find yourself more "keyed up," nervous, or tense than you would like to be when you are ready to sleep?

What do you usually think about before you fall asleep? (e.g., replay events of day, think about things that happened a long time ago, thinking about tomorrow, etc.).

When you go to bed, do you ever have the fear that you might not wake up the next morning, does it ever cross your mind?

If yes, please describe.

In general, do you consider your getting-ready-to-sleep time as (from "very comfortable" to "often uncomfortable").

3. *Sleeping*
Do you usually wake up at about the same time every morning?

What time to you usually wake up?

How often do you wake up during the night? (How often per night, and whether every night, occasionally, or what)

How long do you usually stay up when you awaken during the night?

How difficult is it for you to get back to sleep (usually?)

Do you consider yourself a "light" or a "deep" sleeper (usually?)

How many hours sleep do you need each night to feel at your best?

How many hours sleep do you usually have each night?

In general, do you sleep as soundly, as long, and as well as you would like to?

How have your sleeping patterns changed—these days as compared with earlier in your life?

How important is a good night's sleep to you these days?

4. *Dreaming*

How often do you have dreams that you can remember when you wake up?

How often do you have nightmares?

Have you had a dream that you could remember—at least temporarily—during the past week?

Have you had a nightmare that you could remember—at least temporarily—during the past week?

Do you think dreams have any meaning?

Should dreams be taken seriously?

Have you ever had a dream that foretold the future?

Have you ever dreamt of being reunited with somebody who has been separated from you?

Have you dreamt recently (within the past three months or so) of being reunited with somebody who has been separated from you?

Do your dreams seem to make sense as they go along, or are they confusing?

5. *During the day*

How much energy did you have when you were quite a young person?

How much energy do you have now as compared with others of your age?

How much energy have you lost as compared with yourself when younger?

Do you have enough energy to get through the demands and opportunities of the day?

Do you have enough energy to do all that you would like to do during the day?

What time of the day do you feel at your best?

What time of the day do you feel at your lowest ebb?

Draw a line to show your energy pattern through a typical day ("Energy-o-Gram" form provided to the respondent).

Over the past year, has your energy level changed?

Do you take a nap?

Would you like to nap more than you do?

Are there any activities you would do—or do more of—if you felt more "up to it"?

If yes, please describe.

Are there any activities you would like to cut out or cut down on?

If yes, please describe.

6. *Your general situation*

How would you describe your health these days?

How often do you find yourself blue or depressed?

How often do you find yourself irritable or angry?

How often do you have difficulty in concentration or paying attention?

How often do you have trouble with your memory?

How often do you feel that life is not worthwhile?

How much of your time is spent with worries on your mind?

In general, how do you feel about your life these days?

Are you now under a physician's care?

If yes, please describe (including current medications, if any).

DAILY REPORT INSTRUMENTS

The participants were then instructed in the use of two forms, the *Snooze News* (SN), and the *Early Bird's Report* (EBR). Each of these self-report forms was to be completed on a daily basis, placed in the stamped, addressed envelope provided for the purpose, and mailed promptly to the project director. This method of data collection was intended to (1) maintain the participant's interest in the study by requesting an action to perform every day, (2) assure that the self-report was made promptly rather than by delayed retrospections, and (3) minimize the likelihood that the participant might fall into a pattern of automatically giving the same responses every day in order to be consistent with previous responses. This latter aim was achieved by promptly "removing" (mailing off) each response soon after it was given.

The SN was a single sheet of paper folded into four pages that were blocked out to resemble a newspaper. On page 1, the participant recorded the "edition" (the date) and wrote a "lead story" on "the kind of day it was." Page 2 was headed, "The Day in Review." The participant circled the appropriate response category for the following items:

Accomplished
     less   more   about the same   as I expected today
Mood in general was
     brighter   darker   about the same   as usual
Mind worked today
     better   worse   about the same as usual
In general:
     great day   good day   fair day   one of those bad days

Page 3 was "Vital Statistics of the Day." This consisted of the Energy-o-Gram, upon which the participant recorded the level of energy he or she had at various points throughout the day and evening.

Page 4 was the "Night Letter," which was completed by the participant just before settling down to sleep. The items were:

Prepared for sleep by: (short answer)
At bedtime, feel
    not very tired   tired   very tired
Mood at bedtime:
    relaxed   tense   else? (short answer)
Time went to bed:

The EBR was completed by the participant shortly after awakening. The items were:

I woke up at:
Got out of bed at:
Feel like I've had a:
    poor night's sleep
    fair night's sleep
    good night's sleep
    very good night's sleep
During the night I woke up
    once
    twice
    more than twice
    up all night
    not at all
I had a dream (yes/no)
    pleasant dream?
    unpleasant dream?

Space was also provided on this form for other comments the participant might wish to make.

DATA COLLECTION

SN and EBR data were obtained for 20 consecutive days and nights, 10 before wine and 10 during. Participants were contacted between both phases of study and again at the end. These interviews were semi-structured, allowing time for the participant to volunteer questions, comments, and observations and for the interviewer to explore a few areas of concern. Although additional information was obtained at times through these interviews, the data analyses per se were limited to the SS, SN, and EBR.

PHASE II

Participants

Participants in Phase II were 40 elderly people, 29 women and 11 men, ranging in age from 60 to 84. The mean age of the women (69) exceeded that of the men (64), but this was not a statistically significant difference. None were residents of nursing homes or other congregate care facilities, but 18 lived in housing units designed especially for the elderly. This sample, as in Phase I, could be characterized as essentially independently functioning older men and women. As compared with the first sample, fewer of the Phase II participants were still active in full-time employment or in other major responsibilities outside of home. The participants in general appeared to be "getting by" financially, but only by watching every penny. Concern about continued survival on fixed incomes during inflationary times was evident among the participants and perhaps constituted the major theme of spontaneous conversation.

Research Design

A before–after design was used, as in Phase I, although some details differed. The baseline phase was expanded from 10 to 15 days. The experimental, or on-wine, phase was also expanded to 15 days.

Procedure

The Sleep Survey (Phase I) was retained but included an expanded background information procedure. The new material consisted of a section on *habits and life-style*. Nine items on use of tobacco and seven on medication and diet were included here. A section on use of alcoholic beverages was also added, based on work done by the project director and other investigators in this field. Because of its particular relevance to this report, the drinking habits items are given below.

Use of alcoholic beverages:
1. Please tell me which of these answers best describes your use of alcoholic beverages:
    (a) I never drink wine, beer, or whiskey or liquor at any time
    (b) I have a drink only on rare occasions
    (c) I usually have no more than three drinks a week
    (d) I often have more than three drinks a week
2.   People drink wine, beer, whiskey or liquor for different reasons. Here are some of the reasons people have given to us. By the way we are referring to people who

do not have drinking problems, but who use alcoholic beverages in moderation, as most people do:

How important would you say that each of the following is to YOU as a reason for drinking—very important, fairly important, or not at all important?

It helps me to relax
I drink to be sociable
I like the taste
I drink because the people I know drink
I drink when I want to forget everything
To celebrate special occasions
Helps me forget my worries
Improves my appetite
The polite thing to do in certain circumstances
Cheers me up when I'm in a bad mood
Helps me sleep better
Helps me when I'm tense or nervous

3. (Asked only of those who report they never drink) What are the main reasons that you don't drink? (Responses were recorded verbatim if they did not fit into one of the following categories. If no reasons are volunteered, each of the following possibilities was raised).

Is it partly for religious reasons?
Is it partly because of the cost?
Is it partly because of your concern for your health? (if "yes," inquire further, especially, if ever advised by a physician not to drink)
Is it partly because other members of your family, or your friends would rather that you didn't drink?
Is it partly because you have had bad experiences with drink?
Is it partly because you have heard that a person of your age should not drink?
Is it partly because you never had a chance to learn whether you would like to drink or not?
Is it partly because you have known people who have had drinking problems?

4. (Asked only of those who report they never drink) Was there ever a time when you drank wine, beer, whiskey or liquor at least a couple of times a year?

At what age did you stop drinking?
Why did you stop drinking at that time?

5. (For those who report current drinking behavior) When are you likely to have a drink of beer, wine, whiskey, or liquor? (More than one answer OK). What type of beverage on each occasion?

before your meals? with your meals? after a meal?
during the evening? before going to bed? other time?
What type of alcoholic beverage is usually your favorite?
beer wine whiskey mixed drink other
In the past month or so, have you had any beer?
In the past month or so, have you had any wine?
In the past month or so, have you had any whiskey or mixed drinks?

NEW BASELINE PROCEDURES

Earliest Memory (EM). The EM was the first mental functioning procedure per se administered to each participant. The EM was used in the first interview as a "warm up" for the procedures that followed later, as well as for the distinctive variables it added to the study.

Participant was asked: "How far back does your memory go? That's what I'd like to find out now. Please think back as far as you can. . . . What is the earliest event or experience you can remember? Can you describe it for me?"

Examiner might encourage the participant to provide more detail but would not otherwise guide memory recall or expression. Follow-up questions were: "About how old were you when that happened?" "Why do you think this particular memory has stayed with you?" "Would you say this is mostly a pleasant, mostly an unpleasant memory, or what?"

Tempo Variability Test (TVT). The TVT provides a measure of the participant's ability to vary in both directions from his or her preferred tempo of functioning, using handwriting as the particular function observed. It is based on a measure introduced by Downey,[1] who included only the slow-down variation from normal tempo. Impulse control is required for individuals to slow down their characteristic behavioral tempo. According to our past research, this control is likely to be difficult for elderly people to exercise. Speeding up requires calling upon the efficiency limits of the central nervous system. A person who already is functioning near the top limits of speed possible within his or her CNS status would find it difficult to exceed the characteristic tempo. The total range between slow and fast time indicates something of the individual's ability to shift functioning intentionally from its usual fixed point. The TVT thus is one measure of adaptive flexibility. It has the advantages of being readily observable and quantifiable, as well as involving a routine kind of behavior (handwriting).

Participant is told: "Here is a card that has some words on it. NEW ENGLAND FLOWER SHOW. The words are printed so they can be read easily. But I would like you to write these words longhand. Please wait until I tell you to begin. The stopwatch will be running, but I don't want you to hurry your writing. Just write the words, NEW ENGLAND FLOWER SHOW at whatever speed feels right and natural to you. Ready? Please begin now." (Elapsed time is recorded for performance.)

"Thank you. Now I would like you to write the same words again, but in a different way. This time, I would like you to write these words as *slowly* as you can. The idea is to slow your writing down, but to keep the pencil and pen moving along. See how slowly you can do it. Ready? Begin." (Time is recorded.)

"One more time now—and again, differently. This time I would like you to write NEW ENGLAND FLOWER SHOW as *fast* as you can. Just as fast as you can! Ready? Begin." (Time is recorded.)

Digit Span Forward. The digit span forward is one of the tasks included on the Wechsler Adult Intelligence Scale (WAIS). It is often interpreted as a measure of concentration/attention and short-term memory. The participant is told: "I am going to say a few numbers. Listen carefully please. When I have finished, you say the same numbers in the same order. This is called the Digit Span. It is an exercise for attention and memory. Are you ready for the first set of numbers?"

Sets of three digits, four digits, five digits, six digits, and seven digits are presented. Three failures at the three-digit level or two failures at any of the higher levels terminates the task.

Digit Span Backward. The digit span backward is also a WAIS task. It is more difficult for most people than DS forward because it requires the reversal operation, and it is especially difficult for people who have CNS impairments. The participant is told: "I am going to say a few numbers. But this time, please say them in the *reverse* order. You start with the last number and go backwards. If I said, '1, 2,' you would say, '2, 1.'"

Series of two, three, four, five, six, and seven digits are presented, with rules similar to those for DS forward.

Similarities. The similarities task is frequently used to assess verbal and abstract thinking. One version of similarities is included in the WAIS. The format is exemplified by Item 1 in our set: "In what way are these two alike: an orange and a banana?"

The other five items in our version are hat and a pair of shoes; dog and lion; train and automobile; eye and ear; bird and tree.

The items vary in difficulty. A person who has difficulties in thinking abstractly is likely to give circumstantial responses, mention differences rather than an essential similarity, or give no response at all.

What Are They Thinking? This measure was developed especially for this research series to give the older person an opportunity to demonstrate social insight or the ability to take another person's perspective. This ability obviously is important in daily life.

Participant is told: "I am going to describe a situation to you. Several people are involved in this situation. I will ask you to tell me what each of these people might be thinking in the situation."

Two situations are used. In this study, Situation A was given to half of the participants during the baseline phase; they were retested with Situation B. The B-A condition was reversed for the other half of the participants. The procedure is illustrated here by Situation A:

Situation: Sam Carter has just retired after working many years for the same company. He and his wife, Mary, have lived in the same neighborhood for almost forty years, and in the same house for thirty years. This is where their children, Diane and Arnold, grew up. Some of the people in the neighborhood are their closest friends, although a lot of "new people" have moved in lately.

The Carters had planned to move to Florida to enjoy the mild climate after he retired. Now they must decide if they are really going to move. From what little I have told you about the situation, *tell me what you think might be going through the minds of the following people:"*

The perspectives of eight different people are then requested:

Mrs. Armstead is the next door neighbor. She is an elderly widow. Her husband was a close friend of the Carters. She and Mrs. Carter often spend time together. What might Mrs. Armstead be thinking?

Mr. Richards is a local real estate broker who has also been a friend of the Carters for a long time. What might Mr. Richards be thinking?

Diane, the Carters' daughter, lives nearby with her husband and two small children. She and her mother are close to each other, although they sometimes give each other a hard time. Diane is in the habit of asking her parents to babysit, especially when she and her husband want to go away for a few days. What might Diane be thinking?

Arnold, the Carters' son, is now a businessman who does a lot of traveling. He has been telling his parents for years that they should enjoy life more and see more of the world. What might Arnold be thinking?

Mr. and Mrs. Sherman have been living in Florida for the past few years. Mr. Sherman worked at the same company with Mr. Carter and retired earlier, because of his age and health. They have been urging the Carters to move to Florida and live near them. Although the Shermans and Carters have known each other for a long time, they were never really the closest of friends. The Shermans seemed to expect the Carters to do things with them and for them and did not always recognize when the Carters had other plans. What might the Shermans be thinking?

Jimmy is a six-year-old boy in the Carters' neighborhood. He has no grandmother or grandfather of his own, and his mother and father do not seem to have much time for him. Jimmy loves coming over to the Carters, telling them of his adventures in school, doing little errands and chores for them, and eating Mrs. Carters' cookies and snacks. What might Jimmy be thinking?

Sam Carter. What might he be thinking?

Mary Carter. What might she be thinking?

What do the Carters decide to do? And why?

Two basic scores are derived from the participant's responses: a *differentiation* score that indicates how many different viewpoints he or she was able to take, and a *qualitative elaboration* score in which further insightful comments are added to the basic viewpoint-taking. A person with low scores on this task probably would have difficulty understanding what is taking place in complex interpersonal situations and in "reading" other people.

Recall Test. The recall test is a standard test of memory in which participants are asked to repeat significant elements of a newspaper-type story that is read to them. The story contains 20 memory units. Participants are credited for accurate recall of each unit and penalized for distorted recollections.

The recall test was given in two forms to each participant: (1) *immediate* recall (right after hearing the test story for the first time), and (2) *delayed* recall (after hearing the story again, and then returning to the task 10 minutes later). The immediate/delayed recall feature of this task makes it especially relevant for the study of mental functioning in later life, given the likelihood that short-term and intermediate-term memory functioning are based on different types of physiological mechanisms, one of which might show more impairment than the other.

Free Recall Memory Card Task. In this task, the participant is told, "I will present a series of cards to you. Each card will have a word on it that you know. I will show you each word card only once, and only for a few seconds. Your task is to try and remember as many of the words I have shown you as you can. After I have gone through the cards once I will ask you to write down as many of the words as you can in any order you please. Don't worry about the spelling, but put down as many words as you can. Do you have any questions? OK. Here we go." The interviewer then presents 24 different word cards.

This task, while it has some elements in common with the recall test, is different enough to constitute an independent measure of memory functioning.

Story Completion. By contrast with the preceding two tasks, story completion requests the participant to construct his or her own response. Both the thematic development of the story and its formal structure provide insights into mental functioning.

The general instructions are: "Let's see what kind of a storyteller you are. I am going to read a sentence that could be used to begin a story. Start off with this sentence, and make it into an interesting story. Any kind of story you want. The more interesting, the better."

When the participant has completed the story, he or she is also asked to provide a title for it (which is separately reated with respect to appropriateness and creativity).

Two story roots were used: "When Bill Davis woke up, he felt that this was going to be a very special day." (Now, you take it from there.) And "It had been a long time since Marie Ellsworth and Gary Burns had seen each other." The differences in the story roots (solitary vs. interpersonal beginnings) were intended to sample a wider variety of possible thought operations.

Sorting Task. The sorting task is intended to assess the ability to group or classify items. This is one type of basic logical operation. It requires considerable development during the early years of life and may show impairment later. The particular technique used here is similar to those frequently employed in laboratory studies.

The participant was told: "Here is a set of 48 cards. Each has a word that you know on it. These words name various things. What I would like you to do is to simply look through the deck of these word cards, and then place them into piles that seem to go together, to belong together. There is no right or wrong way of doing it. Just put together into one pile those words that seem—to you—to belong together. You can use as many piles as you like and they do not have to be equal. Take your time. There is no rush. Do you have any questions?"

The word cards themselves represented 12 different categories with four examples of each. The categories were body parts, flowers, four-legged animals, professions, clothes, house parts, insects, vegetables, birds, countries, fruits, and materials (example: body parts—nose, knee, ear, toe). The categories were not marked as such but were shuffled into a random arrangement for each presentation. Participants could either use the categories that had been preestablished or develop other categories of their own devising (e.g., things to eat, animals, words that begin with vowels, etc.).

Twenty Questions (Inquiry Strategy Test). The participant was shown a large sheet of photographic paper on which 42 familiar objects were displayed in small color pictures. These included items such as a shoe, a hammer, a doll, and a bumblebee. The photographs were arranged in a grid, six down and seven across. It was first ascertained that the participant could see them clearly enough to identify them. The task then was to discover which of the pictures the examiner had selected as the "correct" answer. The participant was encouraged to arrive at the correct answer by asking questions of the examiner, as in the "Twenty Questions" game format. The participant could ask any question that might be answered with a "yes" or a "no."

The purpose of this task was to learn what processes of inquiry strategy the older person uses and whether the experimental treatment (wine) could result in an improved strategy. Much of daily life activities consists of selecting out and making sense of a relatively few bits of information from among all the stimuli that confront us. A person with a purposeful and flexible "search" approach is more likely to arrive at the information he really needs. The inquiry strategy test provides a small, controlled sampling of how a person goes about this selecting, sorting, and grouping process with a goal (getting the right answer) in mind.

Incidental Observations Task. The purpose of this task is to learn something about the older person's ability to notice and register information apart from the material that is directly confronting him. Can he "see out of the corner of his eye," so to speak? Although seldom studied in an older population, this ability to make incidental observations is important for adaptation and creativity.

The task itself is a simple one. The participant is asked to tell the interviewer what he or she remembers observing on the way to the current appointment. Clarity and precision, as well as extent, of observation are noted.

Life Gestalt. The life gestalt task assesses the participant's ability to put his or her own life into perspective. Both the formal characteristics of the individual's approach and the nature or content of the particular perspective that is applied are evaluated.

This is a semistructured interview within an interview. It is organized around a graphic form that displays six representative "life gestalts." These are briefly explained to the participants as examples of how other people have described the trajectory and shape of their lives. "The person who made this sketch, for example, saw his life as having improved steadily throughout the years. . . . This person had just the opposite view of his life." When the participant has had a good opportunity to comprehend the task, he is asked either to select whichever of the six presented graphs comes closest to his own view of his life or to sketch another graph that would do better justice to his own circumstances and view. (The interviewer can assist the individual to make the sketch if necessary, following the participant's instructions.) During this life-mapping process, the participant is encouraged to discuss his total view of his own life—past, present, and future. Part of the task includes specifying the point along the total life gestalt where the person sees himself at the moment and the likely course of his life in the future.

Maze Test. Performance on a paper-and-pencil maze test requires concentration, foresight, control of hand action, and the ability to find the only correct pathway in a situation where there is more than one way to go wrong. It is a behavioral situation that calls upon some important human abilities, basically, perhaps, the ability to coordinate thought and action without the intrusion of emotional impulses.

For this study, a set of four mazes was prepared, each of a different level of difficulty. Maze A is quite easy. Each of the other mazes is progressively challenging, although even the most difficult, Maze D, is only of moderate difficulty. The format of these mazes and their inspiration and research background derive from the Porteus Maze Test.[2]

Participants begin with Maze B. If this maze is failed, Maze A is presented. Failure on both B and A terminates the task. Success with Maze A is followed by a second chance at Maze B and on up through C and D. Initial success with B is followed by presentation of C and D.

Performances on maze tests conventionally are scored in terms of complete success or failure. For this study, an intermediate category was also used, "flawed success" (1 error, corrected).

Dart Throwing. The game of throwing darts was adapted for this experiment as a measure of both the level of aspiration and visual-motor coordination and energy. A regulation dart board with bull's-eye target is mounted at the appropriate height. Both participant and interviewer warm up by throwing six darts each from a distance of 6 feet. The interviewer then goes over to the dart board and calls attention to the scores that are printed in the various target rings. The participant is asked to estimate how many of the first six darts he or she will land in each of the three major sectors. The participant then throws the six darts. The level of aspiration prediction is made again, and the participant throws another six darts.

From this procedure, we have the opportunity to observe the older person engaged in an activity that does not exclusively involve sitting down and answering questions or solving problems. We can also see how the participant's self-expectations and esteem either are influenced by his own performance or remain impervious to the performance feedback. In addition, we have, of course, data on the actual performances themselves.

All of these test procedures were given before wine was introduced and were subsequently repeated when the participant was using wine regularly.

PHASE III

Method

PARTICIPANTS

The 48 participants in Phase III consisted of equal numbers of men and women. The total sample was divided into two groups on the basis of functional status, with equal number and sex distribution. Level A participants were relatively unimpaired men and women who were still able to maintain their characteristic adult life-styles. They were not free from problems and limitations but could be considered to be making life adjustments within the "normal" range. Level B participants were residents of two institutions for the elderly. As a group, the Level B subsample had more physical and psychosocial problems and limitations. The institutionalized group, however, did not include individuals with impairments we would classify as severe. This was, then, a group intermediate between the normal, community-functioning elders and geriatric patients who are heavily dependent upon others for daily care and life-support measures.

The Level A participants were intended to be comparable in general characteristics to the men and women who took part in Phases I and II. The level B participants were intended to represent a significantly more impaired (although not severely) population of elders. Further information regarding the panel is given in Table A-1.

The institutionalized (Level B) participants were slightly older as a group. No person in either group was younger than 67 or older than 82. We therefore sampled the elderly but not the very old in this study. It should be noted that to achieve equal representation of the sexes from a population in which females predominate does, in some sense, result in an unrepresentative sample. We know of no way both to sample the sexes equally and to represent actual male/female proportions in the general population within the same study, and we selected in this case the alternative most relevant to our aims.

Table A.1
Description of Participants: Age-by-Sex-by-Functional Level

	Level A	Level B	Level C
N	24	24	48
Men	12	12	24
Women	12	12	24
Mean age, men	72.3	76.6	74.4
Mean age, women	70.9	77.0	73.9
Mean age, N	71.6	76.8	74.1

RESEARCH DESIGN

A before–after design was used, as in Phases I and II. Unlike the previous phases in this series, however, the existence of two different groups of participants made cross-comparisons possible as well. Both Level A and B groups were examined first prior to the introduction of the wine condition and retested when on wine.

PROCEDURES

Most of the assessment procedures used in this study had also been employed in Phase II. These were: habits and life-style questionnaire; sleep and activity patterns questionnaire; Snooze News, Early Bird Report; earliest memory; Tempo Variability Test; digit span forward; digit span backward; similarities; free recall memory card task; story completion; sorting task; life gestalt; and dart throwing.

Introduced into this research series for the first time was the Lawton Morale Scale,[3] one of the standard techniques for assessing the mood and self-esteem of older people. The morale scale consists of self-descriptive items such as "I sometimes feel that life isn't worth living" and "Little things bother me more this year."

PHASE IV

Method

PARTICIPANTS

The final panel of participants for Phase IV consisted of 30 elderly adults: 14 men and 16 women. We were not quite able to obtain an equal number of men and women as in previous phases. The mean age of the men was 73.5, the mean age of the women was 77.2, and the mean age of the combined sample was 75.5.

All participants were residents of congregate living facilities but varied in their general functional levels. Individuals with severe impairments and limitations in daily functioning were not included, but the sample did include an appreciable range of functioning.

RESEARCH DESIGN

The same basic design as in the previous phases was used here as well. This time, however, the participants were also cross-classified on the basis of the prewine data to accord with the Phase IV emphasis on individual differences. Each participant was classified with respect to each of four characteristics: *quality of sleep, level of cognitive functioning, morale-hope index,* and *sex* (male or female). This was to facilitate determination of which of these characteristics (taken separately or in any combination) most adequately predicted the response to wine.

PROCEDURES

Assessment procedures retained from previous phases included: Habits and life-style questionnaire; sleep and activity patterns questionnaire; Snooze News; Early Bird Report; similarities; digit span forward; digit span backward; free recall memory card task; Tempo Variability Test; Lawton Morale Scale.

Two new procedures were added for Phase IV. The *Rehearsal-Recall Test* provided the participants with the opportunity to practice skills and strategies in order to improve memory performance. This type of technique has been found to offer a usefully different approach to the study of memory, especially in those who have some impairments.[4] This technique was included here on the possibility that use of wine might help old people make better use of psychological and environmental help, in addition to whatever directly favorable results might possibly be attributable to wine.

The *Beck Hope Scale*[5] derives from the important clinical research of A. T. Beck and his colleagues. It is more of a psychiatrically oriented instrument than the morale scale and is concerned with depression in particular. It has proved useful in distinguishing between people with self-destructive, suicidal, or bleak future orientations and those with more optimism about the future.

All the procedures in this phase were scored objectively. This particular battery was assembled with several factors in mind: (1) the need to repeat enough measures previously used in this series to allow both for cross-validation and the continued buildup of standardized data; (2) the need to keep the data-gathering procedures within the time-and-effort limits of the elderly people themselves and of the research team; and (3) the desirability of refining and improving the measurement of key variables. (Nine of the less productive items from the sleep and activity patterns questionnaire were dropped.)

PHASE V

Method

PARTICIPANTS

The mean age of the 27 elderly people in this sample (18 women, 9 men) was 76.3. There was no significant difference between the ages of the women and the men. The participants were residents of local nursing homes at the time of Phase V. None were at a functional level requiring total care. All had some combination of physical, behavioral, and social problems typical of an elderly institutionalized population.

RESEARCH DESIGN

All participants were given the same battery of assessment procedures during the baseline period, as in previous phases. All participants also completed the daily self-report forms throughout the entire course of Phase V. The postbaseline period was extended from 15 to 20 days.

Unlike previous phases, the sample was divided into experimental and control subgroups, in addition to the before–after design. Eighteen participants (12 women, 6 men) were randomly assigned to the experimental or wine condition. These people used wine after completion of the baseline period. Another 9 participants (6 women, 3 men) were randomly assigned to the control group, which was asked to use a nonalcoholic beverage of their own choice. The random assignment of individuals into wine and control groups was not made until completion of the baseline phase.

All participants were retested with the same assessment procedures.

PROCEDURES

The habits and life-style and sleep and activity patterns questionnaires were supplemented by health information provided to us through the courtesy of the participating institutions and their medical consultants.

Assessment procedures retained from previous phases also included: Lawton Morale Scale; Beck Hope Scale; similarities; digit span; and Tempo Variability Test.

Procedures introduced for the first time in Phase V were the *disassembly test* of the General Aptitude Test Battery, the *Turning Test* of the General Aptitude Test Battery, and a modified form of the *Personal Age Scale*.[6]

The Disassembly and Turning Tests are behavioral tasks that have been widely administered to adult populations in the United States and lately have been found of value in behavioral studies of the elderly.[7] The Personal Age Scale is a self-descriptive procedure that relates chronological age to a set of self-perceptions of age status.

All procedures in this battery were scored by objective means.

PHASE VI

Method

PARTICIPANTS

The participants were 36 elders (21 women, 15 men) residing in nursing homes and sheltered, congregate housing arrangements. Mean age for the sample was 72.4. Men and women did not differ significantly in age. (It should be noted that more than twice the number of people included in the final sample had to be interviewed before enough could be found who were both willing and able to take the complete Wechsler Adult Intelligence Scale.)

Table A.2
Overall Research Design

Group	N	Baseline Testing	Immediate Retesting	Time-Lag Retesting
A	12	yes	yes	yes
B	12	yes	yes	no
C	12	yes	no	yes

RESEARCH DESIGN

All participants were interviewed and started on their self-report forms for sleep, energy, mood, and sense of achievement. The other procedures were administered in a second baseline session. After a 20-day baseline period, the participants were randomly assigned to one of three subgroups. The female/male mix was identical: 7 women and 5 men in each. All subgroups were placed on wine. The differences among the groups pertained to the schedule of retesting (see Table A-2).

The immediate retesting cycle took place within the last week of the usual 20-day on-wine phase. This, then, was equivalent to the retesting sessions carried out in previous phases. The time-lag retesting was introduced in Phase VI for the first time. It was intended to be conducted approximately 30 days after the first retesting period. In practice, the sessions varied from 27 to 36 days after the date of initial retesting (or the dates for which retesting would have been held in the case of Group C).

This design made it possible to explore the possibility that favorable effects associated with wine use might either fade or increase further with time. It would have been most direct to include all participants in the design specified for Group A. But this would have raised the question, even more than previous phases have, of possible practice effects. In other words, the observed improvements in performance might result more from the opportunity to take the same procedures again than from any effects that might otherwise be attributed to wine. While there were some internal indices in previous data that practice effects would not be a thoroughly convincing alternative explanation, it was considered both necessary and desirable to test this alternative explanation more directly, and the present design appear to be the simplest way of doing so. Other permutations than those used here would have added further information (a no-test baseline condition, e.g.), but this would have exceeded our ability to recruit and test participants in sufficient number to fill all the research design cells.

PROCEDURES

The instruments used here included, once again, the habits and life-style and sleep and activity patterns questionnaires, as well as the Snooze News and Early Bird Reports. The Tempo Variability Test was retained from the battery used in the previous phases.

In addition, the full-scale WAIS was individually administered. The WAIS is the most widely used individually administered omnibus "intelligence test" in the United States, the descendant of the once equally popular Wechsler-Bellevue Intelligence Scale.

REFERENCES

1. Downey, J. E. *The will temperament and its testing*. New York: World Book Company, 1923.
2. Porteus, S. D. *The maze test and its clinical applications in psychology*. San Francisco: Horizons Press, 1957.
3. Lawton, M. P. *The dimensions of morale*. In D. P. Kent, R. Kastenbaum, and S. Sherwood (Eds.), *Research, planning and action for the elderly*. New York: Behavioral Publications, 1972, pp. 144–165.
4. Botwinick, J. *Cognitive processes in maturity and old age*. New York: Springer, 1967.
5. Beck, A. T. *Depression: Clinical, experiential, and theoretical aspects*. New York: Hoeber, 1967.
6. Kastenbaum, R., Derbin, V., Sabatini, P. & Artt, S. "The ages of me": Toward personal and interpersonal definitions of functional aging. *International Journal of Aging and Human Development*, 1972, *3*, 197–212.
7. Fozard, J. L., & Thomas, J. C. Psychology of aging. In J. G. Howells (Ed.), *Modern perspectives in the psychiatry of old age*. New York: Bruner-Mazel, 1975, pp. 107–169.

9
Summary and Recommendations

The data on alcohol use in old age suggest that a balanced perspective could be achieved if society were willing to abandon some of its assumptions and stereotypes. Alcohol use appears to be more moderate among the elderly when compared with other age groups. Furthermore, few if any detrimental effects have been associated with moderate consumption levels. Those who regard alcohol as an unqualified menace for elderly men and women and for society in general will not find their views well supported by evidence of this type. There is evidence, however, that heavy use of alcohol in old age does pose a serious threat to health and well-being. Furthermore, older problem drinkers may not be coming to the attention of treatment agencies.

There is evidence that moderate use of alcohol (particularly wine and beer) can be of positive value. Most of these observations come from studies of morale and related variables in the institutionalized elderly (Chapter 6). New data reported in this book (Chapter 8) suggest that benefits may also be experienced by elderly people who live in the community and that these benefits may also extend to some cognitive and coping functions. Such findings appear to support a long historic tradition (Chapter 1) that has regarded alcoholic beverages as a source of comfort in a troubled and uncertain world.

Nevertheless, the negative case cannot be entirely dismissed. It is clear that alcohol abuse is a serious problem in our society. Although survey data suggest that the elderly in general do not appear to be among those most frequently ravaged by inordinate use of alcohol, there are alcoholics at all age levels. Moreover, elderly people who are not themselves abusers may be deprived or jeopardized indirectly. The loss of productivity and the increased burden of alcohol-related illness, unemployment, and interpersonal disorder in our society in general reduces the resources that might be made available to the elderly. This can be seen not only on a national level but also within the family circle, where instability can jeopardize all family members, including the elderly, when one person has a serious drinking problem. In addition, the survey data indicating that elderly people are less likely to be alcohol abusers (Chapter 3) are not beyond criticism. It is possible that the true incidence is underreported. Another possibility is that the relatively low incidence of alcohol abuse among the elderly carries a message quite opposite from the surface findings. The destructive effects of alcohol might result in the death of many heavy drinkers before they reach old age. Massive intake of alcohol has serious consequences for biological integrity (Chapter 2).

A key distinction must be made between moderate and heavy use of alcoholic beverages, especially when exhibited over an extended period of time. This distinction has been urged by many researchers and clinicians who are concerned with the use of alcohol in general. It applies with at least equal force to the elderly. The same facts and interpretations just do not fit both the 80-year-old who is enjoying a glass of wine in good company with dinner and the age-peer who is turning in desperation to any beverage at any time as part of a still-deepening pattern of trying to cope with problems he finds overwhelming.

It is also useful to distinguish between the elderly alcoholic who has been drinking heavily for many years and the individual who has turned to the bottle for the first time in old age in reaction to adverse life circumstances. The lifelong alcoholic who manages to reach old age may be so debilitated that he or she is no longer able to procure drink or perform daily care and survival functions. But those who have a long history of heavy drinking and are still around in reasonable shape at an advanced age may possess some remarkable characteristics. It requires an unusual physiology to endure that much abuse; in addition, it may also require distinctive social skills to survive so long in a society that looks down upon chronic alcoholics and frequently has little use even for intact elders. Because of these possibly distinctive characteristics, the aged longtime alcoholic may be either more resistant to anxiety or have a better prognosis than many younger chronic alcoholics. Data on the prognosis of such people is not clear at this point, but there is no evidence, as yet, that they have a poorer prognosis than the young. As seen earlier (Chapter 7), treatment prospects for elderly alcoholics do not seem to be nearly as discouraging as some might have expected.

The essentially *reactive* elderly alcoholic is harder to identify and is much less likely than either other old people with problems or younger alcoholics to receive help. Outreach programs and the desire to locate and help the reactive elderly alcoholic seem to be indicated here.

Obvious though they may be, several other recommendations should also be made at this time:

1. Educational efforts should be directed not only to the general public but also to agencies charged with responsibilities for care of the elderly and for treatment of alcohol-related problems. Those who work with the elderly often are not well informed about the total spectrum of alcohol effects, both positive and negative, psychosocial and physical, while those involved in alcohol treatment programs often hold assumptions about old age that owe more to culturally determined stereotypes than to scientific and clinical evidence.

2. In sifting through evidence and opinions about alcohol effects in old age, a clear distinction must be made not only between anecdoctal reports and controlled research but also between two rather different methodologies that are in use: (1) the laboratory type of experiment in which alcohol is administered in a well-controlled but emotionally sterile and unrealistic manner, and (2) studies conducted in real-life situations. Each type of study is legitimate and has its advantages and disadvantages. However, the "social psychology of the experiment" cannot properly be ignored if we are to put the results in useful perspective.

3. There is a pressing need to develop methods of identifying and finding older problem drinkers. A variety of appropriate treatment programs to meet the different needs of various subgroups with alcohol-related problems must be developed. Such programs must consider and respond to the specific physical, social, and economic needs of the client in order to be truly effective.

4. Well-designed treatment outcome studies of alcohol-related problems in old age should receive high priority. Such studies should compare a variety of treatment modalities and evaluate change along several dimensions.

5. It is important to recognize the context or sociophysical setting in which the alcoholic beverage is used. What are the implicit expectations for behavior in this setting? Is the setting conducive to mutual gratification and mature behavior or to isolation and heightened vulnerability?

6. The individual's general health (including any current use of medication) must be considered before coming to a conclusion about the advisability of alcohol use.

7. The individual's life-style (including ethnic group roots and current affiliations) also must be considered before coming to a conclusion about alcohol use.

8. The differences among various types of alcoholic beverages should be recognized. Each beverage has its characteristic percentage of ethanol and a more or less distinctive configuration of other components. A particular elderly person might find one beverage acceptable but not another, or experience a sense of benefit from one but disagreeable sensations from another.

9. Consideration might be given to educational and attitudinal programs with the purpose of helping people to integrate the use of alcoholic beverages into their life-styles. This will probably be a controversial suggestion. Some people are completely opposed to any use of alcoholic beverages. We are not advocating that everybody should drink or that everybody should think that drinking is a good idea. The point is that some people have, in fact, developed patterns of alcohol use throughout their lives that seem to yield no problems either to themselves or others. Other individuals have developed patterns of alcohol use that are associated with substantial hazards. Family education could be useful in helping to develop patterns of drinking that in a sense "inoculate" against the possibility of subsequent misuse. Somewhat parallel reasoning could be applied to the development of eating and nutrition habits that begin to form very early in life. There are people, for example, who run into difficulties later in life because they have not learned how to provide themselves with well-balanced nutrition. Instead of leaving the development of drinking patterns to circumstances that unfold outside the home, parents may be able to shape more constructive attitudes and habits if they themselves are in possession of accurate information about the psychosocial and physical effects of alcohol. Prevention of alcohol abuse in adulthood and old age might well begin with the availability of more comprehensive and accurate information to those who will be raising and educating children.

It is probable that both the positive and negative effects of alcoholic beverages are mediated to some extent by the total socioenvironmental context. Positive effects will probably prove to be more positive when supplemented by other therapeutic efforts. A person who feels more relaxed, better rested, and in general more comfortable with himself through the moderate use of alcoholic beverages may also be ready to respond favorably to a variety of other opportunities for improved functioning. Problem drinkers may generate negative responses from others, thereby increasing their difficulties and leading to further abuse of alcohol or to other maladaptive actions. It is helpful when we can see beyond the problem drinking as such and discover the anxieties, insecurities, and maladaptive behavioral patterns that have led to this situation. It is, after all, the problem, not the drinker, that needs to be attacked.

Finally, we must return to one of the most pervasive stereotypes afloat in our society. Old age is often viewed as a grim, unrewarding time of life, and old people are considered to be, in effect, second-class citizens. Those who remain captive to this stereotype may have a difficult time in attending to some of the distinctions made in this book. Why talk about improving the quality of life in old age by the moderate use of alcohol, or why talk about treatment efforts for elders who have drinking problems? Neither of these options is likely to impress itself on those who continue to assume that old age is and must be an undesirable condition. This deeply pessimistic and essentially do-nothing view is at variance with the facts[1,2,3,4] and even more at variance with the potentialities of human experience throughout the total life span. The example of a "promising" wine reaching full maturity through the years is itself an appropriate image to keep in mind.

REFERENCES

1. Hendricks, J., & Hendricks, C. D. *Aging in mass society.* Cambridge, Mass.: Winthrop Publishers, Inc., 1977.
2. Kastenbaum, R. *Growing old: Years of fulfillment.* New York: Harper and Row, 1979.
3. Knopf, O. *Successful aging.* New York: Viking Press, 1975.
4. Riedel, R., and Mishara, B. L. *Social psychology of later life.* Dubuque, Iowa: Wm. C. Brown, in press.

Index

Page numbers followed by *t* indicate tables.